THE POETICS AND POLITICS OF YOUTH IN MILTON'S ENGLAND

As the notion of government by consent took hold in early modern England, many authors used childhood and maturity to address contentious questions of political representation – about who has a voice and who can speak on his or her own behalf. For John Milton, Ben Jonson, William Prynne, Thomas Hobbes, and others, the period between infancy and adulthood became a site of intense scrutiny, especially as they examined the role of a literary education in turning children into political actors. Drawing on new archival evidence, Blaine Greteman argues that coming of age in the seventeenth century was a uniquely political act. His study makes a compelling case for understanding childhood as a decisive factor in debates over consent, autonomy, and political voice, and will offer graduate students and scholars a new perspective on the emergence of apolitical children's literature in the eighteenth century.

BLAINE GRETEMAN is an assistant professor of English at the University of Iowa. A Rhodes Scholar and former contributor to *Time* magazine, he continues to publish in both scholarly and popular publications, including *The New Republic, Milton Quarterly, Renaissance Quarterly, ELH*, and *Philological Quarterly*. He earned his PhD from the University of California, Berkeley.

THE POETICS AND POLITICS OF YOUTH IN MILTON'S ENGLAND

BLAINE GRETEMAN

University of Iowa

CAMBRIDGE
UNIVERSITY PRESS

CAMBRIDGE
UNIVERSITY PRESS

32 Avenue of the Americas, New York, NY 10013-2473, USA

Cambridge University Press is part of the University of Cambridge.

It furthers the University's mission by disseminating knowledge in the pursuit of
education, learning, and research at the highest international levels of excellence.

www.cambridge.org
Information on this title: www.cambridge.org/9781107038080

© Blaine Greteman 2013

First published 2013

Printed in the United States of America

A catalog record for this publication is available from the British Library.

Library of Congress Cataloging in Publication data
Greteman, Blaine.
The poetics and politics of youth in Milton's England / Blaine Greteman, University of Iowa.
p. cm.
Includes index.
ISBN 978-1-107-03808-0 (hardback)
1. English literature – 17th century – History and criticism.   2. Children in literature.
3. Youth in literature.   4. Children and politics – England – History – 17th century.
5. Literature and society – England – History – 17th century.   I. Title.
PR438.C55G74 2013
820.9′354–dc23   2013008594
ISBN 978-1-107-03808-0 Hardback

For Finn, Jo, Whit, and Beck,
my parliamentum puerorum

Contents

Acknowledgments

Families must usually wait for the end of the acknowledgments to get their due, but in a book about children it seems only fitting to mention them first. This project would not have happened without my own children, who inspired and complicated it, and their mother, Mandi Bozarth, who made it possible. My parents provided a model of faith and support that I can only hope to emulate. I owe all of them a "debt immense of endless gratitude" that, as I argue later, would be downright Satanic to forget.

My scholarly debts begin and end with Edward Jones, who introduced me to early modern literature and who continues to play Raphael to my Adam. The efforts and influence of Robert Graalman helped make my studies a reality. Another irreplaceable mentor, John Carey, helped suggest the topic, and the generous insights and advice of Victoria Kahn, James Grantham Turner, Alvin Snider, and David Landreth helped bring it to fruition. Daniel Shore and Joanna Picciotto provided encouragement and expertise at the times I needed them the most.

The collegial and intellectually stimulating atmosphere provided by the members of my department, especially Claire Sponsler, Miriam Gilbert, Adam Hooks, Kathy Lavezzo, Tom Simmons, and Jonathan Wilcox, made the experience a pleasure. Financial support and research leave from the University of Iowa allowed me to visit archives at the Newberry Library, the Bodleian, the British Library, the Lambeth Palace Library, and the UK National Archives, where the expertise and patience of the staff have been greatly appreciated. A Judith Popovich Aikin Award for extended study at the Folger Shakespeare Library provided valuable time to read and write and was made possible by the affiliation of the College of Liberal Arts and Sciences at the University of Iowa with the Newberry Library Center for Renaissance Studies. Austin Burke, Matthew Barrow, and Jatinder Padda, in their own ways, each helped make those research trips a success.

Conversations and debates with many wonderful scholars and friends have left their imprint on the following pages, especially Michael Witmore,

Nigel Smith, Brendan Prawdzik, Ann Baynes Coiro, David Loewenstein, John Rumrich, Michael Schoenfeldt, Debora Shuger, Stephen Fallon, Sharon O'Dair, Julia Smith, and the late John Shawcross, A.D. Nuttall, and Huston Diehl. Special thanks are also due to my editor at Cambridge, Ray Ryan, and to the Press's anonymous readers, whose astute suggestions made for a better book.

Parts of Chapter 1 appeared as "Coming of Age on Stage: Jonson's *Epicoene* and the Politics of Childhood in Early Stuart England," *ELH* 79 (2012): 135–60; © 2012 The Johns Hopkins University Press. Parts of Chapter 4 appeared as "'Perplex't Paths': Youth and Authority in Milton's *Mask*," *Renaissance Quarterly* 62 (2009): 410–43; © 2009 The University of Chicago Press. I am grateful for the permission to reprint them.

Abbreviations

Milton's poetry is cited parenthetically and quoted from the companion editions *John Milton: Complete Shorter Poems*, ed. Stella Revard (Chichester: Wiley-Blackwell, 2009) and *John Milton: Paradise Lost*, ed. Barbara K. Lewalski (Oxford: Blackwell, 2008). Unless otherwise noted, Ben Jonson's works are cited from *Ben Jonson*, ed. C. H. Herford, Percy Simpson, and Evelyn Simpson, 11 vols. (Oxford: Clarendon, 1925–52), the bible is quoted from the Authorized (King James) version, and translations of Latin texts are my own, with the original provided in the notes. For other frequently cited texts I use the following abbreviations:

C   John Milton, *The Works of John Milton*, ed. Frank Allen Patterson et al., 20 vols. (New York: Columbia University Press, 1923–40).

CPW   John Milton, *The Complete Prose Works of John Milton*, ed. Don M. Wolfe et al., 8 vols. (New Haven: Yale University Press, 1953–82).

DC   Thomas Hobbes, *De Cive: The Latin Version*, ed. Howard Warrender (Oxford: Clarendon Press, 1983).

EL   *Elements of Law Natural and Politic*, ed. Ferdinand Tönnies (London: Frank Case, 1969).

L   Thomas Hobbes, *Leviathan*, ed. C. B. Macpherson (New York: Penguin, 1987).

Notes will be used for other references, with each chapter's initial citation given in full.

Introduction
Childish Things

By 1618, the mayor of Exeter, Ignatius Jordan, was fast gaining a reputation as an "Arch-Puritan," but he preferred to think of himself as a close reader.[1] He regularly rose at two o'clock in the morning to reread and annotate his bible, and on the June day when the Children of Her Majesty's Royal Chamber of Bristol presented him with their license to perform "comedies, histories, Enterludes, morralls, pastorals, [and] stageplays" in his city, he studied it, scrutinized the boys, then called an emergency meeting of his aldermen.[2] The mayor chafed at the poor of his city spending their hard-earned money on plays, and like the other elders of Exeter, who later erected a cage to confine children who disrupted church services, he had no truck with irreverent, childish play.[3] But what disturbed Jordan the most about the Children of Her Majesty's Royal Chamber was the disjunction between their overripe appearance and their attempt to present themselves as children. "I perused their patent," he explained in a letter to Secretary of State Thomas Lake, "and finding that it is only for children and youths (for so are the words) I did with advice of some of the aldermen of this city restrain them from playing here, for that there being fifteen of their company there are but only five youths among them, and all the rest are men, some about 30 and 40 and 50 years, as they have confessed."[4] Fifty-year-old boys seemed fundamentally perverse to a man who had been a devout and responsible merchant since age fifteen. By contrast, the men and youths of this children's company were willfully forsaking adulthood to take advantage of a license and liberty granted to the young.[5] Jordan and his aldermen decided to pay them four angels to get out of town.

Some uncertainty remained, however, about whether the players or the mayor had abused their authority. Hearing that the troupe intended to appeal their case to the Privy Council, Jordan dispatched his letter to the Council in advance, "that they may not think I have done anything of contempt, but to keep myself within the compass of the statute," and he enclosed a copy of the players' warrant, "that you may see the words of it."[6] Surprisingly, however, the words did not convince the King and his Council that the company had done anything wrong. Rather than revoking the patent, the Council reaffirmed that the company's master John Daniel (brother of the poet Samuel Daniel) had full "authority to bring up a companie of children and youths in the quality of playing" and firmly rebuked "your letts, troubles, [and] molestations."[7] Whatever their actual age, the players were now children by royal fiat, and Jordan held his tongue. But such encounters had a radicalizing effect, and after winning a seat to Parliament two years later, Jordan became one of the crown's most intractable Puritan critics. In seventeenth-century England, the question of what it meant to speak as a child, and when one should put away child-ish things, was charged with literary and political significance.

This book argues that the ambiguous cultural space that allowed thirty-year-old men to tour the country as children is crucial to under-standing early modern formulations of poetic and political voice. The central problem in all politics, argues the philosopher Jacques Rancière, is knowing "whether the subjects who count in the interlocution … are speaking or just making a noise," and this certainly seems to have been the case in seventeenth-century England, where consent was explicitly fig-ured as voice.[8] Voters, often simply called "voices," shouted names to elect members of Parliament, and prospective Parliamentarians made sure they collected ample voices in advance, trotting "up and down / To every *Inne* and *Alehouse* in the Town / To gain a *Voice*," as the satirist George Wither complained in 1646.[9] Once they came of age, even those unqualified to vote took oral oaths and protested injuries with oral depositions, and in this context the "constitutive" political clashes Rancière describes often played out across lines of youth and authority.[10] To be an infant under age twenty-one, after all, was to be legally "voiceless," a term derived from the Latin root *infans*, implying not only silence but speech so inconsequen-tial that it registers only as babble. The Exeter mayor had reasons beyond Puritan anti-theatricality for asserting a strict divide between infancy and adulthood, because the voices of the city's freemen authorized his own power. The thirty-year-old boy players, for their part, had reason to strad-dle this line, performing childhood to leverage the special mimetic, theat-rical, and legal status that it bestowed.

The following chapters focus on works by John Milton (1608–74) and his contemporaries that interrogate the threshold between childhood and adulthood, asking how voice emerges from infancy and how childish speech before that moment complicates human agency and obligation.

In each case, the ability of poets and dramatists to produce and reproduce powerful voices is key. The earliest English humanist educational text, Thomas Elyot's *Boke Named the Governor* (1531), illuminates the basic tenet that made childhood the nexus between political and poetic discourse:

> Poetry was the first philosophy that ever was knowen, wherby men from their childhode were brought to the raison, how to lyve wel, lernyng therby not only maners and naturall affections, but also the wonderful werkes of nature, mixing serious matter with thynges that were plesaunt.... In poetes was supposed to be science misticall and inspired, and therefore in latine thei were called Vates, which woorde signifieth as muche as prophetes.[11]

The mature subject's authoritative speech might seem mundane next to the semi-magical furor of the *vates*, but according to the most prominent educational reformers, poets, and political thinkers of the sixteenth and seventeenth centuries, they were intimately related. In the infancy of the race, poetry taught all humankind what it continues to teach children, how to "lyve wel," as part of a moral human society. Adulthood emerges as an act of voice, inspired by the child's engagement with poetic and rhetorical delight. Although they all approach and value this moment differently, I argue that works as diverse as Ben Jonson's *Epicoene* (1609–10), William Prynne's *Histrio-Mastix* (1633), Milton's *Comus* (1634) and *Paradise Lost* (1667), and Thomas Hobbes's *Leviathan* (1651) all grapple with its possibilities and problems to formulate their views on art, education, and society. As they interrogate the relationship between childish mimesis and adult subjectivity, such works demonstrate the central role played by childhood in the early modern theorization of consent and political representation.

Discovering Childhood

To make that argument, this book draws on recent historical and literary scholarship that has utterly reversed the earlier consensus that childhood was an unknown concept in Renaissance Europe, where children were supposedly either neglected or "hated as agents of sin within the household" by parents who "beat them mercilessly," as Lawrence Stone memorably explained.[12] The remainder of the introduction discusses the state of scholarship on early modern childhood and the way this book's attention to "childish" figures like the boy players of Bristol changes our understanding of the relationship between childhood, literature, and political voice.

Stone's work, like most historical treatments of childhood in the 1960s and 1970s, follows the path blazed by Philippe Ariès in his still-influential *Centuries of Childhood*. Children in medieval paintings tend to look like shrunken adults, and Ariès uses such evidence to suggest that early European cultures did not recognize childhood as a distinct stage of life, while high infant mortality rates discouraged parents from investing emotionally in their offspring. When childhood finally began to be "discovered" in the sixteenth and seventeenth centuries, Ariès claims, things only got worse: children lost what freedom they had and became the targets for harsh discipline and strict moral reform.[13] "The history of childhood," according to this first wave of scholarship, "is a nightmare from which we have only recently begun to awaken."[14]

Such studies remain useful for reminding us just how alien seventeenth-century sentiments about childhood can seem to our post-Victorian sensibility. John Donne (1572–1631), a father of twelve, claimed, for example, that unborn children learn "cruelty, by being fed with blood, and may be damned," while Richard Baxter (1615–91) elaborated the doctrine of original sin by proclaiming children "as hateful in the eyes of God, as any Toads or Serpents."[15] Nevertheless, a new generation of revisionist historians has demonstrated that affective bonds and paternal instincts ultimately trumped strict theology, and not the other way around, as Baxter himself learned when enraged parents responded to his sermon by harrying him through the streets.[16] Linda Pollock was among the first to produce evidence from the diaries of besotted and bereaved parents to show that scholarly reliance on proscriptive materials like sermons, conduct books, and legal regulations had given us a distorted view of attitudes toward premodern children.[17] By the turn of the twenty-first century, Nicholas Orme completed the demolition of Ariès's idea that childhood did not exist as a separate state in medieval Europe, producing evidence that adults built toys for children, played with them, and happily engaged in "baby-talk" with them.[18] Margaret King has more recently described even the strictest Puritans, who were once caricatured as dour child haters, as ancestors of today's "helicopter parents," intensely focused on the well-being of children who would carry forward their religious mission.[19] Early modern parents loved and nurtured their offspring, and they had a clear concept of childhood, although it was different from our own and was to undergo profound historical and ideological shifts during the era of the English Civil War.

Literary scholars have been particularly attentive to early modern depictions of the child as a figure of submission and passive imitation, "a rich and complex symbol," as Leah Marcus puts it, "not only for humility and anti-intellectualism, but for a whole range of values associated with an England of the past and rapidly disappearing under

Puritan attack in the divided England of their own time."[20] Sixteenth-
and seventeenth-century authors regularly described the child as a text
ready for inscription, a blank book, or as John Earle (1598–1665) wrote in
one of the era's most popular character sketches, "a man in small letter,
yet the best Copie of *Adam* before hee tasted of *Eve*, or the Apple ... his
soul a white paper unscribled with observations of the world, wherewith
at length it becomes a blurr'd Note-booke."[21] The persistent early modern association of children and books derives from Aristotle's idea of the
mind as a tabula rasa in *De Anima* and his suggestion, in the *Poetics*, that
the child's blank, mimetic consciousness demonstrates that poetry had
natural origins: "[I]t is an instinct of human beings from childhood to
engage in mimesis (indeed, this distinguishes them from other animals:
man is the most mimetic of all, and it is through mimesis that he develops
his earliest understanding)."[22] As Michael Witmore explains, for many
early modern writers this implies that the child is a "medium without
a motive," easily caught up in "feedback loops" of automatic mimesis.[23]
Performing on stage and in royal processions, such children are "agents
without interests," like automatons or puppets, and thus convenient vessels for expressing monarchical power.[24]

Since the 1980s, such concepts of childhood have made it a key subject
for scholars interested in describing the way institutions and discourses
inscribe values on their subjects. The "age of eloquence," as the early modern explosion of literary activity has been called, was according to many
historicist and materialist critics largely a by-product of an educational
philosophy that aimed to immerse children in great works of literature in
order to turn them into more serviceable subjects and competent bureau-
crats.[25] Work by scholars such as Richard Halpern, Anthony Grafton, and
Lisa Jardine has fundamentally challenged the classic interpretation of
humanist learning as a triumph of literary style and a liberation of the
individualist self; we are now more likely to see early modern classrooms as
a site of what Pierre Bourdieu and Jean-Claude Passeron describe as "symbolic violence."[26] In this view, the humanist pedagogue imparts arcane
knowledge and an elevated style to his students, simultaneously imbuing
them with elite status and obsequious habits, while imitative children gain
cultural capital by producing writing that reinforces conservative social
values.

Most humanist pedagogues, it should be said, would have embraced
this description without reservation. The famed master of the Merchant
Taylors' School, Richard Mulcaster (1531–1611), invokes the learned slave
to exemplify education's ability to create "such an utterer, as is part of the

state, and capable of best state," while the influential Elizabethan tutor Roger Ascham's (1514–68) ideally eloquent student is nonetheless "a quiet subject to his Prince," and the prolific seventeenth-century pedagogue Charles Hoole (1610–67) claimed students may be "taught with delight" to become "serviceable instruments" of Church and Commonwealth.[27] As John Donne summed up this ambitious project of subject formation, "The *School* will receive a pregnant child from his parents, and work upon him; The *University* will receive a grounded Scholar from the School, and work upon him; The *State*, or the *Church*, will receive a qualified person from the University, and worke by him."[28] In view of such ambitions, it is small surprise that critics like Halpern have observed that children in theatres and schools were at the center of "a mode of indoctrination based on hegemony and consent rather than force and coercion."[29]

Such studies reveal the cultural and pedagogical imbrications of sovereign power in many ways that inform this book. Alongside political histories such as Gordon Schochet's *Patriarchalism in Political Thought*, which shows how models of fatherly power and childlike obedience were used to justify seventeenth-century absolutism, they have helped establish an indispensable connection between childhood, mimesis, and political obligation that I wish to elaborate.[30] But childhood was a contested territory, especially in the latter, youthful period that Ascham called "the most dangerous tyme of all a mans life, and most slipperie to stay well in," and existing scholarship has failed to recognize the ways in which it complicated and was complicated by shifting notions of hegemony and consent.[31] My approach remains historicist in its occupation with the interplay between discourse and governance, but it recognizes that New Historicism's familiar emphasis on sovereign power needs substantial revision to account for actual modes of authority in the divided, parliamentary English polity, especially as we turn away from the sixteenth century and toward the era of civil war.[32] During this period of profound political upheaval, the children who were the elusive and sometimes resistant objects of humanist pedagogy became the center of the debate over the nature of consent, dissent, and whether a literary education instilled obedience or inspired rebellion.

At the beginning of the seventeenth century, elections served primarily to confirm social and kinship bonds and voting was less about making choices than about affirming a social order based on birth and inheritance – a government by assent, to use Mark Kishlansky's distinction, rather than consent. But with surprising speed, "assent would become choice," and elections would become genuine contests of conflicting ideologies and allegiances.[33] "Political consensus and the patronage system broke down," Derek Hirst explains, "elections and contests ensued, and a surprisingly large social group became involved in legitimate politics."[34] An important body of recent scholarship shows that such shifts had a complex and little-noted impact on the patriarchal metaphors commonly used to conceptualize government as a family with a father-king at its head. If the commonwealth was a family, as scholars such as Su Fang Ng, Erin Murphy, and Melissa Sanchez have shown, the king's fatherly power might be invoked to demand passivity, conservatism, and obedience, but the relations of brothers or mothers could also model competing modes of fraternal equity and feminine power.[35] Such works have significantly enlarged our understanding of the period's politics, especially with regards to gender, but they largely concentrate on adult siblings, wives, and mothers.[36] By contrast, this study contends that children, as figures of mimetic response, were the crucial point of contact for conceptualizing the way art could reinforce patriarchal obedience or cultivate independent voice.

Indeed, one downside of the otherwise fruitful preoccupation with questions of gender in early modern studies is that it has often led us to overlook or misunderstand the depiction of weakness, powerlessness, or silence, which childishness inflects in a very different way from femininity, both in terms of poetics and politics. This is because, unlike the other "muted groups" to whom they were often compared, particularly "*women, Lunaticks, and Ideots,*" children's political condition was expected to change.[37] Trained up in an expanding educational system, many children would develop politically significant voices, learning to speak for themselves and others.[38] Some would use these powers to stir passions, create obligations, and even catalyze new social formations. Countering much recent work on humanist pedagogy, Rebecca Bushnell has argued that early modern classrooms sometimes allowed for "functional ambivalence" and debate rather than simple social reproduction.[39] The following chapters show, however, that during the era of civil war we must go still further, recognizing the ways that childhood, both inside and outside the classroom, could be a site not only of debate and ethical inquiry but also of radical opposition.

The Digger Gerrard Winstanley (1609–76), for example, looked to childhood during the tumultuous 1640s to insist that each generation held the possibility of Edenic return, because "*Adams* innocency is the time of child-hood; and there is a time in the entering of the understanding age, wherein every branch of man-kinde is put to his choice, whether he will follow the Law of Righteousnesse."[40] Winstanley described the dawning, empowered, collective self that he hoped to cultivate as a "Man-Child," and the following chapters explore the way this liminal state was performed on stage in works like Jonson's *Epicoene*, worried about in William Prynne's political and anti-theatrical writings, and exorcised from the political discourse, after a long struggle, by Hobbes's *Leviathan*.[41] As we shall see in Part II of the book, Milton no less than Winstanley drew heavily on concepts of childhood to construct an evolutionary society in his greatest works, and I argue that many of his most fascinating and politically significant figures are, in important ways, childish – from the Lady in *Comus* to Adam, Eve, and their angelic consorts in *Paradise Lost*.

Previous discussions of childhood simply cannot account for such cases, in part because they have focused on extremely young, "physically slight" children who are explicitly cut off from questions of consent and dissent.[42] Marcus, for example, writes about neonate consciousness and the poetic "celebration of little things," while Witmore discusses the uncanny aesthetics of "diminutive" child performers, and nearly all the work on boy actors assumes they were prepubescent imps with unbroken voices.[43] As my opening anecdote about the strapping Children of Bristol suggests, this is a major point of departure for the current study, and one that requires some explanation.

Many of the figures in the following chapters are "childish" rather than children in a sense we would normally understand, and might also be called "youths," a term often employed in the early modern period to label the disputed territory between the onset of puberty and marriage or freedom from apprenticeship. Paul Griffiths has in fact insisted on this term in his study of apprentices and servants between puberty and adulthood, lamenting the way "an ill-defined border between childhood and youth is crossed with worrying ease by historians in their use of age-titles."[44] Early modern writers also worried about these fluid boundaries, but to carve out a discreet period of youth disconnected from childhood is to achieve something they found impossible. As Ilana Krausman Ben-Amos notes, maturation "did not occur at a specific point in the lives of the young, nor was it a steady, uniform set of gradual stages."[45] Across the discourses that define the ages of life, sixteenth- and seventeenth-century lawyers, poets, and preachers often speak with some precision, and in ascending order, of babies, boys, adolescents, youths, and youngmen; the most famous example is Shakespeare's Jaques, who describes the "infant, / Mewling and puking in the nurse's arms," the "whining schoolboy," and the youthful lover "Sighing like a furnace."[46] But such specific categories collapse just as readily into the nebulous category of "childhood," which legal, medical, and religious sources described as lasting until at least age twenty-one and often much longer.[47] The present study focuses specifically on the aspects of the boundary between childhood and adulthood that allowed it to be crossed with "worrying ease" in the age of Milton, and for that reason I stubbornly persist in using the terms "child" and "youth" in situations that sometimes strained credulity even in the seventeenth century. As Anna Davin has noted, "if any definition of childhood is feasible it must be made in relation to adulthood. Children are always, in any culture or society, those who are not yet recognized as adult."[48] In seventeenth-century England, this made "childhood" a shifting category: one could be considered a child in one context and an adult in another. I retain the terminology of my sources when speaking of boys, children, or youths, while reserving "childish" to describe behaviors or traits that mark one as less than adult. As we shall see, it was precisely the ambiguity surrounding childhood and its terminus that made it crucial to theorizing consent.

Definitions of Childhood: Innocence, Imitation, and the Birth of Consent

It is hard to overstate the amount of legal and cultural gray area surrounding childhood in the early modern period. In a popular text that draws on the best medical and classical authority, Henry Cuffe (1563–1601) says "*childhood is the first part and age of a man's life, wherein their generation and growth is perfected* and this lasteth (for the most part) untill wee be five and twentie yeeres old, and this age is proportionable unto the *Spring*, hot and moist."[49] Cuffe goes on to distinguish various stages of childhood – infancy; boyhood; the "*budding and blossoming* age, when our cheeks and other more hidden parts begin to be clothed with that mossie excrement of haire;" and finally, youth.[50] But for understanding the status and signification of boy actors and other children in this society, two elements of Cuffe's description are more important than these deceptively systematic divisions. First, the age of maturation is hedged and uncertain: Cuffe places it at age twenty-five, but his parenthetical "(for the most part)" expresses an indeterminacy that saturated legal, religious, and medical discussions of maturation during the period. Second, youths of twenty and even older share the same conceptual and even physiological status as neonates. Historians sometimes use the onset of puberty to establish the end of childhood and the beginning of adolescence, but for Cuffe and contemporaries who sought such a physical threshold, childhood was defined by a moist, warm, humoural constitution that could last far beyond puberty. In *A Short Compendium of Chirurgery*, for example, the doctor John Shirley (fl. 1678–82) agrees that "[c]hildhood, comprehending the first five and twenty years of our age, is of a hot and moist temper. From thence Youth, proceeding to five and thirty or fourty years, of a hot and dry; Manhood, consisting in the ten or fifteen next years, is esteemed cold and dry."[51] The best medical authorities agreed that at age thirty-five the flames of youth were just beginning to abate and that a twenty-five-year-old boy was more constitutionally inclined to respond to his environment with a child's passion than an adult's cool resolve.[52]

Neither legal nor cultural institutions like the church did much to clarify the resulting ambiguity about when childhood ended, but both identified this moment as the birth of consent. Legally, "infancy" lasted until age twenty-one, but the influential jurist Matthew Hale (1609–76) admitted that both civil and common law were "very uncertain" about setting absolute markers for adulthood, while Sir Edward Coke (1552–1634) agreed that "Man by the Law, for several purposes hath divers ages assigned unto him," and this made the child's will the subject of fascinated scrutiny in legal questions of wardship, indentures, marriage, and rape.[53] The English church, in the throes of the Protestant Reformation, similarly generated much heat but little light about the limits of childhood. In many ways, Protestant reformers deliberately extended the time to full adulthood, contributing to a phenomenon Keith Thomas describes as a large-scale "prolongation of childhood."[54] Where traditional church law insisted (à la Friar Laurence in *Romeo and Juliet*) that a very young couple's mutual consent could make a marriage despite parental objections, the reformed ecclesiastical laws drafted during Henry VI's reign required even adult children to obtain parental consent for marriage.[55] Moreover, Protestant moralists and divines frequently insisted that adult children were bound to a whole set of deferential filial behaviors, such as bowing and removing their hats.[56] Such demands may have partly been wishful thinking, but John Aubrey (1626–97) affirmed that, in the years before the Civil War, children of thirty and forty "were to stand like great mutes and fools bare headed before their Parents."[57]

Protestantism also rekindled debates over baptism that focused attention on the earliest possible moment that children could consent and whether their membership in the church could be guaranteed without this act.[58] The English church held that the infant's baptism sufficed for salvation, but only until "children come to that age, that partly by the frailtie of their own flesh, partly through the assaultes of the world & the Devil, they begyn to be in daunger to fall into sin."[59] Definitive proofs of adulthood, as this language implies, traditionally came more certainly from transgression than from an extended spring of innocence. The doctrine, as it was first expressed in the common law during the fourteenth century, was *malitia supplet aetatem*, or "malice supplies the age."[60]

This dictum crossed over into the law from theological treatments of genesis during the medieval period as the solution to one of the first "tests" of legal responsibility in English law – the "knowledge of good and evil test."[61] "An infant of ten years of age killed his companion and concealed him," according to the account of the precedent-setting trial, "and [the judge] caused him to be hung, because by concealment he showed that he knew how to distinguish between good and evil. And so malice supplies the age."[62] Here, church and court agreed: wrongdoing – specifically the attempt, like Adam and Eve's, to conceal the crime – could supersede conventions and uncertainty about when childhood ended. Guilt is how we grow up. "Our first Parents for an apple lost Paradise, and woon hell," wrote the clergyman and schoolteacher Thomas Granger in 1621, "so every child of *Adam*, like *Esau*, for a sweet bit will sell his soule to the Divell, and his brother to a lying bribing thiefe."[63] Mankind's fall is reiterated with each generation, and in a troubling way it is precisely this fall that enters the child into full adult society.

To be innocent was of course preferable to being guilty, but it was also, as the Oxford English Dictionary has it since the sixteenth century, to be "deficient in intelligence or sense," to lack the ability to speak or act with purpose.[64] And this, as a popular sixteenth-century translation of the medieval scholar Bartholomaeus Anglicus (c.1203–72) explained, created another inauspicious link with Adam, as even innocent children would "make more sorrow and woe and weepe more for the losse of an apple, than for the losse of their heritage."[65] The principle was reputedly even formalized in legal practice to determine if a young heir was fit to receive his inheritance: if in doubt, the judge commanded "an *apple* or a *counter*, with a piece of *gold* to be set before him, to *try* which he will take; If he take the apple or the counter, and leave the gold … he knowes not the *valew of things*, or how to make a true *election* of what is fittest for him."[66] If the Adamic child represented mankind's potential, he also represented his proclivity to fall, to succumb to passion and take the forbidden fruit. Understandably then, many parents became anxious about waiting for the traditional age of thirteen to confirm their children, enthusiastically catechizing them as young as age two and monitoring their deathbed comportment for signs of grace. Such anxiety obliquely responds to the question the various sects known as Anabaptists began asking openly when censorship lapsed during the Civil War: "How then do children Covenant at baptisme, or enter into Covenant who yeeld no consent?"[67] The Anabaptist idea that infant baptism offered only an illusion of salvation remained marginal and heterodox, but it responded to a broader, and growing, sense of the insufficiency of signs and symbols to replace consent.

For this same reason, children in public life began to make the gaps in political representation painfully obvious. While thirty-year-old men performed in children's theatrical companies, ten-year-olds signed indentures and contracts, and children as young as twelve served in the House of Commons. The presence of these children exercising adult responsibilities indicates a culture where "status trumped age," notes Holly Brewer.[68] When pressed, many contract theorists would argue that adult women had rational capabilities and that their familial and political status derived from consent.[69] But children, by definition, lacked the rational machinery to make informed choices, and as the basis of political authority shifted from status to contract, they would in many ways be driven out of public life, allocated a "separate space," and singled out as "the main example of the group for whom consent should not apply."[70]

Brewer's work chiefly describes shifts in early American governance, but we can see the beginnings of the same process at work in England during the years leading up to the Civil War and Interregnum. Here the liminal position of child parliamentarians and elderly boy actors exposed the kinds of attenuated agency that could pass for consent, while the country's demographics gave questions of childhood and consent special urgency. England was a nation of the young: at any given time during the seventeenth century, 40 percent to 50 percent of the population was under the age of twenty-four, when apprentices typically gained their freedom.[71] At what point did their voices become more than babble or noise? This question animated not only the work of political theorists but also the performances of child actors and the efforts of poets and teachers to cultivate voices that would do real work in the world. It involved poetry and drama on a fundamental level because the same qualities that made the child incapable of rational consent – his passion, his irrationality, and his imitative compulsion – made him the ultimate exemplar of poetic response.

The child's unthinking mimesis had been a truism, and a problem, at least since Plato invoked it to justify the expulsion of poets from his ideal republic, reasoning that "imitations, if continued from youth far into life, settle down into habits and second nature."[72] The child imitates the good along with the bad, becoming a slave to these imitations rather than a free and rational agent, and the commonplace that "[c]hildren will do like parrots, without understanding what they say," continued to haunt early modern attempts to formulate doctrines of government by consent.[73] The child's imitative nature, noted John Locke (1632–1704), introduced an epistemic problem to all philosophical and ontological systems, because "by familiar use from our cradles, we come to learn certain articulate sounds very perfectly ... but yet are not always careful to examine, or settle their significations perfectly.... Not only children, but men, speak several words, no otherwise than parrots do."[74] So acculturated, how or when did anyone ever exercise choice in his own government?

In his early notes on political obligation, this dilemma caused Locke to reject the notion of the autonomous consenting subject in favor of a patriarchal theory.[75] Eventually he invoked the idea of "tacit consent" to work around the problem, arguing that it is "easie, and almost natural, for Children by a tacit, and scarce avoidable consent to make way for the *Father's Authority and Government*," and this laid the foundation for his suggestion that adult subjects could also consent even by silent and half-conscious acts like walking on the public highway.[76] Tacit consent requires "no Expressions" of agreement; it merely assumes that any rational person would agree to the conditions of a given contract if given the choice.[77] Rather than a decisive coming of age, the Lockean subject "makes way" for authority through a series of such tacit agreements, beginning in childhood. Later generations of liberal theorists have accepted and expanded upon this idea, but the value of "scarce avoidable consent" was the subject of fierce contention throughout the seventeenth century.[78]

To end this contention, the fraught coming-of-age moment that is the subject of this book needed to be erased from the center of the political discourse – an erasure that precipitated the rise of the eighteenth-century "cult of childhood" and facilitated the development of a distinct, "apolitical" but didactic children's literature.[79] "Long before they became a distinct object of the book trade," notes Warren Wooden, "English children read avidly of whatever literature was available to them."[80] In the new paradigm that developed in the eighteenth century, however, the child's innocence would be protected and enforced with moralistic works like the anonymous but wildly popular *Goody Two Shoes* (1765) and Eliza Weaver Bradburn's redaction of Milton's epic, *Paradise Lost for Children* (1828).[81] Where Edmund Spenser had once set out to "fashion a gentleman" in the *Faerie Queene* by leading both young and old readers through Error's Cave and the Bower of Bliss, these later works rather sternly set out to purge young readers of error and strip bliss of its wayward potential.[82] We can see results of this erasure even in Romantic works that use the child as a figure of cultural critique: the child as a unified "ideology-proof, organic sensibility" in such works stands apart from society rather than at the center of its authorization.[83] The same development erased poesy, as an art of becoming, from the center of political culture. Wordsworth's rhapsodic "Child among his new-born blisses" offers childhood and its "endless imitation" as an escape from adult society rather than a twisting path into it.[84]

Exercising of the Voice

In the liminal moment examined in the following chapters, however, the child draws on his native mimetic powers to emulate and internalize adult authority, even if he must ultimately subdue those powers or leave them behind. This gave poetry and drama a central role in "the gentle exercising of the voice," as Mulcaster described his efforts to cultivate adults who could speak as both dramatic actors and political agents.[85] The emphasis on "gentle exercising," even by teachers like Mulcaster who reserved a prominent place for the rod in their classrooms, was the most innovative aspect of the humanist pedagogy during the dramatic sixteenth- and seventeenth-century expansion of the English educational system, and we find its legacy everywhere in the era's poetry and drama.[86] Educators should "use discretlie the best allurements ye can," Ascham recommended, because "love is fitter than feare, and gentlenes better than beating, to bring up a childe rightlie in learninge."[87] The belief that "children and the products of the imagination have interchangeable qualities" made the allurements of poetry and drama especially discreet.[88] Erasmus (1466–1536), easily the most influential humanist educator in Europe and England during the sixteenth and seventeenth centuries, explains that because children are like "starlings and parrots," they can be "drawn to study by their natural delight in imitation," especially the imitation of "charming poetic fictions."[89]

Pre-rational and pre-moral, the child's immersion within language was a sensual experience of sound creating sense, beautifully described in 1598 by the unluckily named clergyman and poet Thomas Bastard:

> Me thinkes 'tis pretie sport to heare a childe,
> Rocking a worde in mouth yet undefild.
> The tender racket rudely playes the sound,
> Which weakely banded cannot backe rebound,

And the soft ayre the softer roofe doth kisse.

. . . . .

The alphabet is searcht for letters soft,
To trye a worde before it can be wrought.[90]

The child plays with language, rocking a word in her mouth as she might rock a doll in a cradle, for the sheer thrill of imitative representation. The gentle rhymes and rhythms of poetry made learning "a very pastime," claimed Henry Peacham (1578–c.1644), endorsing an educational theory and practice that immersed students in Terence, Horace, Juvenal, and Virgil, while making dramatic performance a classroom staple far outside the elite circle of schools like St. Paul's and Eton.[91] Even the "meaner and ruder" country schools were advised to harness the child's ludic drive in this way.[92]

Local records show that such performances regularly spilled out of the classroom and into the wider community, providing schoolmasters with a valuable supplemental income and a forum to "better exercyse" the boys as they made a trial of the public voices they would one day claim as adults.[93] The same logic justified the "play days" mandated in school charters throughout the country, as well as the university drama, which was performed by students who ranged in age from twelve to their late twenties but who were thought to embody the same qualities of childish mimesis as much younger children.[94] Hobbes, for example, describes the minds of university students as "white paper," while John Lyly (1554–1606) describes Euphues, a marriageable young heir who travels abroad independently, in the terms that Aristotle, Ascham, and Erasmus use for the smallest infants: he is a "younge Impe" with a "witte beeinge lyke waxe apte to receive any impression."[95] Milton's "At a Vacation Exercise," performed at Cambridge in 1628, similarly recalls the very young child of Bastard's poem:

> Hail native Language, that by sinews weak
> Didst move my first endeavouring tongue to speak,
> And mad'st imperfect words with childish tripps,
> Half unpronounc't, slide through my infant-lipps. (1–4)

Milton plays the role of "father" to his fellow students, and part of his point is that he no longer speaks with childish trips. But at age nineteen he also remains a legal infant, and he later prints this work as juvenilia delivered "*in Collegio Adolescentis*" (*C* 12:118); the disconnect between adult role and infant status is part of the joke.[96] Milton plays with language throughout this performance of travestied paternity, punning with salty and sometimes vulgar wit, cracking fart jokes, and fully indulging in an "exercise" meant to cultivate students' voices by engaging their childishly ludic sensibilities.[97]

A brief example from one of Erasmus's colloquies shows how such methods were supposed to create self-disciplined subjects and will also help exemplify the oppositional potential I wish to explore. *De Lusu* ("Of Play") is a witty little drama about "begging," or literally "extorting" (*extorqueat*) a "play day" from a strict master – a highly ritualized and regular form of licensed misrule in early modern schooling.[98] In Erasmus's version, the schoolboy has learned his lessons well and invokes Quintilian as he promises that the boys will study more vigorously later if allowed to play now. This play now, pay later proposal sets up a joke and a concession:

PAEDAGOGUS: Who will act as security [*fideiussor*] for fulfillment of this promise?
COCLES: I'll venture my head on it.
PAEDAGOGUS: No, you'll rather venture your tail – I know not to put too much trust in your word. But this time I'll see if you can be faithful. Mind you, if you break your word, you'll never receive anything from me afterwards. Let them play, but they must stay together in the field.[99]

The gesture toward corporal punishment is really just a teasing bit of wordplay on heads and tails; the teacher's real threat is withholding pleasure. In fact, the whole episode has been a kind of play, with banter doing the work of negotiation and the boy enacting a legal role for which he is really ineligible (*fideiussor* is a law term for a surety, who cannot be a minor).[100] The boys gain their victory, but their play is now contractually bounded within set physical and moral limits – they are not to leave the field, "go drinking, or anything worse."[101] Play channels the boys' desires into a discipline they willingly embrace: to get what they want, they learn to speak in the master's language (Latin) and in his style (which is governed by wit). At every level of the educational system, from translating Terence to public performances by much older scholars, this is how the child's encounter with poetic and dramatic material was meant to work.

Fictional schoolboys, however, often bore little resemblance to their historical counterparts, who were so notoriously unruly that their play days sometimes turned into genuinely violent insurrections.[102] Even the colloquies' playful energy sometimes overflows and challenges their disciplinary ends: the boys in *De Lusu* who win a play day are rewarded not merely for agreeing to a set of self-imposed rules but for mocking their teacher's authority and exploiting a weakness for play they know he has secretly harbored since childhood.[103] This dynamic recurs regularly in texts produced for humanist classrooms, where the drowsy, half-drunk apprentices are simply more entertaining than their strict masters, and the lazy, sarcastic schoolboys run circles around their moralizing peers. The apparent incongruities help constitute what Robert Weimann has called "the noncoercive space" of reading, leaving readers free to interpret and judge in a way that didactic works typically deny (or at least claim to deny).[104] Such ludic unpredictability helped make the colloquies wildly popular in forms that bore no relation to their professed purpose of Latin instruction, with hundreds of editions printed in London during the seventeenth century, often in English.[105] In his edition of colloquies, Hoole boasted that he could teach children "as we do parrots, to speak they know not what," but at least one early reader and annotator seems to have ignored Hoole's pieties and morals while carefully marking salty phrases like "Dii perdant phrontisterium una cum magistro" ("hang the school and the master too") and "Quid precar? imprecari libeat magis" ("what, shall I pray? I have more mind to curse").[106]

In short, children were never wholly passive or innocent readers, and in cases like this they seem to have been downright malicious. It is in this sense, I want to suggest, that Seth Lerer's conclusion about children's marginalia in medieval books could also apply here: "[O]n the margins of the pages, we may see the shards of childish reading or, on rare occasion, children acting like the authors of their age."[107] Throughout this book I explore such moments not only in the margins of books but also in children's theatrical performances, in the legal records they left behind, and in the way adult writers depict and seek to foster processes of maturation and development.

Part I establishes childish liminality as a site of political discipline and disruption before turning to John Milton's sustained engagement with this stage of life in Part II. Chapter 1 argues that the perilous threshold moment between childhood and adulthood was the great metatheatrical subject of the Jacobean theatre companies, as we see most clearly in Ben Jonson's *Epicoene*. Jonson's play is a felicitous place to begin, roughly bookending the historical period under investigation: it debuted in 1609/10, when Milton was still a toddler, performed by a group of actors in their late teens and early twenties, who would shortly graduate into adult companies; it was also the first play revived at the Restoration, when the child actor who is silenced at the play's conclusion served to exemplify the disciplinary power of "state-sponsored mirth."[108] Childhood and adulthood, we begin to see in Jonson's play, are power relations as much as developmental stages. But even as the play presents the silent child as an idealized subject of the absolutist state, its transgressive play across the lines of innocence and experience reveals the destabilizing poetic potential of childish things.

The writers in the rest of Part I attempted to purge this instability from the political discourse. Chapter 2 suggests that William Prynne makes this effort particularly clear in both his famous anti-theatrical polemic, *Histrio-Mastix*, and his little-known polemic against children serving as members of the House of Commons, *Minors No Senators* (1646). Justifying parliamentary authority, Prynne insisted, necessitated severing the link between poetic and political representation that was embodied by the presence of child actors in both the Parliament and the playhouse. To claim an authoritative voice, English voters and their representatives would need to leave childish things behind and make rational adulthood the sole basis of political speech.

Prynne was by no means alone in this effort to eliminate the ambiguities of childhood from contractual obligation. Chapter 3 argues, however, that the era's most important political thinker, Thomas Hobbes, approached the same problem from the opposite end: while Prynne and most other Parliament men attempted to base consent on the voices of the decidedly mature, Hobbes downgraded the meaning of consent itself until it could be comprehended by the neonate's most basic acceptance of sustenance. Consent, in Hobbes's absolutist system, operates without choice and obligates without the possibility of dissent. Rather than a dramatic and unpredictable coming-of-age moment, the child signals his membership in society by participating in a "culture" of education and nurture that promises to mobilize humanist education's disciplinary power without its transgressive potential.

Milton's resistance to such efforts defines his work, which is the subject of Part II. The critical heritage has essentially given us two, seemingly distinct Miltons. The first, as Nigel Smith puts it, is dedicated to "positive transformation in all spheres of human activity," an advocate of political liberty, religious freedom, and an emancipated experience of reading even (or especially) when this creates tensions within his theological worldview.[109] The second Milton is the more conservative figure who has found his most powerful recent advocate in Stanley Fish: for him, all external concerns are secondary to a simple insistence on "faith, obedience, chastity of mind and deed" that erases tension and ambiguity from his work.[110] I argue that Milton's embrace of the fraught, complicated coming-of-age moment tracks a course between these two poles.

More than any other writer in this book, Milton is obsessed with the moment when malice supplies the age and with the possibility that one might seize the ability to speak without seizing the inheritance of sin. To do so would be to regain Paradise and speak without subjugation. At the same time, Milton fully recognizes that this is not possible in this life, where we can only "know in part," as the apostle Paul makes clear in a scripture that echoes throughout Milton's oeuvre:

> When I was a child, I spake as a child, I understood as a child, I thought as a child: but when I became a man, I put away childish things. For now we see through a glass, darkly: but then face to face: now I know in part, but then shall I know even as also I am known. (1 Corinthians 13.11–12)

As Augustine glossed the scripture, this means that even "the prophesie of admirable men is to bee compared to that life, as children to a young man."[III] The ultimate goal of existence for those who accept such a view is, as Fish suggests, the annihilation of the childish, individual self at the apocalyptic moment when we finally come face to face with the divine. But for Milton this does not make the childish state one of passive obedience; rather, it is a field of tremendous action, a secular age of vigorous, free endeavor where virtue is formed and prophetic voices arise from silence.

Chapter 4 argues that *Comus*'s engagement with this possibility marks a major turning point both in Milton's career and in the conceptual possibilities of childish voice, realizing the potential that the authors in Part I of the book tried to limit – that the child could actualize a radical, powerful, and independent voice through play. This goal inspired Milton's lifelong engagement with education, and Chapter 5 turns to Milton's pedagogical and political writings to suggest that these works make the childish sensibility a locus of revolutionary reform. Chapters 6 and 7 argue that Milton's great epic, *Paradise Lost*, is his most successful realization of these poetic-pedagogical ideas. In its embrace of error, choice, and trial, the poem offers a counter not only to Hobbes but to all theories of representation, monarchical and republican, that would limit the childish freedom to cultivate a world-changing voice through poetic play. Both theologically and politically unorthodox, Milton populates his poem with fully sexualized, physically adult beings whom he nevertheless endows with all the qualities of apprehension and poetic absorption traditionally associated with childhood. Harnessing the powerful affective associations of childhood without endorsing the idea that the child's subservience or helplessness is also an Edenic ideal, Milton presents a world where choice is never tacit but always in the making. This is a world of sheer dynamism, presided over by a God who is neither the overbearing pedant introduced to Milton studies by Fish nor the God of "indeterminacy and incertitude" proposed by much of the "New Milton Criticism."[112] Rather, he enacts Milton's own pedagogy as he offers his creatures the liberty to grow and explore their own desires.

While these chapters progress chronologically and trace genuine developments in the notions of consent, they avoid the strict trajectory of infancy to voice that we might expect in a triumphant Whig history. As my epilogue makes clear, if I hint at such a narrative, it is strictly a failed one, because the liberal settlement that emerges from this period rests not on the realization of the child's voice but on the occlusion of the child as a speaking subject – the forgetting or repression of children's voices is key to supporting what Carole Pateman has called "the myth of consent."[113] Liberal societies speak for and in the name of children all the time, protecting, educating, and disciplining them. But the problematic voices of children themselves are formally and necessarily excluded from the discussion by this same apparatus, which arose in conjunction with a determined reconceptualization of children as angelic, fragile, and quiet. This book, then, is ultimately a prehistory of consent, where the most powerful voices often emerge not by putting away but by embracing childish things.

PART I

The Growth of Consent and Discipline of Childhood in Early Modern England

CHAPTER I

Coming of Age on Stage
Jonson's Epicoene *and the Politics of Childhood in Early Stuart England*

To begin exploring the relationship between early modern poetics, the child's voice, and the possibility of consent, I want to turn to a very noisy play about a supposedly silent woman – Ben Jonson's *Epicoene*. The play was one of the last performed by the Children of the Blackfriars before the boy actors became official adults and the company disbanded, and this might be enough to call it to our attention. But the play is also about the disruptive power of childish speech, reveling in the torment of the aged and pathologically noise-averse Morose, who discovers to his horror that his young and supposedly silent bride "hath a voice" (5.4.36). As it turns out, "she" is really a boy playing a woman's part, and this fact eventually allows Morose to nullify and escape his onerous marriage. The boy's transformation from silence to speech also allows Jonson to explore theatre's capacity to fashion political subjects by shaping or silencing the child's voice. By attending to this transformation, we can see that transgression and subjugation in *Epicoene* and other children's company productions take place not exclusively or even primarily in the gendered terms that have fascinated recent critics, but across the lines of youth and authority.

As explained in the introduction, children younger than the age of majority were legally "voiceless," from the Latin *infans*, although contemporaries readily acknowledged that despite their "nominal silence," they were capable of making all kinds of noise.[1] Such unmotivated speech is the great metatheatrical subject of the Jacobean children's companies, and it was charged with political significance when *Epicoene* debuted in 1609/10, as James I wrestled with an increasingly vocal Parliament by aggressively promoting the image of himself as a "natural father" to his people and advertising his role as "the virtuous government of his children."[2]

This is the context for a host of Jacobean children's company productions that repeatedly and self-consciously explore the limited agency of their performers, demonstrating the ways drama could test the boundaries of consent and develop self-disciplined subjects. *Epicoene* embraces the idea that dramatic play functions as a gentle discipline, preparing the child for his role in adult society, and I argue that the play eroticizes both this discipline and its resulting, childish subjectivity. Indeed, after two decades of republican upheaval, this aspect of the play made it a suitable choice to be the first play revived at the restoration, as Charles II reasserted his monarchical rights by pointedly reissuing the founding documents of Jacobean patriarchalism.[3] But *Epicoene's* early stage history also demonstrates that such discipline was always problematic, because much of the boy players' popular appeal clearly derived from the way they strode the line between childhood and adulthood, innocence and malice. As it tests that line, *Epicoene* serves as a kind of bookend for the current study: it both demonstrates the counterintuitive theory that a rambunctious play can instill discipline and exemplifies the oppositional potential of childish things that Milton and his fellow radicals would later develop.

To understand these aspects of the play, we must first move away from the critical misprision of the boy players as diminutive, passive performers. They were, instead, young men on the limen between childhood and adulthood, dramatizing a very real crisis of agency at the heart of their society both through their physical presence and through the roles that were written for them (and, in some cases, that they wrote for themselves). Although they were physically and sometimes even legally capable of adult behavior, they remained children in important legal and cultural senses, and as they came of age in public they modeled the possibilities and paradoxes of a populace that would, over the next century, fitfully claim the right to government by consent.

Mannish Women and Childish Men

To understand the political and poetic agency and desires bodied forth by child actors who performed plays like George Chapman, John Marston, and Ben Jonson's *Eastward Ho!* (1605), Francis Beaumont's *Knight of the Burning Pestle* (1607–10), and Jonson's *Epicoene* (1609/10), we first need a much better sense of just how "childish" they really were. Since Lisa Jardine identified the erotic object in Shakespeare's plays not as a woman but a "potentially rapeable boy," an extensive critical tradition has examined the boy actor's body as a site of erotic desire and transvestized transgression, a stage for the performance of gender.[4] But whether the cause is discomfort over what Stephen Orgel has called "the pederastic component of the Elizabethan erotic imagination," or whether the boys' sometimes-advanced age has occluded their conceptual and legal infancy, the specific relationship of the boys' childishness to their eroticization has been little studied and still less understood.[5] Studies of the boys as erotic objects, like Orgel's, tend to suggest that "the fact of transvestite boys is really only incidental" to the reactions they provoked and their function in constructing and deconstructing gender – both boys and women are equally "treated as a medium of exchange within the patriarchal structure, and both are (perhaps in consequence) constructed as objects of erotic attraction for adult men."[6] Likewise, studies of the boys' childishness have generally either steered well clear of their eroticization or seen erotic moments in the plays as heavily ironized or burlesqued, as in Michael Shapiro's influential argument that the children's companies used erotic material "to remind the audience of the obvious disparity between child actors and adult characters."[7] Shapiro's sense of the "visible disparity" between child actors and their adult roles relies on the critical common-place that boy actors were very young, physically slight, and markedly different from the adults who came to see them perform.[8] Michael Witmore likewise claims that the children's companies showcased the "unique capac-ities and cultural connotations of their diminutive performers," while Claire M. Busse contends that "the children's size and youth marks them as vulnerable" both in early plays like *Cynthia's Revels* (1600) and in later ones like *Knight of the Burning Pestle* (1607–10).[9] Peter Stallybrass, que-rying the materiality of Renaissance stage transvestism, assumes that the "body beneath" the female costume includes a "boy's small parts," which are "at variance with the symbolic weight of *the* phallus."[10] In their own ways, each of these critics, and many more, have indicated an ironizing effect as characteristic of children's performance – a disjunction between the actors' appearance as children and the roles they personated, a physical alienation that opened their performance to metatheatrical and discursive play. I want both to affirm and to complicate that analysis by pointing out that most "children" on the English stage in this period were far from the diminutive boys we often imagine. If it seems like I'm having it both ways – arguing that the boys were both physically older and conceptually more childish than we usually realize – that is because the potential to have it both ways was key to the boys' appeal as performers, as subjects, and as erotic objects.

The company that performed *Epicoene* was variously known as the Children of the Blackfriars, Children of Her Majesties Revels, and Children of the Whitefriars.[11] By the time they staged Jonson's play in 1609/10, the actors were no longer young. We have information about the ages of four of the eight actors listed in the folio edition of the play. Nathan

Field, the company's leading player and a possible candidate for *Epicoene*'s title role, was baptized in October 1587, making him twenty-two at the first performance.[12] Based on Field's advanced age, Richard Dutton argues that he probably did not play the childish Epicoene, whom Dauphine describes in the final denouement as "a boy: a gentleman's son" (5.4.199). Dutton proposes Giles Cary (or Gary) instead.[13] A few months earlier, in April 1609, Cary appeared in Jonson's *Entertainment at Britain's Burse* in the role of the Shop Boy, a small part that probably called for singing and that clearly calls attention to the actor's childishness as his master rebukes the untutored boy for his clumsy sales technique.[14] We must, however, qualify Dutton's sense that what set Cary apart from the other actors and qualified him for this role was his unbroken voice and diminutive size. On August 29, 1611, one year after *Epicoene*'s earliest performances, we find a record of "Gilles Gary" signing a 500 pound bond to theatrical financier Philip Henslow along with fellow *Epicoene* actor William Barksted.[15] This is almost certainly the same actor, now in a new company that formed under the patronage of Princess Elizabeth in April 1611. The fact that he signed the bond implies he was at least twenty-one years old by this date and a minimum of nineteen or twenty when *Epicoene* premiered in late 1609 or early 1610, because a bond signed before full adult age would typically be no good.

For example, the former manager of the Children of the Whitefriars, Robert Keysar, sued Cary's fellow actor Barksted for nonpayment of two bonds signed in January 1608/09, almost exactly a year before Barksted performed in *Epicoene*. The bonds came due, and Barksted defaulted, simultaneously with the play's first performance, in January 1609/10. To avoid payment, Barksted argued in court that he was under age twenty-one when he signed the bonds, while Keysar maintained the boy was of full legal age and therefore liable.[16] If Keysar was right, Barksted must have been twenty-two by the time he debuted in Jonson's play, taking the role of Morose according to one early annotator of Jonson's folio.[17] If Barksted was telling the truth, he must have been at least twenty, but was certainly no innocent, because another legal record shows he was arrested in a notorious bawdy house in Field Lane the year *Epicoene* was performed.[18] By September 8, 1610, at the very latest, Barksted seems to have been unquestionably adult, because Richard Graves won a judgment against him for a bond signed on that date.[19] Finally, Hugh Attawell, who likely played Sir Amorous la Foole, was at least seventeen and probably older when the play premiered, because he gave sureties for a friend in a legal document of 1613 that also described him at that date as a "gentleman."[20] In short, the youngest performer we can identify with any certainty was at least seventeen and, even if a slow starter, well down the path to puberty and sexual maturity. The others ranged from nineteen to their early twenties, and this is wholly in line with other known members of the "children's" companies from 1604 to 1610, when they performed many of their most iconic plays.[21] Younger boys may, of course, have been in the play, but much internal evidence points in the direction of age and maturity rather than diminutive childishness.

Truewit, for example, describes Epicoene as an "Amazon" (5.4.230), while Morose chastises his formerly silent wife's surprisingly noisy speech as "Amazonian impudence" (3.5.39), referring to him/her as both Penthesilea (3.4.54), the Amazon Queen who fought against Greeks at Troy, and Semiramis (3.4.54), the Assyrian warrior queen who dressed in male clothes to govern as a man. Any early-seventeenth-century woman who engaged in a traditional male pursuit, like writing, was liable to be charged with Amazonian behavior. But as Kathryn Schwarz has shown, in Renaissance literature these female warriors typically upset gender boundaries not primarily because they are delicate, feminine creatures engaged in male behavior, but because they look like men – strapping, vigorous, yet strangely erotic.[22] In all of *Epicoene*'s references this seems to be the case, as the joke depends on the overt masculinity of this supposed woman. The actor playing Epicoene is not alone in this category – Truewit describes the noisy, aggressive ladies known collectively in the play as the "Collegiates" as "masculine, or rather *hermaphroditicall*" (1.1.79–80), and lest we miss the point, one is named "Centaure," alluding to the mythological beast that was both sexually voracious and half-man. The verbal jabs at mannish women both call attention to their loud, indecorous behavior and wink at actors who are old enough to shave but still playing female roles.

Others have noticed the boys' advanced age, although without always highlighting the ways it disrupts our model of the children's company. Andrew Gurr, for example, notes that "by 1608, there was only one company, no longer boys but young adult players," but without registering the dissonance, he adds that Jonson "obviously valued the children because he could order them to do what he wanted more easily than he could his adult employers."[23] Setting aside, for a moment, the seeming contradiction that Jonson apparently valued these "adult" players for their childlike malleability, the advancing age of the Blackfriar's company raises two possibilities. In the first scenario, as time went by, they became children's companies in name only, a little younger than adult companies like the King's Men, but fundamentally just another group of professional actors. But plays like

Epicoene and *The Knight of the Burning Pestle*, performed two years earlier, clearly market themselves as children's company productions, with generous metatheatrical references to the actors' minority. This raises a second possibility: that the child actor himself was, as Edel Lamb suggests, a kind of "rhetorical and theatrical construct."[24] Drawing from Judith Butler's theories of gender performativity, Lamb calls our attention to the fact that childhood is always a social and discursive construct that bears no absolute relationship to children themselves. Accordingly, child actors were able to "perform" childhood as an institutional fiction even as they aged.[25]

This seems true of *Epicoene*, which routinely reminds the audience to think of the youths on stage as children. *Epicoene*'s Clerimont, for example, displays a flamboyant schoolboyish pique when he accuses Truewit of lecturing him with lessons "from PLUTARCHS moralls, now, or some such tedious fellow" (1.1.62–3). Plutarch's text was a classroom standard and a key humanist source text. It expresses both the view that childhood was "prodigal in its pleasures, restive, and in need of a curb" and the equally central humanist idea that poetry and drama could provide that curb, playfully alluring youths to a greater moral awareness, because "children, if they be rightly nurtured amid poetry, will in some way or other learn to draw some wholesome and profitable doctrine even from passages that are suspect."[26] Clerimont's determination to forsake such lessons in favor of baubles like "pins and feathers" (1.1.64–5) satirizes the life of a dandy by making it seem distinctly childish, like the proverbial infants who would forsake their inheritance for an apple or a bit of ribbon.

Such rhetorical positioning is everywhere in the play. Both Epicoene and Clerimont's boy, who could have been doubled by a single actor, appear prepubescent: Truewit says Epicoene is "a'most of yeers, & will make a good visitant within this twelve-month" (5.4.248), while Lady Haughty and her companions call the boy "innocent" (1.1.18), kissing, carrying, and tossing him around in a way that implies a diminutive presence. Still more surprising, when Otter poses as a lawyer secured to pry Morose out of his marriage, he proposes "That a *boy, or child, under yeeres, is not fit for marriage, because he cannot reddere debitum*. So your *omnipotentes* – " (5.3.184–5). Otter is a fool, so perhaps the joke, as he trails off into incoherence, is how wildly inapplicable such a principle would be to the aged Morose, who was surely played by one of the company's older boys. But while Truewit corrects Otter's confusion of "omnipotentes" for "impotentes," he does not correct the legal principle invoked – the idea that children below a certain age are incapable of certain adult, sexual, acts.

Morose too embraces this absurdity in another moment of metatheatrical flair, proclaiming "I am no man, ladies," as he attempts to use Otter's principle to void his marriage (5.4.44). Jonson seems to be playing here with a metatheatrical indication that the aging actor playing the aged Morose really is a child, and quite a young one.

The canon law generally set a minimum marital age of fourteen for boys and twelve for girls, but only marriages below age seven were deemed absolute nullities owing to sexual and intellectual incapacity. Between ages seven and fourteen, puberty could be proved by inspection (which Truewit and Mrs. Otter propose), or the marriage could be considered valid but "imperfect," giving both parties a way out once they finally reached the age of discretion.[27] The prominent seventeenth-century jurist Edward Coke calls such marriages "inchoate," and gives a good indication of just how diminutive a bride and groom would need to be for a marriage to become automatically invalidated when he proposes that a nine-year-old widow can receive full dowry, "what age soever her husband be, albeit he were but four yeares old."[28] As much as Jonson is poking fun at Otter and playing on his actors' identification as children by asking us to imagine them in these terms, he seems also to be taking advantage of the absurd disjunction between capacity and social expectation that such legal principles imply.

At such moments Jonson's play points very directly to the child's body even as it represents that body in more diminutive terms than was the actual case. The result must have been something like what Bertolt Brecht called *verfremdung*, an alienation effect that arises from the deliberate obtrusion of artifice into a play, as the child actor suddenly shows the audience that he is also an actor playing a child.[29] For Brecht, such moments make the ordinary seem suddenly strange, demystifying the hidden workings of the world. But because this artifice works in the opposite way from what we have traditionally understood – not with tiny children enacting adult roles, but with grown men performing infantile disability – it could be politically dangerous on the Jacobean stage at a time when the king actively promoted his reign as the government of childish subjects.

This patriarchal governance depended on what Jonathan Goldberg has described as a "mystification" of James's body that conflated the king's political and personal identities, making even unprecedented absolutist claims seem "naturalized, familiarized, supported by hierarchies of head and body, husband and wife, father and child."[30] We can see the infantilizing effect of such mystification in the doggerel verse that James penned shortly after he dismissed Parliament in 1621, encouraging an Epicoene-like silence from his people and their representatives:

> Oh stay your teares, you whoe complaine
> And cry as babes doe all in vaine
> Turbulent people why doe you prate
> Too shallow for the depth of state
> You cannot judge what's truly mine.[31]

James circulated his manuscript in response to an anonymous verse libel entitled "The Commons' Tears" that expressed some parliamentarians' increasingly vocal demands on taxation and foreign policy. By turns menacing and condescending, the king's paternalism deliberately renders such demands voiceless, their dissent only an infantile prating or subhuman "houleinge sounde / That rise as vapours from the grounde."[32] As noted in the introduction, during this era Britain underwent an uneven transition to a government based on consent rather than birth. But as the stirrings of this change clashed with his absolutist ambitions, it is easy to imagine James in the guise of Jonson's Morose, with dozens of caps pulled over his ears to stop the noise – and easier still to understand why actors performing childhood or shedding their silent infancy on stage could carry a political charge.

These legal and political dimensions of age make it necessary to qualify Lamb's important argument that companies like the Queen's Revels performed childhood. While she correctly notes that "the physical age of the players is, to an extent, incidental to the representation of them as children," it does not follow that "whether or not the parts of Morose and Epicoene are played by young boys is not important."[33] As this book's opening anecdote about the thirty- and forty-year-old boys in the Children of the Queens Revels of Bristol shows, contemporaries paid close attention to the physical age of children, and Henry Cuffe's well-documented assertion that childhood "lasteth (for the most part) untill wee be five and twentie yeeres old" should warn us against understanding childhood as merely a theatrical fiction.[34] For Cuffe and his contemporaries, childhood was also a visible, physical state, "proportionable unto the *Spring*, hot and moist."[35] The grey area surrounding childhood was vast, but writers like Coke and Hale show this heightened rather than eliminated scrutiny, making the boundary between childhood and adulthood the proving ground for questions of consent and self-determination.

We need only look at the Barksted lawsuit to begin to see how the boys' very specific ages allowed them to perform the vexed status of childhood with all its possibilities and perils. Recall that Robert Keysar, the theatrical manager of the Blackfriar's Children, signed two bonds with Barksted around a year before the boy took the stage in *Epicoene*, probably as the litigious Morose. The amount of money – 29 pounds – was not negligible; 10 pounds was a decent yearly wage for a skilled laborer and 20 was a good salary for a schoolmaster. Keysar was a member of the Goldsmith's guild and a sharp financier, unlikely to sign a bond without proper assurances that he would receive a return on his investment: his testimony that he believed Barksted was twenty-one seems entirely credible. So was the infant Barksted performing adulthood when he signed the bonds? If we take his word, he seems slyly to have undertaken an action that the law granted him no power to do, using his status as a voiceless *infant* who cannot speak a binding oath as a kind of privileged license to borrow money with immunity from repayment. Put another way, he recognized that the ability to speak, to give an oath and so to leave voiceless infancy behind, represented both freedom and fall. To speak with authority, as subject rather than object, was to bind oneself into debts and obligations that childhood performances potentially evaded.

Another possibility exists: when he stood before the judge, did Barksted use maturational ambiguity to slip back across the line from adult to child? For our purposes, the answer does not matter so much as it matters that we recognize his deliberate exploitation of the legal and cultural ambiguities surrounding childhood, both to participate in his society and to evade its strictures. These were the same ambiguities the boys exploited on stage in *Epicoene* and that Keysar himself leveraged when he marketed the performances of a man he thought was twenty-one as part of his "children's company." Rather than the boys wearily performing a tired fiction of childhood, every indication points to a much more dynamic situation, with both the boys and the playwrights who wrote for them exploiting their liminal status for maximum effect. In plays performed by the Children of the Blackfriars, the boys' specific age on the cusp of adulthood made their performance of childhood a site of profound anxiety, irony, and energy – a space for determining when voices became more than noise.

Objects and Subjects

Tracking the boys' maturation as part of her larger repertory history, Lucy Munro suggests that "during the first decade of James's reign the Queen's Revels' actors gradually stopped being objects – boy actors controlled by a managing syndicate or the passive cause of lust in an audience – and became subjects, taking a progressively more active role in the company."³⁶ Munro's company "biography" does not explain how this dynamic relates to broader political developments, but I would argue that *Epicoene* enacts this process of objects becoming subjects at a moment when coming of age on stage could not fail to be political.³⁷ For the subject within James's patriarchal structure, as for the child actor performing in and presented by *Epicoene*, subjectivity was tremendously vexed, defined both by the ability to speak and by the limitations imposed on that speech. In the year of *Epicoene*'s debut, for example, James emphasized this aspect of his fatherly authority as he encouraged reluctant Members of Parliament (MPs) to assure a fixed royal income by accepting his conditions on the Great Contract. "I would not willingly press you," he told the Parliament on May 20, 1610, and "neither would I have you press me ... I shewed you in a glass my intention. My motion to you is not to abuse my mirror nor to break it. Come with those motions to me that yourselves may have no fear of a contrary success."³⁸ In his pose as a gentle disciplinarian, James draws here on the familiar model of mimetic childhood education to argue that the role of parliamentarians was not to speak their own desires but to learn to reflect and internalize his own. His approach shows why careful historians generally speak of government by "assent" rather than "consent" in Jacobean England.³⁹

James's warning that the parliament must not "abuse" his glass refers not only to the proverbial idea that children learn by mirroring but also to the notion that these prerational creatures were apt to play with (and break) mirrors as they attempted to touch or talk to the images reflected there, looking "behinde the Glasse, to finde out the Babe that [they] seeth."⁴⁰ Such references were surely not lost on Parliament, where, as I discuss in the following chapter, actual children elected as MPs served as a constant reminder that the representative body's role was as much symbolic and theatrical as authoritative.⁴¹ Far from passively accepting the model of child-like subservience, however, parliamentarians increasingly began calling on one another to grow up and leave childish things behind. The member for Arundel, John Tey, accordingly responded to James's call for childish mimesis by defiantly noting that "If we should retorne into our contry with nothing for the good of our common wealth, they would say that [we have] bene all this while like children in ketching butterflies."⁴² In his diary, another MP anonymously echoed this fear of returning "empty-handed like children" as if "we had voices in parliament only to give subsidies or give subsidies to have voices in parliament."⁴³ But growing up without guilt was easier said than done. As the king's staunch parliamentary ally George

More reminded his fellow MPs, "*Conscientia*, was *frenum ante peccatum, and flagrum post peccatum*, and *omne sub regno*": conscience was a curb to prevent transgression and a whip afterwards.[44] His point is that to act as a loyal subject one must internalize the whip – a pedagogical model embraced by even the staunchest advocates of Humanist soft discipline, like Juan Luis Vives, who argued that the rod should be kept in sight at all times ("*disciplinae virga perpetuo ante oculos pueri*"), even in a classroom governed by love and play rather than corporal punishment.[45]

Taking the stage in the midst of such debates, what kind of subjectivity did the boys in *Epicoene* embody? Or, to put that question in the terms that *Epicoene* itself suggests, what is the difference between speaking as an object and as a subject, and what role does performance play in the transformation? First, it helps clarify the boys' status in the eyes of law and civic society. In brief, children of any age were essentially conceptualized as chattel, which is Coke's closest analogue for wards until age twenty-one. Some "chattels reals," Coke notes, "cannot be severed, as in the case aforesaid, where two be possessed of the wardship of the bodie of an infant within age."[46] Like the very young infants who were sometimes married before they could speak, with adults ventriloquizing their vows, such children could make binding agreements, but "disagree they cannot," Coke explains – a very limited form of consent without the possibility of dissent.[47]

The trail of lawsuits and indentures they left in their wake makes it abundantly clear that the boy actors shared this status. Henry Evans, proprietor of the Blackfriars, supplied his company with boys by partnering with Nathaniel Giles, the Master of the Children of the Chapel Royal, who held a royal commission allowing him to "take such and so Children as he or his Deputie shall think meete in all Cathedrall Collegiat parish Churches Chappells and schooles" to furnish the Royal chapel with "well singing Children."[48] This was effectively a license to kidnap, and it became problematic only when the men slipped up and kidnapped someone whose elevated social status trumped his age-related identity as an object ripe for exploitation. This was the case in 1600 when, evidently according to their normal technique, the entrepreneurial kidnappers conspired "vyolently and unlawfully to surprise … Thomas Clifton," snatching the thirteen-year-old as he passed between his father's house and his grammar school, "and with like violence and force to carry unto the … play howse in the blackfryers."[49] The description comes from the deposition given by the boy's father, Henry Clifton, a member of the Norfolk gentry who argued that it was "not fitt that a gentleman of his sort should have his sonne & heire ... to be so basely used" and so took the case to the Star Chamber.[50] The affront is to the father, although the son was the one kidnapped and ordered to learn his parts "by harte" or "be surely whipped."[51]

The deposition names several other boys abducted in this manner, including Salomon Pavy, whose death in 1602 inspired Jonson's "Epitaph on S.P.," where he described the boy as "a child that so did thrive / In grace and feature, / As Heaven and Nature seem'd to strive / Which own'd the creature" (5–8). The deposition also names Nathan Field, who was fortunate enough to escape being owned by heaven but who was essentially owned by his theatrical company for the next eight years and was a legal adult still being presented as a child when he took the stage in *Epicoene*. Such cases were not unique to this company or its managers: at the Canterbury grammar school, for example, where Christopher Marlowe was a student in 1578–79, the children were apparently so adept at presenting their yearly "tragedies, Commedyes and interludes" that two scoundrels "inveigled the scolars ... to go abrode in the cuntrey to play plays contrary to lawe and good order."[52] Again, the children were caught between competing authorities – although the boys in this case were faulted for their disorderly ways, the adults who seduced them away were ultimately held responsible. The whole affair was akin to a property dispute: the boys' performances were valuable commodities and their voices readily alienable for profit.[53]

Perhaps because of high-profile scandals like the Clifton case, Giles received a new patent in 1606 specifying that boys conscripted for the chapel should not be "used or imployed as Comedians or Stage players," but by this point the company that performed *Epicoene* had established its core personnel and this did not change their condition. Indeed, two decades later the career of Stephen Hammerton with the revived Children of the Revels provides a striking reminder of the boy players' continuing status as objects. Hammerton, who went on to a successful career with the King's Men, was one of fourteen boys caught up in a legal dispute over the Children of the Revels' control in 1632. An investor named Christopher Babham bought a share in the company from the actor Richard Gunnell, who promised to deliver the boy actors and other theatrical properties. But Babham later explained that he was unable to meet his financial commitments because the theatre's assets were in much worse shape than he had been led to believe:

> The boys were delivered to your subject in far worse plight than he hoped, for amongst fourteen of them there was not found seven shirts, and but

five sheets and a half to lodge them in, their apparel so ragged and so altogether unprovided of fitting necessaries that being in the time of pestilence
it might have endangered your subject's life that was constrained to look
over and provide a supply to their wants. Divers of them were likewise sick,
and one of them died occasioned by an ill diet, some of them being forced
to steal, others to beg for want of sustenance. He likewise further showeth
that of the goods whereof he had an inventory delivered, there were divers
things wanting.[54]

Gunnell denied that the boys had been forced to steal and beg their
bread, but his defense of their treatment further emphasizes the sense that
they were essentially chattel. According to Gunnell, before his purchase,
Babham "did take a view of all the boys and the said complainant did very
well approve and like of them and did desire that he might have them."[55]
As we consider the boy players' capacity to present estranged agency in
works like *Epicoene*, the most interesting thing about this lawsuit is the
way the plaintiff describes the boys as just another part of the inventory.
Indeed, as a star performer and valuable theatrical property, Hammerton
was later singled out in a countersuit by one of the company's original
owners, who asserted that Babham had unjustly "possessed himself not
only of the said apparel bands, cuffs, gorgettes, lawn, two pieces of arras
and other commodities so bought by your subject ... but also of the said
apprentice."[56]

This objectified status was not merely incidental to the children's performance, but constituted a key part of its dramatic appeal. The company that performed *Epicoene* was essentially the same one that Mary
Bly has described, during its brief run at the Whitefriars Theatre from
1607–08, openly advertising its "sodomitical boy" actors.[57] They performed *Epicoene* under a different name and in a different location, but
Jonson's play makes it clear both that their erotic identity remains intact
and that it derives from their objectification. In the opening scene, for
example, Clerimont's boy announces that when he visits Lady Haughty
he is the "welcomest thing under a man" (1.1.9.10), and Lamb is surely
being uncharacteristically naive when she reads this only as an imaginative
"return to the state of the unbreeched child."[58] No doubt the idea that the
boy is "under a man" works, on one level, as part of the performance of
an artfully and imaginatively diminutive childhood. But the boy is also a
"thing," an object clearly subjugated to the other men and women in the
play. And not just any object: a "thing" is a familiar pun on the penis – as
in Shakespeare's Sonnet 20, where the male beloved has "one thing to my
purpose nothing."[59] Lest we forget the pun, Truewit enters a few lines later

and calls the boy an "engle" (1.1.24), or male prostitute, and all of this, combined with the fact that the boy was played by an actor in his late teens or early twenties, would have made it clear that he was capable of at least one kind of adult action. To be "under" a man is to be an object of both power and desire.

The way *Epicoene* orients these forces on the limen between object and subject, youth and adulthood, suggests the fundamentally political dynamics of the play's erotic content. Bruce Smith notes that "Renaissance Englishmen, like the ancient Greeks and Romans, eroticized the power distinctions that set one male above another in society. Sexual desire took shape in the persons of master and minion; sexual energy found release in the power play between them."[60] In the Jacobean period these erotic power relationships most commonly played out across the lines of youth and authority. "Thy dear dad sends thee his blessing," writes King James in a series of unsettlingly erotic letters to his "dear sweet child," the Duke of Buckingham (1592–1628), frankly urging the royal favorite to return to court or to produce offspring so "that I may have sweet bedchamber boys to play with me."[61] To call such language "homoerotic" or even "sodomitical" is accurate, but only when we recognize that when Edward Coke writes about the crime of sodomy in the seventeenth century, as Smith notes, he "treats the forcible rape of an underaged boy as the only kind of act in which the law takes an interest."[62] Coke, in his own words, does not seem to identify a crime of "buggery" that is not also what he calls "*paederastes*" or "*amator puerorum*."[63] Sodomy, so defined, depends specifically on a lack of consent or even the impossibility of consent, and the most common paradigm for understanding that impossibility in early modern England is infancy.

In fact, one qualification needed in Bly's account of the stage ingle is that the term can imply not merely a catamite or homosexual prostitute but a childish sexual plaything adaptable to all uses, enflaming both male and female desire. The wholly mimetic Ape of Pleasure in Richard Brathwaite's (1588–1673) bizarre *Age for Apes* exemplifies the type. "Trained for Ladies Secrets" since his "first infancy," he becomes a lady's "*Ingle, Gue,* her *Sparrow bill,* / And in a word, my *Ladies* what you will."[64] The boy plays his part – any part – to perfection, but his part provides pleasures that are not his own. This is exactly the kind of scene Clerimont's boy describes when he visits Lady Haughty and her mannish, sexually voracious women: "The gentlewomen play with me, and throw me o' the bed, and carry me in to my lady; and she kisses me with her oil'd face; and puts a perruke o' my head and asks me an I will weare her gowne" (1.1.12–15).

Ultimately, Lady Haughty releases the boy and calls him "innocent," and this innocence and the potential to violate it constitutes his appeal. Whether or not this is the same boy who, in the final scene, will stand passively as Dauphine "*takes off Epicoene's perruke*" (5.4.198), the play highlights the forces that determine the young actors' roles and direct their speech.

From his first experiments with the children's companies Jonson had explored the way the child actors' mimetic capacities allowed them to fulfill such roles, as we see in *Cynthia's Revels*, which was performed in 1600 by a freshly kidnapped Nathaniel Field. In the very metatheatrical induction the boy actors play themselves, arguing with a pretended audience member who desires to speak with the author. "Wee are not so officiously befriended by him, as to have his presence in the tiring house," one boy explains, but he makes it clear that the young actors are "fine engles," and "if you please to conferre with our Author, by atturney, you may, sir: our proper self here, stands for him" (ind. 165, 168–70). To be an ingle here does not only mean that the boys can be bought and sold or that they are the blank slate on which others may project their desires. It also seems to be connected to their ability to represent those others. The author accordingly voices his disgust, by attorney, with the kind of audience member who lacks adequate learning to appreciate his plays, who has more fashion than sense, who calls "all by the name of fustian, that his grounded capacitie cannot aspire to" (ind. 121–2, 214–15).

Even when the children appear to offer us a peek behind the mask, these "unscripted" moments are still, with a wink and a nudge, part of a script that claims to dictate their every move. The boys may claim the "Author" is conspicuously absent, but we hear him or his actual attorney just off stage, chiding the children for every misstep and deviation: "Why Children," this disembodied voice asks at one point in *Cynthia's Revels*, "are you not asham'd?" (ind. 11). The children's representational power derives from their blank status, lack of agency, and passive ability to be inscribed and reinscribed at will. Even when they pretend to respond spontaneously to the audience, their actions are predetermined. These are children representing child actors representing their author, a dizzying series of refractions that present the boy player as a purely imaginary or symbolic figure, tossed from one masterful imitation to the next.

This is "play," in its most pure, childish form, but it could not be more different from the way we usually think of play as a kind of freedom, or as Johan Huizinga defines it, "a free activity standing quite consciously outside 'ordinary' life."[65] Instead, in Jonson's works, play is a radically limited kind of agency; as we shall see in Chapter 3, Thomas Hobbes drew on a related notion of play, or "the absence of obstacles to motion," to suggest that there was no conflict between "liberty" and the most abject forms of servitude, as long as slaves, children, or other subjects are not physically bound (*DC* 9.9.167). The child's ludic sensibility was characteristic of a time of life that was, as Plutarch describes it, "prodigal in its pleasures, restive, and in need of a curb," and the brilliance of the humanistic pedagogy was to propose that play itself could provide this curb.[66]

It is no wonder that many "Puritan moralists" reacted instinctively against play, as Leah Marcus notes, especially when they identified forms of it in the liturgy.[67] Such contemporaries recognized the erotic potential of these displays of subjugating power, and this became a key part of the most virulent anti-theatrical attacks. The self-described "scourge" of stage plays, William Prynne, claims that the child actor's appeal lies partly in the satanic thrill of seeing innocence corrupted.[68] The Christian child's acting of wanton parts amounts to the misuse of a sacred body "devoted unto God in baptism," and this misappropriation works to "exhilerate a confluence of unchaste, effeminate, vaine companions."[69] Prynne's language implies a kind of delirium, expressing the familiar anti-theatrical concern that the evacuation of agency performed by the boys was not only erotic but also infectious. If the boys were blank slates onto which an audience could write its desires, they also incited dangerous desires and "sparkles of lust" in the audience, according to John Rainolds (1549–1607), who worried that this "flame of lust may bee kindled in the hearts of men, as redie for the most part to conceve this fire, as flaxe is the other."[70] Rather than becoming active subjects, the boys inspire irresistible lust, an infectious irrationality that replicates their own objectification. As we shall see in the next chapter, Prynne describes this subjugating power specifically as infantilization and he believes it unites poetic and political representation in an unholy alliance that prevents men from exercising authoritative consent.

This age-inflected power dynamic has major implications for our understanding of sex and gender on the stage. When Truewit casually refers to the boy as Clerimont's "engle" in *Epicoene's* opening moments (1.1.25) it is not quite accurate to say that "the fact serves as nothing more than one of a number of indications of the easy and pleasant life of a London playboy," as Orgel's influential account has it.[71] Quite the contrary, the opening scene stages a forced performance and insists on its force. Clerimont has written a satirical song, which he orders the reluctant boy to perform in a scene that must have been familiar not only to boy actors but to other survivors of the English educational system:

CLERIMONT: Ha' you got the song yet perfect I ga' you, boy?
BOY: Yes, sir.
CLERIMONT: Let me hear it.
BOY: You shall, sir, but, I'faith, let nobody else. (1.1.1–4)

Clerimont's imperious tone reeks of the pedagogue, and the boy's life as an ingle must be understood in this disciplinary context as well as in his role as a childish object of unbounded desire.

Indeed, when we consider the force behind the performance, we can see more clearly why proponents of theatrical, humanistic education had long identified the theater, even in its apparently transgressive moments, as essentially disciplinary. In his 1592 defense of cross-dressed boy actors against Puritan attacks, William Gager wrote that the practice was meant "honestly to embowlden owre yuthe; to trye their voyces, and confirme their memoryes; to frame their speeche; to conforme them to convenient action; to trye what mettel is in everye one."[72] Gager's primary intention here is to defend school and university drama, not the public stage. But the same educational and disciplinary logic facilitated the emergence of child companies on London's public stage, which drew their actors from grammar schools and, even in the charters that allowed for the worst abuses of impressment, framed the children's service as part of their ongoing education. Nathanial Giles's commission of 1604, for example, claims the enterprise is for the "advancement helpe and futherance of such Children as shalbe taken," and provides for a seamless transition to a university or other appropriate educational institution to continue this education at the end of their service.[73]

This disciplinary role is pronounced in *Epicoene*, which ultimately frames the performance of the cross-dressed boy at its center not as an act of rebellion but as a study in discretion. "Let it not trouble you that you have discover'd any mysteries to this yong gentleman," says Truewit, in the lines that end the play, "He is (a'most) of yeeres, & will make a good visitant within this twelve-month. In the meane time wee'll all undertake for his secrecie, that can speak so well of his silence" (5.4.242–46). The boy's performance functions like the play as a whole, as a carefully released and modulated display of transgressive energy. The parenthetical "(a'most)" continues to emphasize his liminality, the bare technical qualification that prevents this star performer from being "of yeers" right now. It is enough to keep him silent.

Of course the boy has not been silent in any conventional sense at all, and the claim for his discretion rests on the ironies of this disciplinary strategy. Epicoene's usefulness as part of Dauphine's plan to thwart his uncle's marriage and remain the older man's sole heir depends on nonstop garrulity that drives Morose to desperation. The boy has been silent in that he has performed another voice at the expense of his own, suppressed any expression of self that was not part of the role that Dauphine crafted as he instructed and trained the boy "this half year at my great charges" (5.4.200). All actors perform the voices of others, but the child actor does so with a peculiar irony that is one of the most remarkable and least remarked features of the play: the boy who has successfully *acted* the part of a silent woman truly and finally becomes voiceless only when Dauphine removes the female costume and the fiction ends. From this point in the play, he never speaks another word. Becoming a subject, in this regime, means neither gaining nor losing rights so much as confirming the transfer of disciplinary power from parents or masters to the state and, ultimately, to the self. To learn to speak is to assent to this transfer, to recognize the boundaries of fiction within which one can act and be heard.

That, at least, was the ideal, although like all ideals it was imperfectly realized. The boys performing *Epicoene* were near the very end of this educational trajectory, and as the lawsuit between Barksted and Keyser indicates, they had begun to act outside and even against the paternal structure provided by the company, which theoretically was expected both to reap the profits of their labor and to meet their tutorial and physical needs. In most cases they remained legally voiceless, but their performances on and off stage demanded careful scrutiny to determine the moment when childhood innocence fell away. In the same year as *Epicoene*, we even find records of the boys receiving payment independently of the company for their roles performing and coauthoring Jonson's *Entertainment at Britain's Burse*. For Field in particular, this shift in the economics of his work would seem to mark a seamless transition from object to subject, as he was paid for staying "up all night wryting the speeches, songes and inscriptions" that he would speak.[74] Field would soon become a shareholder in the King's Men and author of independent works, his career an apparent validation of the educational ambitions of both the children's theatre system and the core humanist tenant that adult voice develops through poetic immersion and play. In conversations with Drummond, Jonson in fact singled Field out as "his Schollar," describing a loving tutorial relationship in which the older dramatist "read to him the Satires of Horace and some Epigrams of Martial" (1:137).

But even after he began to be paid for his efforts, Field continued to characterize his early authorial attempts as child's labor. In the tribute he wrote, at nearly the same time, for the 1610 printing of John Fletcher's *Faithful Shepherdess*, Field deferentially protests that his "name and muse (in swathing clowtes) / Is not yet growne to strength."[75] This is not mere rhetoric, but an acknowledgment that childhood as a cultural and conceptual category could last beyond even the legal threshold that Field had by this point crossed. Law was too blunt an instrument to deal with a concept of such flickering uncertainty as age and authority, and Field navigates this terrain more subtly in a poem that simultaneously protests his infancy and announces the birth of a new voice. In relation to parents or other authority figures, one could remain a child indefinitely – a fact Field acknowledges in the quarto of the first play he wrote himself, *A Woman is a Weathercock* (1612), which gives pride of place to a poem by George Chapman identifying Field as his "loved Sonne."[76] Even later, in *Bartholomew Fair* (1614), when the hapless Bartholomew Cokes (perhaps played by Field) encounters a puppet show, he quickly asks which of the "minors" is the star of the "young company": "Your best actor, your Field?" (5.4.87). As Witmore has shown, part of the child actor's appeal was precisely his identity as a kind of puppet or "pretty creature" – a purely alienated agency. All grown up, Field and the author were still trading on his identity as a childish thing, given voice by the master who holds the strings.

Such late references may be partly ironic, banking on the audience's knowledge of Field's previous career. But they also acknowledge something that seventeenth-century legal scholars like Matthew Hale had made clear: it was nearly impossible to draw a fixed line between childhood and adulthood in a culture that registered power and authority in terms of age. Hale shows that neither positive achievements nor a set age of discretion were able to account for inceptive agency with real clarity in borderline cases: only the doctrine of *malitia supplet aetatem*, or "malice supplies the age," could close the door on childish things once and for all.[77]

Jonson's theatre, however, explicitly disclaims such malice, as does the humanistic tradition that inspires it, by recommending mimetic play to effect a seamless transition from object to subject. The title page of *Epicoene* includes an epigram from one of the Horatian satires that Jonson had shared with Field to this effect: "*cur metuas me?*" ("why should you fear me?"). The passage comes from Horace's fourth satire, in which the poet famously defends his poems by highlighting their educational function and disclaiming their subversive intent, claiming that "malice shall be far from my pages" (*vitium procul afore chartis*).[78] But despite such protestations, Jonson's Horatian ambitions were often in dramatic conflict with the realities of his theatre: on the most basic level, Horace claims his satires are innocent because they are private, whereas the theatre is very public, and malice seems to have been a hot ticket on the Blackfriar's stage.[79]

Boys Gone Bad

The company that performed *Epicoene* was famous, or infamous, for testing the limen that divided youth and innocence from transgressive adulthood, pushing as far as possible before authority pushed back. In 1605, Samuel Daniel was hauled before the Privy Council after the boys performed his *Philotas*, a play that dangerously invoked a romanticized Essex in its young, prodigal, and rebellious hero.[80] Ironically, the episode cost Daniel his position as Master of the Revels – the person in charge of licensing and censoring plays – but the company itself does not seem to have suffered much from the affair. Nor did they shy from controversy, and by the next year the boys' performance of Jonson, Marston, and Chapman's *Eastward Ho!* landed two of its authors in prison for its barely veiled satire of the king and his Scottish entourage (Marston went into hiding to avoid the threatened physical mutilation). Still the boys themselves were unscathed and continued to play, taking the stage in 1606 with yet another play that provoked the authorities' wrath, John Day's *Isle of Gulls*. The play's depiction of a king smitten by love for a boyish Amazon glanced at James's own penchant for attractive young men, but this time the performance as much as the subject matter seems to have been at issue. Although the plot is an Arcadian romance, the boys adopted thick Scottish accents in what must have been a campy, travestied production, and this may finally have demonstrated the malice that supplied the age. Sir Edward Hoby wrote to the diplomat Sir Thomas Edmondes describing the whole affair and noting that "sundry were committed to Bride-well," with the implication that the actors themselves were held culpable.[81] The episode certainly provoked a minor crisis in the Children of the Queen's Revels, which lost the queen's patronage and was quickly reconstituted as the "Children of the Blackfriars." In this guise they performed *The Knight of the Burning Pestle* and other fare that ironically showcased the aging boys' childishness before again running afoul of the authorities in 1608.

At this time they performed both Chapman's *Conspiracy and Tragedy of Charles, Duke of Byron*, which gave offense to the French ambassador, and a lost play that openly mocked King James. As the French ambassador Antoine de la Boderie made clear in a letter, the boys themselves had now definitely crossed the line into bad agency and were held accountable:

> About mid-Lent those very actors whom I had barred from playing the history of the late Marshal de Biron, noting all the court to be away, did so nonetheless.... I went to see the Earl of Salisbury and made a complaint to him that not only were those members of the troupe contravening the prohibition made against them but they were adding to it things not only more serious, but ... all false, at which in truth he showed great anger. And at once he sent orders to arrest them. However only three were found, who were at once put into prison where they are still; but the principal culprit, the author, escaped. A day or two before, they had slandered their King, his mine in Scotland and all his Favorites in a most pointed fashion; for having made him rail against heaven over the flight of a bird and have a gentleman beaten for calling off his dogs, they portrayed him as drunk at least once a day.[82]

The author remains the principal culprit, but the boys are more than passive channels for his voice, and the fact that they must be ferreted out of hiding helps confirm their guilt according to the legal precedents governing young offenders. Another report, by Sir Thomas Lake, who was travelling with the king, confirms that James was so incensed over the behavior by "the children of the blackfriars" that he "had vowed they should never play more, but should first begg their bred."[83]

Throughout all the turmoil, the company retained a core group of actors, boys like Field who were impressed into service in the earlier 1600s. Over the period leading up to *Epicoene* they went by various names – The Children of the Revels, The Children of the Queen's Revels, The Children of the Blackfriars – and even changed location to the Whitefriars theatre, but despite these changes, their brand only seems to have solidified. Their plays pushed sexual and political boundaries and offered a constant risk of transgression, a display of juvenescence that walked a tightrope between innocent object and malicious subject. This must have registered as a profound metatheatrical moment in the scene where a horrified Morose realizes that his new bride has a voice:

MOROSE: You can speak then!
EPICOENE: Yes, sir.
MOROSE: Speak out I mean.
EPICOENE: I sir. Why, did you think you had married a statue? or a motion, onely? one of the *French* puppets, with the eyes turn'd with a wire? or some innocent out of the hospitall? (3.4.34–40)

The puppet talks back at the same moment the boys had begun taking an active role in the company and the authorities had begun questioning who was pulling the strings. As late as 1612, long after the early, diminutive performers were a distant memory, Thomas Heywood famously complained about "the liberty which some arrogate to themselves, committing their bitternesse, and liberall invectives against all estates, to the mouthes of Children, supposing their juniority to be a priviledge for any rayling."[84] He advised a stricter discipline, "to curbe and limit this presumed liberty within the bands of discretion and government," but watching the youths and their authors navigate and violate those disciplinary bands was clearly part of the appeal.[85]

Despite the king's threat, the boys were playing again within the year, in a work whose very title, *Epicoene*, promised another dazzling tightrope walk. The term derives from Latin and Greek grammar, referring to nouns that can denote either the masculine or feminine gender or, as Charles Hoole put it in his popular Latin textbook, that "signifieth both sexes under one Article."[86] The epicene was also popular shorthand for sexual indeterminacy, and Otter's discussion of the sexual incapacity of children reminds us that this indeterminacy, in the period, was characteristic of childhood.[87] From the beginning, the play showcases this liminal ambiguity. In the opening scene, when Clerimont's boy claims to be the "welcomest thing under a man," he prompts Clerimont's bemused "I think, and above a man, too, if the truth were racked out of you" (1.1.9.10–11). In part, this repartee merely extends the eroticization discussed earlier – but it carefully orients that eroticization on the threshold of youth, neither over nor under the age of adulthood. It is this liminality, rather than the mere fact of the homoeroticism, that opens up real transgressive potential.

Clerimont's suspicion that the boy may really be "above a man" invites several readings: he is an adult pretending to be a child, he is a "top" rather than a "bottom," he is the seducer rather than the seduced. *Epicoene* explores and tests such possibilities in the same ways the company's earlier performances tested boundaries between innocent comedy and politically culpable satire. Accordingly, the main plot displays the disruptive potential of youth, perhaps most obviously when Dauphine outwits and usurps his uncle, a contest pitting youth against age. The contrast is made clear by Truewit, who repeatedly refers to Dauphine as an "innocent" (1.2.54), and most dramatically by the aged Morose himself, who in his moment of surrender offers to switch places with Dauphine: "My whole estate is thine. Manage it, I will become thy ward" (5.4.170). Even as it upends the relationship, the scene's invocation of the wardship system brings this private moment into conversation with an issue of real public urgency: James's typical response to parliamentary recalcitrance was to eke more money out of the Court of Wards, making this the most visible and controversial area where the crown exploited children's utter lack of agency to raise money (this exploitation also had an erotic valence, as the king and the MPs referred to wardships as "the fair Helen" that all sides wooed).[88] Using the theatrical tools of cross-dressing and performance, Dauphine seems to have found a way to upset the social order that makes such exploitation possible and to appropriate it for himself.

On a metatheatrical level, too, the play parades youth's disruptive power in the camp sexuality of the boy actors who play the Collegiates. The Collegiates draw their members from both court and city, and their sexual voraciousness simultaneously emblematizes both the traditional decadence of the court and the undesirable upward mobility of the city wives and their merchant milieu. Their sexual availability also suggestively advertises boy actors whose "deere acquaintance," Thomas Dekker hinted in a contemporary pamphlet, "you may (with small cost) purchase."[89] "My chamber, sir, my Page shall show you," Haughty whispers to Dauphine (5.2.20–21), while Mavis offers Dauphine an "Italian riddle," which reads in part "if I might be so honor'd, as to appear at any end of so noble a worke, I would enter into a fame of taking physique to morrow, and continue it foure or five dayes, or longer, for your visitation" (5.2.60–63). Her "riddle" is simply a bald invitation for sex – an escapade totally in line with her debauched and intellectually defunct character – but the lines about appearing at "any end of so noble a worke" must have carried an extra charge when delivered by a boy, to a boy, at a time when the Italian was shorthand for the sodomitical.[90] It is only in this sense, as it points back to the boy's body, hidden beneath yet displayed by female clothes, that Mavis's invitation can be called a riddle. Indeed in this sense the moment delivers exactly what an audience would expect from Italian riddles, which Michele De Filippis notes were famed "for their obscenity," especially as they highlighted the barely disguised phallus that almost invariably serves as one wrong-but-right answer to the set of clues they offer.[91] (The form persists: what's hard and dry when you put it in, and wet and limp when you take it out? Spaghetti, of course.[92])

This ability to provoke unlicensed thoughts and their subsequent behaviors is precisely why anti-theatrical critics saw boy players as a threat to moral order. Even for a prolific playwright like Thomas Middleton, in his *Father Hubburds Tales* (1604), the boys function as part of London's well-oiled machine for corrupting and ruining morals: young rustics thrust into the urban den of vice soon learn that at the Blackfriars they will find "a nest of boys able to ravish a man."[93] This is why, from the sixteenth century, critics like Phillip Stubbes had questioned drama's educational function on the humanists' own terms, labeling theatres "schooles of mischeef" that encouraged audience members to disperse to their "secret conclaves, covertly, to play the *Sodomits*, or worse" after the play ended.[94] The metaphor of theatres as "schools of mischeef" or "schools of abuse" reflects not only the concern that plays destroyed children, as moralists since St. Cyprian had warned, but also the fear, which Chapter 2 explores in greater depth, that they have this effect on adults.[95] Such fears imply a dynamic quite different from the critical commonplace that *Epicoene* and other children's company productions defused sexually and politically risky material by virtue of the boys' innocence and inexperience.[96] No longer merely objects, the boys become malicious subjects, exerting power by secret and covert means.

The reaction to *Epicoene*'s first performance implies that such malice was not merely a matter of sex, as we would expect from a culture where sex and politics share the same vocabulary. Despite the play's claims for discretion, James's cousin Arabella Stuart appears to have decided that it transgressed, crossing the line and defaming her. The disputed passage, which mentions the "Prince of Moldovia," seems innocent enough. But delivered with a wink and a nod it may have elicited some quick, transgressive laughter by recalling the recent humiliation suffered by the royal family and especially the *pater patriae* at the hands of the shady adventurer Stephano Janiculo. Posing as the prince of Moldavia, Janiculo extracted a large loan from James, fled to Italy, and fueled London's gossip mill by proclaiming he would marry Arabella after a courtship rumored to have been conducted secretly and without the king's consent.[97] The affair was an affront to James's image as a father who was always in control, an embarrassment to the patriarchal order.

As always, Jonson disclaimed any such ideas and protested his enduring innocence. But the play and its young performers were evidently deemed malicious anyway and suppressed. Whatever the specific offense, the breakdown of *Epicoene*'s own disciplinary model may finally be the play's most significant, if unintended, contribution to early modern debates over public voice, indicating that simple assent may not be the only alternative to silence. Children playing with mirrors, it seems, may have the power to remake or break the image of authority rather than just reflect it, and as we shall see in later chapters, this is the potential that Milton seized in both his pedagogical and poetic writing.

But *Epicoene*'s Restoration history, when it was drained of political malice and became a more overt instrument of infantilization, usefully reminds us that the history of childish things in literature after Milton is not one of radical empowerment and critique. As Jonathan Sawday has explained, when Charles II reclaimed the English throne after nearly two decades in exile, his supporters' sense of both "the power of symbolic forms" and their "desperate need to re-affirm some form of historical continuity" led them not only to exhume and punish the bodies of the regicides but also to exhume and reinstate the texts of patriarchalism.[98] The goal was to forget the decade of rule without a king, silencing and forgetting the disruptive voices of the 1640s and 1650s that made this historical rupture possible. *Epicoene*'s return to the stage as the first play produced when the theatres reopened in 1660 should be understood as part of this exhumation. Although Charles's proclivity for siring bastards led some wags to quip that he was "the truest *Pater Patriae* e're was yet, / For all, or most of's subjects, does beget," the assertion of his fatherly role in the Restoration was serious and pervasive.[99] In the parades, poems, and plays that greeted his return, the king's subjects hailed him as a father and asserted their loyalty and devotion by embracing the idea of their own voiceless infancy. As one contemporary put it:

> Our Innocence (which to the test was put)
> Must shine like that of Infants, ere they shoot
> Up, to their dangerous years; or else no man
> Of our poor *Israel* enters *Canaan;*
> None are restored.[100]

Restoration in works like these depends on an assertion of innocence that is inseparable from infancy and silence.

Appropriately then, in November 1660, Jonson's play was chosen to be the first presented at the new court, in a performance sponsored by George Monk, the army commander who facilitated the Restoration by allowing the secluded, Royalist members of Parliament to retake their seats in February.[101] The play appeared with a new broadsheet prologue explicitly linking the king's authority and *Epicoene*'s disciplinary function while dismissing the revolutionary voices as so much noise. Likely written by William Davenant (1606–68), the new prologue asserts that the king and the play are one, restoring the damage done when the radicals "broke the Mirror of the times" – a phrase that associates once more the theatre's mimetic discipline with the monarchical injunction "not to abuse my mirror nor to break it."[102] As the rebels performed that malicious iconoclastic act, they fooled themselves and others into believing they were coming of age:

> When the Lyons dreadful skin they took,
> They roar'd so loud that the whole Forrest shook;
> The noise kept all the Neighborhood in awe
> Who thought 'twas the true Lyon by his paw.[103]

Despite the terror they inspired, such voices were really only animalistic noise. For a culture working very hard to believe such things, *Epicoene*'s framing of the boy actor's disruptive garrulity as authoritatively sanctioned play – actually proof of his discretion – held obvious appeal. Indeed, the play made Edward Kynaston, who appeared in the title role at age seventeen, something of a sex symbol by adoring fans who apparently conflated the actor with his role as an object to "play with" (1.1.12–15). One of the last boys to perform women's parts on the stage, Kynaston was "so beautiful a Youth," said Colly Cibber, "that the Ladies of Quality prided themselves in taking him with them in their Coaches, to *Hyde-Park*, in his Theatrical Habit, after the Play."[104] When Samuel Pepys saw "Kinaston, a boy," in a 1660 production of *The Loyal Subject*, he too thought Kynaston was "the loveliest lady that ever I saw in my life – only, her voice not very good."[105] Pepys's slippage between the "boy" and "her voice" and Cibber's image of Kynaston being carted around in costume seem to efface any real agency, absorbing the boy completely in his roles. But the failure of the voice described by Pepys is more complicated. Pepys hears the man's voice stubbornly disrupting the theatrical illusion; he desires a complete erasure of voice that the boy's status on the cusp of adulthood makes impossible. As we shall see in the following chapter, in the years before the Civil War, many playwrights and their critics lent more credence than Pepys to the idea of theatre's complete representational power. In fact, some parliamentary reformers began to argue that both theatrical and political representation erased authoritative voice by using the same mimetic strategies – and this is why the link between them needed to be destroyed.

CHAPTER 2

Children, Literature, and the Problem of Consent

In the sixteenth and seventeenth centuries, the representation of adults by children was not confined to the playhouse: it was also surprisingly common for legal infants to represent constituents as elected Members of Parliament. They were qualified less by their rational abilities than by their lineage, and this suited a form of representative government that could operate in the absence of consent. But as the nation inched toward war, their presence increasingly raised uncomfortable questions about whether the voices actors performed on stage differed meaningfully from the voices that constituted Britain's representative government, or whether performers in both venues were merely objects and instruments of subtle disciplinary power. By turning our attention to these questions we can begin to correct what Oliver Arnold has described as the "near effacement of Parliament from new historicist accounts of early modern England" in favor of a scholarly fixation on literary representations of monarchical, absolutist rule.[1] Arnold argues that the "missing term" in such accounts is consent, although he also rejects the opposing tendency to treat the theatre as a proto-democratic outlet for the popular voice.[2] Instead, parliamentary representation in his account is really no more liberating than monarchical absolutism: it is characterized by "the loss of power, the fall from dignity, the false consciousness, the grief peculiar to the experience of representing and being represented."[3] The character known only as the "Third Citizen" in Shakespeare's late, cynical tragedy *Coriolanus* (c. 1608–09) embodies this radically alienated subjectivity as he describes the limits of his fellow citizens' ability to dissent when they are asked to give their voices to elect Coriolanus as tribune: "We have power in ourselves to do it, but it is a power that we have no power to do."[4]

Arnold insightfully describes the Third Citizen's "fog" as the "psychic state peculiar to representationalism," but I have been arguing that the infant, who was nominally without voice but bound into dense networks of obligation, gave this fog a local habitation and a name.[5] Indeed, immediately after the Third Citizen makes his cryptic analysis the tribunes accuse him and his fellows of "childish friendliness," and when Coriolanus realizes how little the citizens' vote means, he asks a biting paradoxical question: "Have I had children's voices?"[6] The question highlights a problem shared both by Arnold's depiction of early modern political representation as a disciplinary mechanism and those accounts he sets out to correct, like Annabel Patterson's description of early modern theatre as a proto-republican public sphere that "allows the people to speak *for themselves* as a political entity."[7] In both models, the people have a voice, either to use or to lose. But to speak with a child's voice was not to speak at all, which is why James I had characterized his critics as those who "cry as babes do all in vaine," not speaking but making a "houling sound / that rise as vapours from the ground."[8] The Third Citizen's childish voice, in other words, does not highlight a "wonderfully prosaic expression of a tragic fall" or a loss of power, but a failure to realize power in the first place, the impossible situation of being asked to consent, to give your voice, without holding the authority to do so.[9]

As tension between King Charles and Parliament grew during the late 1630s and erupted into open war in 1642, reformers like the polemical firebrand William Prynne began to charge that the presence of children in Parliament proved that this situation was not confined to the stage. The voices of child MPs made a mockery of consent, exposing it as little more than a theatrical fiction. This political critique in turn revealed a pervasive doubt about the shaping power of literary art that went to the heart of the humanist pedagogy – a suspicion that the child's unpredictable encounter with poetic play could lead not to independent voice but to the enslavement of mindless, parroting repetition. To forge a new politics of consent and create the kind of representation that Arnold describes, writers like Prynne deemed it necessary to banish children's voices from Parliament and sever the links between theatrical and poetic representation. Their efforts were an early step toward the removal of children, their performances, and their books from the political discourse.

Children's Voices in Parliament

Far from serving as a ubiquitous form of political power, Parliament sat for barely more than four years between 1603 and 1629. Throughout the Civil War, in fact, parliamentary forces fought not in the name of the people but of the king, and it was not until January 4, 1649, that the Parliament could resolve that "the People are, under God, the Original of all just Power and … the Commons … being chosen by and represent-ing, the People, have the supreme Power in this Nation."[10] That resolution was made, tellingly, only after the Parliament had been purged of the vast majority of its members, leaving a "Rump," as it was derisively called, that finally and rather briefly claimed absolute power to speak for the people.

William Prynne had laid much of the legal groundwork for that claim when he was commissioned to write the official defense of parliamentary sovereignty in 1643.[11] No one was in a more eminent position to do so: when his attacks on the prelates led to a libel conviction in 1637, his pub-lic mutilation galvanized Puritan opposition to the Laudian church and forced the choosing of sides. He was hailed as a martyr, released by par-liamentary order in 1640, and remained an influential voice throughout the 1640s. Considering this prominence, his focus in 1646 may seem quix-otic, because as the Royalist army collapsed and debate raged about who had the right to govern in the ensuing power vacuum, Prynne turned his attention to penning *Minors No Senators*, a tract that energetically pro-claimed that the presence of children in Parliament made him "tremble and feare." "We shall have a *Parliamentum Puerorum, Senatus Infantum*, a Parliament of Children, a Senate of Babes," Prynne announced, "if all Cities, Burgesses, were so Childish, so foolish, and injurious to the pub-like in their elections of such as som (through the importunity of friends) have bin."[12] Prynne was an eccentric, and it is tempting to dismiss such fears as the inventions of a delirious mind, but in fact no early Stuart Parliament sat without its share of minors. Forty-six were elected between 1604 and the beginning of Charles's personal rule in 1629.[13] Although infants were temporarily excluded from serving during the Interregnum, the bill that banned them was revoked with the rest of the Interregnum legislation at the Restoration, and forty-three more infants were elected to the House of Commons before their final banishment shortly after the Glorious Revolution of 1688.[14]

As Prynne's language implies, some were indeed very young. The bor-ough of Wigan, for example, elected Richard Molyneux II in 1572, when he was only twelve, and the town of Callington elected James Wriothesley, the son of Shakespeare's patron, in 1621, when he was only fifteen. But *Minors No Senators* was probably provoked by the case of parliamen-tary army captain Sir Christopher Wray, who used his superior influence with the Lincolnshire gentry to outmaneuver Colonel Edward King and procure a seat for his twenty-year-old, expatriate son, William Wray, as MP for Grimsby.[15] Despite Prynne's depiction of them as babbling neo-nates, most minors serving in Parliament were in fact, like Wray, between the ages of sixteen and twenty and on the threshold of adulthood. But as I have shown previously, boys this age were decidedly not adults, and Prynne's description of childishness is not merely figurative. In language that echoes Shakespeare's Third Citizen, Prynne notes that according to both law and custom, they have "no full power to do or consent to any thing for themselves."[16]

The election of these childish members indicates a culture where status and inheritance trumped age and merit as qualifications for leadership, a patriarchal culture that could, ironically, hand power to mere babes because it had not fully adopted the idea of representation as derived from a form of rational consent. It also highlights a correlative issue: the "authorization view of representation," as Hanna Fenichel Pitkin calls it, had not replaced "symbolic representation" as the dominant political model.[17] In brief, the "authorization view" says that voters authorize a representative to act on their behalf, and this authorization creates an essentially unlimited power to bind and obligate those voters. It makes sense, then, to elect someone whose superior judgment makes him a fit representative. "Symbolic representation," however, "involves no rational, objective, justifiable connection between what represents and what is represented."[18] As with a flag that symbolizes a nation, the connection between symbol and symbolized is arbitrary and takes place only in the mind of an audience. It relies, we could say, on that audience's "belief."[19] The symbol's function is largely ceremonial, its legitimacy based not on "rational persuasion, but on manipulating affective responses and forming habits."[20]

Far from endorsing a notion of symbolic representation, early modern theorists often claimed that parliamentary representation was mimetic, with the Parliament serving as a perfect image or likeness, a *repraesentatio* of the people, as Quentin Skinner has shown.[21] Prynne's occasional ally Henry Parker (1604–52), for example, demonstrates this familiar argument when he suggests that the Parliament reflects the people in a diminutive form: "the Parliament is indeed nothing else, but the very people it self artificially congregated, or reduced by an orderly election, and representation ... from the rude bulk of the universality."[22] Here and elsewhere in his works, Parker clearly draws on notions of artistic representation to make his case for parliamentary power as an uncanny reflection that leaves no gap between the representation and the thing being represented.[23] "It is not rightly supposed," he emphasizes, "that the people and the Parliament are severall."[24] As with symbolic representation, so complete a mirroring would seem to make authoritative representation unnecessary. It might even seem to make children, with their superior powers of mimicry, the perfect representatives.

For Prynne, however, children in Parliament expose mimetic models of governance as a mere mystification of the symbolic manipulation that was really taking place in early modern elections. He disparages young members as "Cyphers," empty signifiers who represent nothing in themselves, and this is exactly the same problem he has in his famous anti-theatrical polemic *Histrio-Mastix* with the "degenerous and Unchristian symbolization" of children on the stage.[25] Children's mimetic nature makes them ideally (or dangerously) suited for such a symbolic role, but the child's apparent ability to act as an agent without interests also makes him a kind of puppet who can be manipulated by powerful, unseen interests who pull the strings. Deluded by this empty show of representation, the people are prevented from exercising truly authoritative voice. "I dare confidently affirm," Prynne hints ominously, "that no Cittie, or Borough, did ever freely of their owne accords make choice of any *Ward*, or *Infant*, to serve in Parliament for them ... but meerly through the over-earnest solicitation, threats, or over ruling power of the Infants friends."[26] This is, likewise, the overwhelming impression left by *Coriolanus:* not that the people lose power, but that even when they take up arms and assault the Capitol they have no power proper to themselves; they are merely blown hither and thither by the various interests that see fit to use them. If their voices are free at all, they are free to assent, not consent – the same kind of freedom the Earl of Suffolk (1561–1626) allowed to local officials in the market town of Saffron Walden after learning they had prematurely pledged their voices to a candidate he did not support: "as I am lord of the Towne & moste of you my tennantes ... give your free consentes & voyces to my good frend Sr Edward Denny knight, which if you shall not ... I will make the prowdest of you all repent it."[27] Before the tragedy that Arnold describes could happen – before the subject could lose his voice in the act of giving it – Prynne recognized that he must find that voice in the first place. This recognition may have been fleeting and only half-realized, but that is what makes him a suitable representative of this vertiginous moment, when consent itself, as a basis of obligation and political action, remained an uncertain concept.

Prynne's efforts had in fact already been anticipated by 1613, according to the physician and polemicist James Welwood, who recounted a speech by Richard Martin decrying the "children elected into the great council of the nation, which came to invade and invert nature, and to enact laws to govern their fathers."[28] Sir Francis Bacon, too, complained that a large number of youths had ruined the "Addled Parliament" of 1614, because they did not possess the "modesty and gravity" needed for parliamentary business and "turneth it into a sport or exercise."[29] By 1621, the year that James wrote his poem chiding state critics who cry like babes and howl like voiceless winds, Richard Weston had introduced a bill to prevent minors from serving in Parliament, announcing that "it is not fit, that they should make Laws for the Kingdom, who are not liable to the law."[30] This brief, fragmentary record of Weston's remarks identifies the fundamental, foggy paradox of child-legislators: they were outside the law, incapable of binding themselves or consenting to the disposal of their own estates or persons, yet their actions could create binding obligations for others.

Weston's prohibition failed in 1621 and was unsuccessfully reintroduced as part of Parliament's campaign to legitimize its use of sovereign power in 1626, a crisis year between Charles's dissolution of his first Parliament and calling of his second, as MPs and the king clashed over which branch of government had the right to choose the king's ministers, collect revenues, and ultimately set foreign policy.[31] Far from quixotic, then, it is only natural that Prynne dedicated himself to the problem of children and representation during the turmoil of 1646, when he claimed that "now the greatest matters ever debated in any Parliament are in agitation" and "a greater reformation is now expected, promised, endeavoured, in Church, State, and Parliaments, then in any precedent times."[32]

Prynne's goal, however, was not the liberation of the individual's voice, as it might seem in a Whig account of this history. He made a powerful and passionate case for parliamentary sovereignty at the outbreak of the Civil War, and in the 1646 edition of *Minors No Senators* he regularly declaims against the "malignant Royall party."[33] But as William Lamont suggests, he "became a symbol of radical aspirations almost by accident: his writings remained resolutely moderate."[34] As Prynne saw it, his 200 pamphlets never intended to roil the British government but to insulate sovereign governmental power against moral decay and clerical encroachments, and he attacked Independents and Anabaptists as passionately as he attacked stage plays, papists, and child parliamentarians. His reconceptualization of parliamentary representation should be understood as part of this attempt to put authority on a firmer ground rather than as the work of a wild-eyed radical. When he published his second edition of *Minors No Senators* at the Restoration, in fact, he silently removed warnings that the presence of children in Parliament "opens the mouthes of Royalists."[35] In the new edition he now advised that child parliamentarians would open "the mouthes of Jesuites, Papists, Malignants, Sectaries, and the Anti-parliamentary party" instead.[36] In both versions, Prynne is at least as interested in the representative body's ability to silence voices as its ability to channel them. His goal, in short, was to create the kind of representation that Arnold describes, in which subjects invest their voices in a representative body that then claims absolute power to speak for them and to them. Nevertheless, such efforts helped shift the center of political gravity from birth and symbolic representation to consent. To invest representative government with new authority based on rational consent, it became necessary to ask what made consent possible, who was capable and who was not, and what markers of age, sex, education, or property could indicate that capability.

Ben Jonson suggestively dramatized the conflicts over such questions in *The Staple of News* (1625), a biting satire of London's burgeoning commercial classes and their thirst for information and power. Jonson's play has regular "Intermeans" in which a group of gossips from the audience takes the stage to express their (mostly negative) opinions of the play, and in one of them the unambiguously named "Censure" expresses her dismay over her country's wayward children and her faith that only authoritative parliamentary representation can restore order:

> *I would have ne'er a cunning* Schoole-Master *in* England. *I meane a* Cunning-Man, *a* Schoole-Master; *that is a* Conjurour, *or a* Poet, *or that had any acquaintance with a* Poet. *They make all their schollers* Play-boyes! *Is't not a fine sight, to see all our children made* Enterluders? *Doe wee pay our money for this? wee send them to learne their* Grammar, *and their* Terence, *and they learne their* play-books? *well, they talke, we shall have no more Parliaments* (*God blesse us) but an' wee have, I hope,* Zeale-of-the-land Buzy, *and my* Gossip, Rabby Trouble-truth *will start up, and see we shall have painfull good Ministers to keepe Schoole.* (344–45)

As Censure spoke these words in 1625, Parliament had been dissolved for attempting to exercise the kind of authoritative representation she envisions. One of the Commons' first acts had been to introduce a petition, nominally directed against recusant Catholics, that effectively would have asserted Parliament's role in dictating matters of church discipline while thwarting the monarchy's proposed French alliance. The monarch's swift reaction suggested to Censure that the country would have "no more Parliaments," but of course this news soon proved wrong. By 1626, Charles was forced to call another Parliament in an attempt to raise funds, and in the brief moment before it was dissolved, Richard Weston joined the efforts to shore up Parliament's power by introducing his legislation to prevent children from serving as MPs. This increased emphasis on authoritative consent, and its close association with questions of minority and majority, helps explain Censure's rather unexpected juxtaposition of poetry, pedagogy, and Parliament. Censure clamors for a firm distinction between political representation and play, and her desire to distinguish adult voice from childish imitation, to put children in their place, requires an intervention in the classrooms and stages that form children into subjects. Her desire for "painful" ministers does not merely imply the institution of strict Puritan beliefs but also punningly insists on rejecting humanistic pedagogy's preferred method of poetic engagement in favor of traditional, painful education – not alluring boys, but beating sense into them. The mystifying magic of poetic representation both results from and enables the collapse of authoritative parliamentary representation.

With his epigraph from 1 Corinthians 13.11, announcing that now is the time to "put away childish things," Prynne in *Minors No Senators* sounds a lot like Censure. As he takes the measure of Parliament, he sees a system corrupted by political fiction and demands its destruction through an iconoclastic act that will expose the hollow idols at its core. He would replace these ciphers with the "most fit and discreet men," whose superior judgment made their representation less a reflection of their constituency than a moral and political exemplum.[37] And fascinatingly, as with Censure, the terms of his argument are intimately related to the ones he uses elsewhere to attack the central role of poetry in humanistic classrooms, where he insists "*amorous wanton Play-bookes*" and a tradition of student acting in grammar schools and universities has "far worse" consequences than even the popular theatre.[38]

The same qualities that render a child unfit for consent, we see in Prynne's attacks, make him a paradigm of poetic responsiveness. Like other writers who drew on the ubiquitous imagery of blank slates, blank notebooks, and unprinted wax tablets, Prynne's *Minors No Senators* defines children by what they lack. They have a complete absence of "experience, wisdom, Learning."[39] They have no "gravity," "sound judgment," or "prudent foresight."[40] Even the child's innocence is constituted not just by his purity but by his very lack of rational capabilities, as Prynne makes clear in *Histrio-Mastix*, warning that children exposed to poetry and drama "know not how to distinguish betweene good and evill, *judgeing onely of the goodnesse of things by sence, by pleasure.*"[41] He repeatedly drives this same point home in *Minors No Senators* to prove that children should not be able to vote on laws while they remain "so indiscreet … that they are incapable to manage or dispose their own estates."[42] To be "indiscreet" in Prynne's sense means both to lack judgment and to lack boundaries. This blank status, in the standard descriptions of childhood we examined in the Introduction, defines not only the child's great mimetic potential but also his dangerous propensity to receive the imprint of all hands or take whatever fruit or bauble is placed before him, even at the peril of his inheritance or eternal salvation. As Michael Witmore describes it, the child "lived in a state of utter absorption in the present, unable to differentiate immediate pleasures from potentially greater pleasures in the future."[43]

This is why Prynne, in his anti-theatrical invective, describes child actors as "apes" and "parrots" and why he claims their presence on stage is so dangerous: they can "act any sinnes or wickedness to the life, as if they were really performed, their minds, their memories, and mouths, full fraught with *amorous, ribaldrous, panderly* Histories, pastorals, jests, discourses, and witty, though filthy, obsenities."[44] The children become utterly immersed in their imitations, mind, memory, and mouth given over to uncanny, all-encompassing mimesis. Prynne uses almost the same terms in *Minors No Senators*, where he claims that children are "void of solid judgment, understanding, and full of folly, apt to be deceived and tossed about with every wind of Doctrine."[45] One might find this endearing, or even pitiable, in a helpless infant, but the capacity for absorption becomes more problematic in the childish figures who speak and act for others, and this is why the worst abuses of school and stage unite in unreformed parliamentary representation. Parliament is used as a "School of Experience to educate, to improve young Gentlemen, and fit them for publick Action," Prynne laments, but this misguided pedagogy really only "bladders them up with Self-conceits."[46] Such representatives are all sound and no substance, blown up with childish self-regard.

In Parliament, on stage, and in classrooms devoted to poetic and dramatic fictions, the indulgence of childishness revealed to Prynne the purely symbolic folly or mirror play at the heart of the English political system. As suggested earlier, neither Prynne's resulting attempt to remove children from Parliament nor his rationale was a private peculiarity: in 1653, the short-lived "Barebones Parliament" quickly moved to heed Prynne's advice and ban minors.[47] And although this ban lapsed at the Restoration, Prynne's ideas found new life when infants were permanently eliminated from Parliament at the century's end.[48] The same unease that drove children from their role in political representation eventually led to attempts to restrict their encounters with poesy to a purely didactic and innocent space outside the political mainstream. The persistence and ultimate victory of Prynne's views in this transition points to an anxiety that always bedeviled humanist pedagogical theory – the fear that mimetic play would not enable consent but would instead short-circuit the rational processes that made consent possible. Even worse, both proponents and critics of humanist education feared poetry's ability to provoke similar responses in adults who, as Prynne put it in *Minors No Senators*, are exposed through the indulgence of these childish things as being "Children, or more indiscreet than those very Infants" themselves.[49]

"Poetical Furie," or the Problem with Play

In accordance with the abiding scholarly interest in questions of gender and sexuality, such fears have sometimes been described as the notion that the arts collectively known as "poesy," including drama, poetry, and the other forms we call "literature," were "feminizing."[50] This was certainly part of the equation, but primarily because the irrational child, who began life and education under the mother's care, was considered a feminized being.[51] When critics charged that poesy compromised "manlike libertie" (as Sidney characterized their argument in his *Defence of Poesie*), their larger political concern was not feminization but infantilization. Indeed, although Sidney's own hugely influential work sets out to counter such charges, it reveals a similar anxiety. Sidney's pedagogical and didactic argument for the value of imaginative literature relies on the utter transparency of fiction, a principle exemplified in the child's encounter with dramatic representation:

> What childe is there, that coming to a play, and seeing *Thebes* written in great Letters upon an old doore, doth beleeve that it is *Thebes*? If then, a man can arrive, at that childs age, to know that the *Poets* persons and dooings, are but pictures, what should be, and not stories what have bin, they will never give the lie, to things not Affirmatively, but Allegorically and figuratively written; and therefore as in historie looking for truth, they go away full fraught with falshood: So in *Poesie*, looking but for fiction, they shal use the narration, but as an imaginative groundplat of a profitable invention.[52]

Even children, with their tendencies for absorption, never lose the distinction between real and unreal. Sidney takes Plato's argument that poetry is a form of lying and turns it on its head: the world is full of falsehoods that we never perceive, as are forms of writing like history that purport to represent the actual truth. The artistic gap between representation and reality, the free play that even a child can appreciate, offers the ground for the "profitable invention" or poetic fashioning that educators from

Erasmus to Brinsley promised. Fictions so obvious offer equally obvious modes of interpretation. The child, to return to Sidney's ground-zero image of consciousness, can only become more grounded in productive forms of subjectivity through these fictional negotiations.

But a few lines earlier, Sidney offers a very different version of the child's encounter with poesy. As he attempts to reconcile the poet's educational mission with his capacity to delight, Sidney describes poetic language as a kind of sugar to make the medicine go down, "even as the childe is often brought to take most wholsom things, by hiding them in such other as have a pleasant tast: which if one should beginne to tell them, the nature of *Aloes*, or *Rubarb* they shoulde receive, woulde sooner take their Phisicke at their eares, then at their mouth."[53] This hardly seems like the kind of transparency or purposive interpretation exemplified by the child who instantly recognizes that "Thebes" written on the wall is a mere representation. But "so is it in men," Sidney continues, "most of which are childish in the best things, till they bee cradled in their graves."[54] Here poesy disguises only "the best things," but reading it still becomes a kind of childishness, the mistaken perception of instruction *as* delight rather than instruction *through* delight. And once the Theban door is opened to this kind of error, there is really no closing it against Prynne's suspicion that poetry and drama are merely forms "sugred, and guilded over with the very quintessence of Art, and Rhetoricke," as he says in language that could be lifted straight from Sidney.[55] But for Prynne, these same features "doeth alienate, and coole our love unto the Sacred, and Soule-saving word of God."[56] Sidney himself acknowledges a similar fear in *Astrophil and Stella*, where he imagines a child reader who "With gilded leaves or coloured vellum plays, / Or at the most, on some fine picture stays / But never heeds the fruit of the writer's mind."[57] This is not just a problem with the reader but with the child's experience of artistic beauty itself, his ecstatic response to the "golden world" that Sidney promised only poetry could create.

As Richard Helgerson argues, this was a recurring worry for poets of the sixteenth and seventeenth centuries, who were plagued by the "suspicion that the golden world might be no more than the deluding product of illicit desire."[58] The "nature of desire," as John Smith emblematized it in his rhetorical handbook of 1656, was a "strange countrey, whereunto the Prodigal child sailed when he forsook his fathers house to undertake a banishment: a countrey where corn is still in grasse; vines in the bud; trees perpetually in blossome, and birds always in the shell."[59] It is easy to see how this strange country could threaten notions of poesy's usefulness in the process of subject formation; it is pure immaturity, unproductive, vainglorious, and perpetually unrealized. As Smith's imagery of green shoots, budding vines, and prodigality makes clear, it is also intimately associated with children, those problematic Adams who will trade their inheritance for an apple, as the scholastic encyclopedist Bartholomaeus Anglicus explained, because "they desire all thinges that they see."[60]

Rather than the profitable invention of profitable subjects, critics like Prynne argued that poetry and drama merely indulged this tendency, and the strong associations between childhood and illicit desire help explain why their reigning metaphor for poetic and dramatic excess was not Lady Poesy but the "School of Abuse." The Oxford scholar and cleric Stephen Gosson, for example, used this educational metaphor for the title of his 1579 polemic against "Poets, Pipers, Plaiers, Jesters, and such like Caterpillers," a work he dedicated, rather surprisingly, to Sidney.[61] In fact, although Sidney and Gosson held similar views about certain "abuses" of the stage, such as "mongrel" forms that mix tragic and comic elements, Gosson's broader attack on poetry may have helped inspire Sidney's *Defence*.[62] Gosson was a firm moralist, but no Puritan, and his *School of Abuse* relentlessly develops the idea that poetic engagement might subvert reason and arrest development, "bewitching the graine in the greene blade."[63] This language of enchantment is not the paranoia of a fanatic, but of a reformed "prodigal" writer who himself had authored plays; in following chapters we will encounter the same sort of imagery in the poems of Milton's youth as they struggle to strike a balance between poetic absorption and self-actualized voice.[64] The child absorbed in his play, the grain bewitched in the blade, are images of desire made tangible, of expectation as perpetual unripeness.

Even humanist-inspired pedagogues who endorsed the use of drama and delight worried it was ultimately impossible to control the child's response – that he might unthinkingly parrot the wrong lessons or that maturation might emerge in wild opposition to authority. As Mulcaster darkly intimated, children were characterized by "uncertain motion, both in soule and in body," and this uncertain motion, or "error," was as proverbial as the child's original innocence.[65] Ascham worried that the quickest-witted children were also "in purpose unconstant, light to promise any thing, readie to forget every thing," while Peacham claimed childish minds were as impressionable as "water spillt on a table, which with a finger wee may draw and direct which way we list; or like the young Hop, which if wanting a poll, taketh hold of the next hedge."[66] Such images of wax, water, and tender young vines may convey an appealing impressionability, but they also suggest a nature that threatens to elude all bounds and flow in every direction.[67]

Consequently, although Mulcaster trained the boys of the Merchant Taylors' School for performances in the Taylors' Guild Hall and at court, he also cautioned that "we plant not any poeticall furie in the childes habit. For that rapt inclination is too ranging of it selfe, though it be not helpt forward."[68] The childish and the poetic imaginations were simply too much the same, tending toward "rapt" absorption in prodigal pleasures. This is the very opposite of the rational acceptance of authority that the humanist pedagogy promised and the kind of authoritative voice it intended to cultivate. The resulting ambivalence underlies the central "contradiction developing within pedagogic theory" that James G. Turner has identified during the seventeenth century, "between discipline as curbing and discipline as fostering, between education as quelling the passions and education as developing the senses."[69] Embodied by the humble but troublesome figure of the child, this contradiction unites early modern theories of poetic and political representation.

Gosson's attack on poetry, music, and other artistic forms, for example, begins with a stark warning about the political consequences of the humanist pedagogy of play. "Are not they accursed thinke you by the mouth of God," he asks, "which having the government of young Princes, with Poetical fantasies draw them to the schooles of their owne abuses?"[70] Gosson's model of government is monarchical, but the educational failure he warns against remains a matter of both political and poetic representation. The grain bewitched in the blade, in the case of young princes, has been "sowed for the sustenance of many thousaunds," and so the corrupting influence of a wayward education has catastrophic implications, reproducing its failure *ad infinitum*.[71] The combined assault on poetry, drama, and humanistic education was so common that it is difficult to find a piece of anti-theatrical writing that does not specifically invoke the dire educational consequences of poetic and dramatic forms. Like Prynne and Gosson, the author of *A Second and Third Blast of Retrait from Plaies and Theaters* deplores seeing "yong boies inclining of themselves unto wickednes, trained up in filthie speeches, unnatural and unseemelie gestures, brought up by these Schoolemasters in bawderie, and in idlenes."[72] Likewise, John Stockwood, who is famous for lamenting that a "fylthye playe, with the blast of a trumpette" could draw a thousand spectators in Elizabethan London, issued his attacks on playgoing not as a discrete attack on theatre but as part of a larger call for educational and disciplinary reform.[73] This schoolmaster, preacher, and publisher of works on Latin accidence and grammar envisions the crowd of London theatergoers as so many prodigal children, and his title page announces that he delivers his complaints squarely to "fathers, householders, and Schole-maisters" who need to tighten the reins on their charges. Stockwood especially laments that play has taken the place of classroom discipline, letting the tender young plants of humanist pedagogy run to seed: if parents "did thoroughly understande what horrible beastly Authors are taught in some schooles," he claims in another pamphlet, they would rather see their children "murthered and slaine before [their] eyes, than that ... their tender minds should be nourished by and infected with such lothsome filthe and deadly poyson."[74] Stockwood puts the pain back into painful discipline in a way that would win the full-throated approval of Jonson's Censure. But as Gosson, Prynne, and Stockwood's shared language of "tender minds" implies, the difference between writers like this and their humanist opponents was not in their concept of the childish mind, or even in their disciplinary intent, but in their opinion of the best way to engage these delicate young shoots without corrupting them.

Still more striking is the fear shared by all these authors that the prodigal imaginations of children are potentially infectious – the concern not merely that poetry and drama will corrupt children but that these literary forms participate in a form of childishness that is itself corrupting even to adults.[75] As spectators are "led awaie with vanitie," anti-theatrical critics routinely warn, boy actors and playwrights effectively become abusive "Schoole-masters" to the adults in their audience.[76] In fact, while Gosson spends ample time talking about the deleterious effects of drama and poetry on actual children, this systematic regression of adults is ultimately the metaphorical "school" of his title:

> You are no sooner entred, but libertie looseth the reynes, and geves you head, placing you with Poetrie in the lowest forme: when his skill is showne to make his Scholer as good as ever twangde, hee preferres you to Pyping, from Pyping to playing, from play to pleasure, from pleasure to slouth, from slouth too sleepe, from sleep to sinne, from sinne to death, from death to the devill, if you take your learning apace, and passe through every forme without revolting.[77]

"Playing" has a special place of infamy as the entry-level class (or form) that begins an education in pleasure and sloth. It seems to tap and enable a natural inclination toward entropy that was notorious among schoolboys and, Gosson implies, only half-suppressed among their elders.

Likewise, Prynne is most exercised not by the threat to children, but the threat posed by childishness to adults. Playing, he argues, is dangerously "childish," and stage players "use such gestures, speeches, rayment, com-plements, and behaviour in jest, which none but children, fooles, or mad-men, doe act."[78] This form of play, in turn, lures audience mem-bers into "childish vanities, as if we were created only to play and follow sports," making theatres "the Schooles, Playes the Lectures which *teach men* how to cheate, to steale; to plot and execute any villany."[79] Indeed, it is a little-noted peculiarity of *Histrio-Mastix* that Prynne describes the theatrical audience largely as "children, those novices, whose ignorance, childishnesse, vanitie, folly, or injudiciousnesse allure them to playes or such like Gugaes, *which men of riper yeares and judgement doe contem.*"[80] This does not appear to be a figurative description; if it requires us to imagine a kind of Circean transformation of men into children, it is worth noting that such metamorphoses were not mere metaphors. Without set boundaries to childhood – irrevocable cultural or legal markers of adult agency – childish incapacity was always a threat, just one indiscretion away. For both Prynne and Jonson's Censure, the answer is to separate poetic play and authoritative representation into very different realms. In the second half of this book I discuss some of the pedagogical attempts to achieve this goal and Milton's resistance to them, but for now I simply want to make it clear that, according to many critics, the same qualities that made the child a figure for mimetic responsiveness marked him as unfit for consent. Painful discipline could help youths set aside childish things and become men, but even poesy's foremost advocates worried that engaging the child's ludic impulses and his imitative nature might make a mockery of adult voice, ultimately infantilizing authority itself.

Flies in the Ointment

Such is Prynne's fear in *Minors No Senators*. His problem with child rep-resentatives is a double one: they are, in themselves, incapable of rational action, and their very presence demonstrates a collapse of rational consent among the electorate. This vicious cycle infantilizes the "whole Kingdom" that Parliament represents, a process of virulent infection that Prynne describes by invoking Ecclesiastes 10.1, "Dead flies cause the ointment of the Apothecary to send forth a stinking savour: so doth a little folly him that is in reputation for Wisdome and honour."[81] The salve meant to sooth a people becomes a principle agent of folly, as only "two or three Infants misguided voices," Prynne warns, "for want of judgement to Vote aright, may infinitely prejudice, endanger our three whole Churches, Kingdoms in a moment."[82]

Arnold insightfully notes that it would be "disappointing" if an increased focus on consent merely led us to substitute the analogy of theatrical and parliamentary representation for the more common New Historicist analogy of theatrical and monarchical power.[83] Yet at the same time, attacks like Prynne's show that, at least in the minds of some critics, the operations of Parliament and theatre shared some genuine, and genuinely disturbing, similarities – not in the way they relied on the audience's consent but in the way they undermined it. The problem with political representation was not that it was secret, but that it was symbolic and extra-rational: this was the debilitating link with the literary imagination, made visible in the figure of the child and in forms of childish folly. According to Prynne, it was necessary to destroy the similarities between political and poetic representation in order to create a chastened, authoritative version of political representation.

Prynne makes the connection explicit in the expanded edition of *Minors No Senators* published in 1661. This edition roughly doubles the size of his original tract and offers more details about the corrupting influences that skew elections and undercut authoritative representation. Specifically, Prynne adds a preface attacking "prodigal Entertainments" that he believes contribute to "Improvident, Indiscreet, Corrupt, Intemperate Elections."[84] According to the traditional model of parliamentary selection by assent and consensus rather than by contested choice, candidates generally secured their voters well before the election, then sealed the deal by paying for supporters' lodging and entertainment before, during, and after the election. These entertainments included not only the copious consumption of food and drink but also displays of music, dancing, and spectacle in a carnivalesque celebration of "institutionalized misrule."[85] Ironically, as the notion of government by consent became more central to the English political culture, bringing with it a corresponding rise in contested elections, the wild lavishness of these entertainments began to exceed all former bounds. In the 1620s, it had already become common to spend hundreds of pounds on drink, bull baiting, and other entertainments; by the late 1670s, candidates could easily spend thousands to provide bell ringers, musicians, and alcohol in what Mark Knights describes as "increasingly sophisticated attempts to seduce [a voter] away from his rational choice."[86] Prynne singles out these prodigal entertainments because he believes they facilitate and demonstrate the failure of agency that child parliamentarians so clearly embody, concluding his preface by utterly conflating childish play with childish political representation: Solomon was surely right "That Childhood and Youth are Vanity."[87] It is impossible to unravel this statement, to decide whether Prynne means it to apply to the child MPs or the childish entertainments that get them elected by deluding and corrupting voters. The simple reason is that childish indulgence and prodigal entertainments demonstrate the same qualities of vanity, foolishness, and imaginative exorbitance as child representatives.

Those qualities are also familiarly infectious, luring adult voters into electing mere children to represent them. They gave the game away to opponents of consent who charged that emboldened parliamentary representation would unleash the forces of anarchy, characterized in contemporary verse libels as an unholy trinity of irrational women, apprentices, and boys:

> There's no such thinge,
> As Bishopp or Kinge,
> Or Peers, but in Name, or shewe,
> Come clownes, come boyes, come hobberdehoyes,
> Come females of each Degree,
> Streach out yor throats, & bring in yor votes,
> To make good this Anarchye.[88]

Prynne answers such charges by emphasizing that his underlying goal is not to give the babbling rabble a voice but to control their noise by drawing a line between political and theatrical representation. The fundamental inability of the church and courts to ascertain when childhood ended and adult will became possible, however, represented a major obstacle to the kind of governance that he proposed. As seen in the previous chapter, boy actors exemplified the problem, slipping back and forth between childhood and adulthood, object and subject, and this liminal instability was routinely on display elsewhere in the culture, from child parliamentarians to figures like John Donne and his brother, who entered Oxford before they entered their teens, Andrew Marvell, who matriculated at Cambridge at age thirteen, and Philip Sidney himself, who became a member of Gray's Inn at age twelve, entered Cambridge at age thirteen, and signed a contract to create a high-powered political alliance, through marriage to Sir William Cecil's daughter, at age fourteen.[89] When did their voices finally demonstrate the kind of authority that Prynne needed to ground absolute obligation in consent?

For patriarchal theorists like Robert Filmer (c.1588–1653), the answer was "never," and the problem itself justified the rejection of consent as a valid ground of obligation.[90] Prynne spurned this strategy, but not because of any principled anti-royalism, given that by the second edition of *Minors No Senators* he was well on his way to becoming a kind of exotic pet of the Restoration regime and would soon produce an exhaustive defense of the king's absolute supremacy "in and over all Matters, Causes, Persons Spiritual as well as Temporal."[91] Rather, Prynne rejected the paternalistic model because of his belief that consent could be a more effective means of control and discipline than the system of birth and patronage; consent required voters actively to "resign up their Lives, Liberties, Estates, Laws, Religion into the hands" of others.[92] Such a view was wholly in the mainstream of political thought during the early 1640s, when parliamentary controversialists like Charles Herle (1598–1659) argued that Parliament's war against the king would never encourage the people to "rise and make resistance" because "the people have reserved no power in themselves from themselves in Parliament."[93] As we shall see in the next chapter, such a view of political representation was in fact surprisingly close to Thomas Hobbes's, and Deborah Baumgold has noted that Hobbes and his parliamentary opponents during this period disagreed not about whether the people were free, but about whether they ceded their freedom to the king or Commons.[94] Accordingly, both Hobbes and Prynne attempted to create more stable versions of authority not by eliminating consent, but by eliminating liminal, "childish" voices from their political systems.

Recognizing the uncertainty about when and how adult voice emerges, Prynne in fact is not really happy even with children who have reached the English age of majority serving in Parliament. He approvingly notes that neither civil nor canon law allows children to serve before the age of twenty-four, a tentative age of adulthood often cited in the medical and legal sources examined earlier. But he also recognizes that even this age is not enough to draw a firm line between childhood and adulthood, and his attempts to avoid all liminality ultimately lead him to the position that representatives and their electors should ideally be "OLD MEN."[95] Following his usual method of piling up biblical and classical sources to win an argumentative war of attrition, Prynne cites Deuteronomy, Numbers, the sixteenth-century Neapolitan Lawyer Alexander ab Alexandro, Jean Bodin, and many others en route to his triumphant proclamation that "no Infants under age, or Children, but Elders, Ancients of the people, for yeares, wisdome and experience, ought to be Members of our supreame Councell especially in such a time as this."[96] Again, in this Prynne was neither odd nor alone: his opinion would be followed by prominent Parliament men like the Earl of Shaftesbury (1621–83), Locke's great patron and a founder of the Whig party, who remained passionately concerned about a system that allowed the election of representatives under the age of "Forty years (whereof twenty five are generally spent in Childhood and vanity)."[97] In retrospect, Prynne's attack on child parliamentarians looks bizarre to us only because such attacks succeeded so completely at situating children and their vain preoccupations in a separate, apolitical world.

In the second half of this book we will see that not everyone embraced a model of authoritative representation that eschewed childish play. A century's worth of performances by children trained in humanist classrooms had proven that symbolic and fictional representation could work powerful effects, and Milton in particular embraced and expanded this tradition – in his hands, childish "poetical furie" becomes a revolutionary resource. But we cannot fully appreciate the originality of his achievement until we understand how the foremost political thinker of his age worked to prevent it. As the following chapter shows, Hobbes struggles with the question of the child's consent and obligation throughout his career, but ultimately his strategy for eliminating the messy coming-of-age moment is opposite to Prynne's, as he makes the diminutive child rather than the old man the basis of consent. Grounding obligation on the preverbal, pre-rational acceptance of nurture by the newborn infant, Hobbes not only redefines the nature of consent but also asserts in a wholly new way the relationship between political representation and art.

CHAPTER 3

Contract's Children
Thomas Hobbes and the Culture of Subjection

From grown boys performing their limited agency on stage to minors dramatizing the failure of authoritative consent in the House of Commons, the previous chapters have shown that childhood figured prominently in early modern formulations of political voice. To return to Jacques Rancière's formulation, if the basic problem of politics is knowing whether subjects "are speaking or just making a noise," then during the era of English revolution this was a question of determining when childish babble became meaningful voice, and it was fundamentally complicated by the messy, protracted grey area between infancy and adulthood.[1] As suggested earlier in the book, attempts to ground obligation on consent accordingly led to the gradual calcification of boundaries around childhood and to the firm distinction of political representation, as the realm of adult rationality, from poetic representation, which became more firmly established as the realm of childish mimesis. The current chapter argues that the era's boldest and most influential political theorist, Thomas Hobbes, also participated in this attempt to erase the disruptive coming-of-age moment from the political system, but in a very different way from Prynne. By redefining consent to include the earliest acts of preverbal infants, he justified a condition of absolute subjection that begins at birth.

Together, the converse approaches represented by Hobbes and Prynne demonstrate the developing tendency to relegate children and their encounters with poesy to the political margins, replacing the potential for transgression that was so pronounced in *Epicoene* with the more prescriptive and politically innocent experience that would be found in the new eighteenth-century genre of children's literature. My goals are to illuminate the origins of this process, to establish it as a useful context for the works explored in the second half of this book, and also to provide a needed revaluation of Hobbes's place in seventeenth-century debates over contract and consent. Although patriarchalism and family structures have been fruitfully explored in Hobbes scholarship, the role of children and childishness has not. In fact, the critical consensus has generally been that Hobbes eliminates the "complex economic, emotive, and social bonds" between parents and children, as Philip Abbot argues, or that "family bonds do not exist in Hobbes," as Su Fang Ng has claimed.[2] There are good reasons for this perception, but it is incomplete. While Hobbes's early works attempt to flatten or eliminate traditional ties between parents and children, this appears to have satisfied neither Hobbes nor his critics. Subsequently, his decades-long struggle to reconceptualize the mimetic child's obligation was key to formulating a theory of representation that replicated complex, authoritarian family bonds on a grand scale while attributing their power not to birth but to consent.

This had a major impact on both the style and substance of Hobbes's work. No less than the humanists and their critics discussed in the previous chapter, Hobbes was troubled by the childish quality of "poetical fury," which, as he explains in one of his final works, can overwhelm "either judgment, or reason, or memory, or any other intellectual virtue," and which was particularly prevalent in fantastic forms like romance.[3] Critical opinion, however, has long been divided over the lingering place of such poetic or rhetorical elements in Hobbes's own philosophy. In one persistent view, the so-called "monster of Malmesbury" was also a monster of modernity, casting off his early humanistic training to embrace the methods and manner of the new natural science.[4] Alternatively, Howard Warrender argues that Hobbes's moral and political conclusions simply do not follow from his natural philosophy but derive instead from an essentially medieval Christian ethics.[5] Few recent scholars have endorsed Warrender's idea that medieval Christianity was the source of these conclusions, but many have been keen to acknowledge the stress lines that he located in Hobbes's thought and to situate them historically and culturally.[6] In accordance with this broader movement, David Johnston and Quentin Skinner have argued that in the wake of the English Civil War, Hobbes fully embraced his humanist roots, inspired by "a new skepticism about men's abilities to perceive and pursue their own interests in a rational manner" and convinced that "in the moral but not in the natural sciences, the methods of demonstrative reasoning need to be supplemented by the moving force of eloquence."[7] As we shall see, Hobbes's attempts to explain the child's place in the commonwealth helped drive this return to eloquence and the idea that art could not only persuade but also generate obligation – especially if it was reformed along properly didactic, authoritarian lines.

Problem Children

For most of Hobbes's contemporaries, filial obligation was the readily available solution to the problem of representing children and other subrational humans. According to the standard line of thought, because parents love their children, they would both nurture them and act in their best interests. This basic affective principle made originary contract unnecessary, explaining not only how families formed but also how they created a framework for political representation that extended to subjects who were not actually children. Such paternalism is a familiar aspect of Stuart and Caroline absolutism, but it was equally germane to the early republican accounts that underpinned the emerging parliamentary opposition in the 1640s. In Cicero's influential etiology, for example, filial affect generates society, and representation of even the most troublesome cases of infants and other voiceless subcategories of subjects within the republican state is just, binding, and appropriate because it is rooted in mankind's natural affections for one another. Those natural affections recapitulate the affective ties of childhood, modeled in the nurturing relationship between parents and their offspring, as Cicero explains in a passage from *De Finibus* that Samuel Pufendorf (1632–94) would later invoke against Hobbes:

> In the whole moral sphere of which we are speaking there is nothing more glorious nor of wider range than the affinity between mankind. That species of alliance and communication of interests and that actual affection which exists between man and man comes into existence instantly upon our birth, owing to the fact that children are loved by their parents and the family as a whole. It is bound together by the ties of marriage and parenthood, and gradually spreads its influence beyond the home, first by blood relationships, then by marriage, later by friendships, afterwards by the bonds of neighborhood, then to fellow-citizens and political allies and friends, and lastly by embracing the whole of the human race. This sentiment ... of which I speak, is called Justice.[8]

The love between parents and children is the basis of all other bonds, radiating by degrees into society as a whole. Even before children are fully rational, their natural affections begin to embody the principle of justice that underlies the distribution of power. Cicero specifically constructs this natural affection between children and parents as a "communication" (*communicatio*) of interests.

As the name implies, this empathic principle is also a rhetorical one. An orator uses the formal device of *communicatio* to invite listeners to take part in his enquiry, activating the mimetic impulse that supposedly came into being the moment the child was born.[9] As Thomas Wilson describes *communicatio* in his *Art of Rhetorique* (1553), the speaker employing it asks, "What would you have doen, if you were in the same case?," appealing to the auditor's "owne conscience" by asking him to mimic the position of another.[10] *Communicatio* does not merely head off objections; it brings listeners into the intellectual and emotional experience. It is in that sense an imaginative act, and this is why children, who had been renowned since Plato for their imaginative mimetic abilities, could engage in it long before they had the capacity to authorize any kind of rational contract or otherwise give their voice in their own government.

As we have seen, establishing a category of subjects with no rights to dispose of themselves, like the children's voices in *Coriolanus*, is even more central to monarchical absolutism, because the extended period of early modern childhood provided an established model of subjection where liberty flourished only within bounds firmly inscribed by authority. During the Civil War, childhood accordingly helped provide a key juridical framework for invalidating action against King Charles, as John Bramhall (1594–1663) demonstrated when he argued that the parliamentary forces who vowed to defend the town of Hull against the king's troops had no capacity to do so under the law: "an Oath made by one that is not *sui juris*, who hath not power over him selfe, in that which he sweares, is voide even when it is made: As for a Child or a Wife to sweare against their Filiall or Conjugall Duty, or for a Subject to swear … against his Allegiance."[11]

In such cases, childhood's value was not only legal but also polemical. As Gordon Schochet has shown, the commandment to "honor thy father and mother" became "a starting point for a discourse concerning obedience to the king" because it allowed that discourse to appeal to a householder's own domestic authority in order to justify his subjection to an even higher paternal power.[12] Rebels against Charles's benevolent paternity were not merely infantilized, but depicted as "monsterous Children," as the Royalist army officer and clergyman Thomas Bayly put it in 1649, "who are borne with teeth in their mouthes, bite off the nipple, and starve themselves for lack of sustenance."[13] Bayly's unforgettable image, drawn from medieval romance and folk belief, graphically literalizes the concept of the king as "nursing father" in Numbers 11.12, where Moses complains that he must carry the Lord's people "as a nursing father beareth the sucking child," and in Isaiah 49.23, where "kings shall be thy nursing fathers."[14] From the time of James I, who made the "nursing father" reference a key part of his divine right rhetoric, it is difficult to overstate the resources Royalists poured into collapsing the distance between the realm of private affect and public rule, perpetuating such images as both history and analogy, biblical proof of the natural monarchical order and metaphorical description of the respective roles of the nurturing king and the passive, childlike subject.[15]

Hobbes was not above using such rhetoric, and beginning with the *Elements of Law* (1640), his works routinely maintain that "all subjects in commonwealths are in the nature of children and servants," citing Colossians 3.20, "children obey your parents in all things," as support for his political theories (*EL* 2.6.4.147).[16] Despite their polemical appeal, however, Hobbes uses these patriarchal materials only to illustrate his theories of obligation rather than to justify them; after he sets out his theory of obligation, he then includes the biblical, patriarchal language "to take away this scruple of conscience concerning obedience to human laws, amongst those that interpret to themselves the word of God in the Holy Scriptures" (*EL* 2.6.3.145). As Ng has shown, Hobbes understood that the family analogy's "universality was a double-edged sword," and that it was simply too easy for clever wordsmiths or dubious orators to turn arguments like Bayly's and Bramhall's on their heads.[17] Milton, for example, devastatingly finesses these patriarchal models as he answers the charge that the regicides have no power over themselves (are "*impotentum*") because they are children of the king and are thus guilty of parricide ("*parricidii crimen*"):

> You are wholly in the dark in failing to distinguish the rights of a father from those of a king: and once you have named kings the fathers of their country [*Patriae Patres*], you believe this metaphor so persuasive that whatever I would admit concerning a father I would at once grant true of a king. But a king and a father are very different things. Our fathers begot us and made us; our king did not make us, but rather we him [*Pater nos genuit; at non rex nos, sed nos regem creavimus*]. Nature gave the people fathers, but the people itself gave itself a king; so the people do not exist because of a king, but a king exists because of the people [*propter populum rex est*]. (*C* 7:44; *CPW* 4:68)[18]

First Milton dismantles the metaphor, distinguishing the private, domestic sphere in which fatherly authority operates from the public sphere. Then he appropriates the affective, familial model to show how far King Charles's behavior had deviated from the principles of natural, affective justice: "we bear with a father, as we do with a king, though he be harsh and severe; but we do not bear with even a father if he is a tyrant" (*C* 7:44; *CPW* 4:327). As father figure, Charles himself is the monster, and just as a "father who murders his son deserves to pay with his head" (*Pater si filium interficit, capite poenas dabit*), so Charles must be held accountable to the public laws of the land as interpreted by the principles of private conscience (*C* 7:46; *CPW* 4:327).

Milton published this aggressive rejoinder to patriarchal absolutism in his *Defense of the English People* (*Pro Populo Anglicano Defensio*) in 1651, the same year Hobbes published *Leviathan*. But from the time Hobbes began circulating the first version of his political philosophy a decade earlier in *The Elements of Law* (1640), he had been working to cut off such arguments by proving that no innate principles of natural morality or government existed. Hobbes warned that holding public authority accountable to private conscience would turn the principles of affective justice into a vehicle for rebellion, and the union of religious belief and political dissent during the Civil War confirmed his deepest fears.[19] The idea that familial relationships demonstrate natural justice was simply an illusion created by classical republican writers who were "passionately addicted to popular government" and wanted to promote it as an organic entity (*EL* 2.9.8.183). These authors "have insinuated their opinions, by eloquent sophistry" in the schools and universities of England where they seduce "young men, who come thither void of prejudice, and whose minds are yet as white paper, capable of any instruction" (*EL* 2.9.8.183–4). This was the root cause of rebellion and bloodshed, and it underwrote Hobbes's early decision to aspire to the "method" of science and to consult "more with logic than with rhetoric" (*EL*, epistle, xvi).

Hobbes would wipe the slate clean by starting with a pre-social state of nature, which is also "an estate of war" of every man against every other man (*EL* 1.19.1.100). As he memorably depicted it later in *Leviathan*, the life of man in this condition would be "solitary, poore, nasty, brutish, and short," and dominated by the overwhelming fear of death (*L* 1.13.186). By beginning here, not with mutual affections but with the most basic drives for self-preservation, Hobbes would replace the language of communication with the language of legally binding contract, demonstrating that "concord amongst men is artificial, and by way of covenant" (*EL* 1.19.5.102–03). Faced with the prospect of continual war, individuals would relinquish their right to fend for themselves and "agree in the will to be directed and governed in the way to that which they desire to attain, namely their own good, which is the work of reason" (*EL* 1.15.75). Such agreements were binding and made it possible for Hobbes to explain with confidence "that no man in any commonwealth whatsoever hath right to resist him or them, on whom they have conferred" the sovereign power (*EL* 2.1.7.111).

But the rational component of contract and covenant made accounting for children in contract theory even more difficult than accounting
for them in the existing positive law, which, as we have seen, was shot
through with ambiguity about when words became more than babble
and misdeeds became more than mischief or indiscretion. In either nature
or the civil state, children's mental deficiency undermined the idea that
their obedience within any system could be explained by a rational choice,
and their relation to adults represented a gross inequality unlike anything
else contract theorists had to deal with. Women, for example, were often
described as irrational, but as Carole Pateman has shown, Hobbes could
quite easily depict marriage as a contract between two competent adults.[20]
By contrast, according to Hobbes's own calculations, the child's ability
to choose its own preservation was absurdly limited: "there be beasts,"
he admits in *Leviathan*, "that at a year old observe more, and pursue
that which is for their good, more prudently, than a child can do at ten"
(*L* 1.3.98).

Even if we focus on youth instead of the neonatal period, children
represent the outward bounds of irrational passion, as Hobbes notes in
one of his earliest works, a "brief" of Aristotle's *Art of Rhetoric* that divides
life into the three stages of youth, middle age, and old age: "young men
are violent in their desires. Incontinent. Inconstant, easily forsaking what
they desired before. Longing mightily, and soon satisfied. Apt to anger,
and in their anger violent. Lovers of Honour, more than of Profit ...
apt to err in the excess, rather than the defect, contrary to that precept
of *Chilon, Ne quid nimis;* for they overdo every thing."[21] As Leo Strauss
showed long ago, Hobbes's early engagement with Aristotle's account of
human motivations and passions remained signally influential throughout
his career for explaining the physical and psychological forces that motivated men to form a society.[22] The child's extreme passion alone, then,
need not be a problem, because Hobbes famously argues that passion,
not reason, drives men toward contract. But contract supposedly constitutes a reasonable response to the most powerful passion, fear of violent
death.[23] As Jean Hampton has explained, "Reason operates as an instrument of the passions" in Hobbes's system; desire determines what is good
and what we should pursue (namely, the preservation of life) and reason
provides the deliberative ability to satisfy that desire.[24] But children and
youth, as we see from Hobbes's free translation of Aristotle, lack both reason and a single, dominant passion. Although their desires are powerful,
they are inconstant, and, contrary to the normative psychology we find
elsewhere in Hobbes's work, they specifically reject self-interest and profit.

In this sense they are very much like the category of people that Hampton describes as "sick" or "insane."[25] Hobbes's own term is "prodigal," a mass of conflicting emotions, making the entire youthful period like "a kind of drunkeness."[26] Unlike the cases of the sick or insane, however, this is the natural condition of youth and, unless such childish things can definitively be put behind, it is deeply embedded in the human condition.

Such innate irrationality was not only a problem for Hobbes, but made "the problem of accounting for the survival of infants part of a general problem in contractarianism."[27] In the account of Hobbes's predecessor and sometimes influence Hugo Grotius (1583–1645), to take the most prominent instance, childhood introduced a hermeneutic dilemma to an otherwise unambiguous account of obligation. Because contract is rational, the Dutch jurist says in *De Jure Belli ac Pacis*, if it "is made without deliberation we do not allow it to have any power of obliging whatsoever."[28] This looks like a simple legal principle when applied to parties with obviously defective judgment. But it requires an act of interpretation when applied to youths – infants under the civil law until at least age twenty-five:

> The promises of madmen, idiots, and infants are void. But the case of minors is not the same, because although they are supposed, like women, not to have stable judgment, yet this condition is not permanent, nor is it of itself sufficient to render their acts invalid. So it is not possible to determine certainly at what age a child begins to use his reason: but this must be judged either from his daily actions, or from the common customs of each nation.[29]

Grotius spoke from experience, having himself entered the University of Leiden at eleven years old and graduated at age fifteen, still a minor for at least a decade under the civil law. By age sixteen he was working as an advocate at the Hague, earning fame for his good judgment within a legal tradition that formally discounted his ability, as a minor, to make rationally binding decisions about the disposal of his own person and property; such decisions remained the prerogative of his father until he was much older.[30] How could contract possibly explain all social relations when familial structures so clearly arose before the age of reason and maintained their binding power long after a child could become rational?

Grotius, who retains elements of Aristotelian essentialism alongside his theory of self-interested contract, gets out of the dilemma by invoking natural sociability. In difficult cases the binding power of promises made by or for youths can always be tested against inherent moral principles, and conveniently, one of those moral principles is that parents have dominion over children "*ex generatione*."[31] Although generation legitimizes the dominion of both father and mother, fathers ultimately have the superior right "due to the superiority of sex" (*ob sexus praestantiam*) – another inherent, natural inequality that closes the door on troublesome questions about divided loyalty and obligation.[32] Acting according to the natural principles of familial affect, fathers can enter into binding contracts that are in the best interest of the children and the family, although children never specifically grant them this power. There is no conflict and no ambiguity, because a child who wished to resist such a contract would be acting irrationally, hence proving himself unfit to act independently. Grotius divides the child's life into three periods: neonatal care, the extended period of life in the parental home, and life as an independent householder. Throughout each of these periods natural principles continue to obligate respect and deference, even if parents lose some rights, such as the ability to sell their children (*vendere*), in the final period.[33] Grotius sharply divides this *ex generatione* dominion from the subsequent dominion that arises *ex consensu* from "either union or subjection."[34]

Despite Hobbes's approval of Aristotle's rhetoric, he roundly rejects Aristotle's essentialism and "dislikes almost everything else Aristotle wrote," as Victoria Silver notes, so it is no surprise that he also rejects this aspect of earlier contract theories.[35] After all, it was precisely such reasoning that led critics of natural equality such as Robert Filmer to fix on the child as a fault line that could undermine the contractual basis of authority altogether. Filmer pounces on Grotius in his *Observations Concerning the Original of Government* (1652): "In that he confesseth in all cases children are bound to study always to please their parents out of piety and duty – 'the cause of which', as he saith, 'is perpetual' – I cannot conceive how in any case children can naturally have any power or moral faculty of doing what they please."[36] Children are their parents' thralls, except where the "transcendent fatherly power" of the prince releases them from their lesser parental obligations.[37] To defer to the natural law of filial devotion and duty weakened contract, not strengthened it. This was, after all, just another way of admitting that some parties needed to have their ability to contract adjudicated by someone else. As Filmer concludes in *The Anarchy of a Limited or Mixed Monarchy* (1648):

> It will be said that infants and children may be concluded by the votes of their parents. This remedy may cure some part of the mischief, but it destroys the whole cause and at last stumbles upon the true original of government. For if it be allowed that the acts of parents bind the children, then farewell the doctrine of the natural freedom of mankind.[38]

This condition is perpetual, because "in nature there is no nonage. If a man be not born free she doth not assign him any other time when he shall attain his freedom."[39] For Filmer, the child, therefore, solves a crucial problem of representation. "Mankind is like the sea," Filmer explains, "ever ebbing or flowing, every minute one is born another dies. Those that are the people this minute, are not the people the next minute."[40] "The people" are unrepresentable because they never form a discrete body that can offer consent. In contrast, writes Filmer, the simple fact of nature is that children are "bound to obey" long "before consent can be given."[41]

Hobbes's Early Solution: Instant Adulthood and Absolute Conquest

Considering the difficulties of accounting for the child's survival and obligation through consent, it is perhaps not surprising that Hobbes avoided the issue as best he could in his earliest works, erasing childhood in favor of a clean fiction of contract in a thoroughly theoretical natural state. The *Elements of Law* begins its discussion of human equality by noting "how little odds there is of strength or knowledge between men of mature age" (*EL* 1.14.2.70) and describing the origins of the state by considering individuals "in the state of nature, without covenants or subjection one to another, as if they were but even now all at once created male and female" (*EL* 2.3.2.127). Both this emphasis on mature age and Hobbes's fantasy of instant adulthood resemble Prynne's proposal to draw all representatives from the ranks of "OLD MEN"; both formulations neatly evade questions about how voice emerges from infancy as a political act.[42] *De Cive* (1642) makes this elision of childhood even starker: "let us return to the state of nature once again and consider men as though they were suddenly sprung from the earth (like mushrooms) as adults right now, without any obligation to one another."[43] Perhaps a bit ironic, this is also Hobbes's most elegant and simple version of the state of nature. In the world Hobbes constructs in these early works, the mushroom men become obligated in moments that seem strangely cut free of history and emptied of any emotional significance besides fear, "suddenly" (*subito*) sprung from the ground "right now" (*iamiam*), spared death by the sword or granted emancipation (*DC* 8.1.160).

Although Hobbes's state of nature in *De Cive* wryly echoes Ovid's account of the dragon's teeth sown by Cadmus that spring up as deadly armed men, it also supports Skinner's sense that this is the high-water mark of Hobbes's attempts to write in a genuinely "scientific" style that rejects the formal arts of rhetoric and anticipates the rigorously axiomatic reasoning of much later contract theory.[44] Not unlike the Euclidean geometry Hobbes so admired, which could postulate a set of conditions, such as points and lines, and then deduce necessary shapes from them, Hobbes's postulation of men like mushrooms, driven by natural reason and overwhelming self-interest, leads to his most methodical account of contractual obligation. From this theoretical starting point of absolute equality, dominion can arise in only one of three ways: contract, conquest, or generation (*DC* 8.1.160).

In the first scenario, equal adult men, driven by the levers of self-protection and fear, agree to some rational transfer of power and goods that serves all. The second and third scenarios, conquest and generation, lead to forms of contractual obligation in exactly the same way. Victims of conquest agree, if only tacitly, to serve their conqueror or cede certain benefits to him in exchange for their lives and freedom from chains, at which point they become participants in contract. Mary Nyquist has shown that Roman war slavery provides the juridical framework for this form of contractual obligation, in which an individual "submitteth to an assailant for fear of death" (*EL* 2.3.2.127).[45] This martial model allows Hobbes to define even the basic social unit of the family in very different terms from his patriarchalist opponents. "Confederations are formed by conquest," Pateman explains, "and once formed, are called 'families.'"[46] Family authority is no different from political authority: families may precede a larger state, or be absorbed by a higher authority, but they cannot stand apart from it. The only exceptions to this model of contract by conquest are the slaves who remain in chains; their physical bondage indicates that they really subsist in the state of war, making it possible for them to "escape, or kill their Master without doing anything against natural laws [*nihil faciunt contra leges naturales*]" (*DC* 8.4.161). Once a slave agrees to be released from his chains or his prison, however, he has contracted for total obedience, and a "master therefore is supposed to have no less right over those, whose bodies he leaveth at liberty, than over those he keepeth in bonds and imprisonment" (*EL* 2.3.4.128). The result, Nyquist notes, is a radical redefinition of liberty that suggests "all servants and subjects who are not in bonds or prison" are free.[47]

This basic outline of Hobbes's early political philosophy hews quite closely to Strauss's model of the Hobbesian psychology of contract, where "it is the fearfulness of death rather than the sweetness of life which makes man cling to existence."[48] From such spare materials, Hobbes achieves the central goal of explaining the obligation of adults to their sovereign, leading him to describe his philosophy, with characteristic modesty, as "the only foundation of such science" (*EL*, epistle, xvi). His attempt to deal with the problem of the child's obligation, however, is less convincing. Hobbes makes it clear that children are identical to other victims of conquest and that "the title to dominion over a child, proceedeth not from the generation, but from the preservation of it" (*EL* 2.4.3.132). The passage Nyquist cites to show Hobbes's reliance on Roman war slavery in fact invokes infants as the primary example of subjects who may be conquered and forced into submission:

> He therefore that hath already subdued his adversary, or gotten into his power any other that either by infancy, or weakness, is unable to resist him, by right of nature may take the best caution, that such infant, or such feeble and subdued person can give him, of being ruled and governed by him for the time to come. (*EL* 1.14.13.73–74)

If Hobbes were using "infant" here to refer to the kind of grown boys that we have encountered in previous chapters, this might not seem bizarre. At nineteen or twenty, it is easy to imagine an infant submitting to conquest, and this would fit reasonably well into traditional juridical models where the freedom to choose and the responsibility to choose wisely emerge at the same moment. It would also fit into traditional patriarchal patterns where the father holds absolute sway in the domestic sphere until the child comes of age and transfers his allegiance to a higher authority. But rather than introduce the prospect of divided power or natural subjection into his system, Hobbes insists that his battlefield scenario takes place during the infant's earliest moments of life.

This is why the mother, "in whose power it is to save or destroy it," first obtains dominion over the child, in a neonatal version of a victor holding his captive at sword's point on the battlefield (*EL* 2.4.3.132). In *De Cive*, Hobbes even specifies that the infant in the state of nature is born into "a state of war" (*status belli*), and that the woman's conquest makes her both a mother and a ruler (*DC* 9.3.164). In neither the *Elements of Law* nor in *De Cive*, however, does Hobbes explain how the child indicates his allegiance, or what advantage the mother gains by conquering a helpless newborn. The closest he comes, in either text, is his argument that feeding the infant somehow procures contractual allegiance that prevents future danger, because "it is to be presumed, that he which giveth sustenance to another, whereby to strengthen him, hath received a promise of obedience in consideration thereof. For else it would be wisdom in men, rather to let their children perish, while they are infants, than to live in their danger or subjection when they are grown" (*EL* 2.4.3.133).

In these early works, Hobbes never actually calls the child's agreement "consent," and this along with the sheer implausibility of applying the model of battlefield conquest to neonatal care would seem to indicate a weak point in his account. Nevertheless, he explains that children are in the "most absolute subjection" to the person who rears them and who may "alienate them ... by selling or giving them in adoption or servitude to others; or may pawn them for hostages, kill them for rebellion, or sacrifice them for peace, by the law of nature" (*EL* 2.4.9.134). Moreover, he makes this condition absolutely central to the radically diminished notion of liberty discussed earlier. The child's subjection, Hobbes insists, is no different from any other subject's, "and this was the reason, that the name that signifieth children, in the Latin tongue is *liberi*, which also signifieth freemen ... and this is all that can be understood by the liberty of the subject" (*EL* 2.4.9.134). In *De Cive*, Hobbes closes the gap between slaves and children even more completely, saying that "children are liberated from subjection in the same way as subjects [*subditus*] and slaves [*servi*]. Emancipation is the same thing as manumission [*eadem enim res est emancipatio cum manumissione*]" (*DC* 9.7.166). The English edition of *De Cive* (1651) translates *servi* as "servant," but as Nyquist makes clear, rather than diminishing the level of servitude, this reflects Hobbes's own habit of "calmly, evenhandedly, obliterating any differences between children, servants, and political subjects."[49]

Yet by the time he writes *Leviathan*, Nyquist notes, Hobbes will obscure the extent to which he models paternal dominion on the slave master's dominion, giving the relationship between master and servant "a more conventionally patriarchal character."[50] Nyquist does not explain how or why Hobbes makes this change, but as we turn to the contemporary criticism of his work, we find a likely answer: Hobbes responds to this criticism by returning to humanism's theories of mimetic education and interpreting them along contractual lines. In *Leviathan*, the diminutive child models the same kind of absolute subjection we find in Hobbes's early works, but Hobbes explicitly calls it consent and describes an educational process that can replicate it in the larger social body.

Contemporary Critiques of Hobbes's "Drowsie Dream"

According to his early critics, Hobbes had replaced felt experience with a particularly implausible kind of "fiction or fancy," as Filmer put it, ignoring biblical and personal history to go "running after the opinions of philosophers and poets."[51] Somewhat surprisingly, such criticism fixated less on Hobbes's equation of subjects and slaves than on his handling of the child's obligation. In particular, Hobbes's critics decried the elision of children from his paradigmatic state of nature, where the model social contract is initiated by adults who spring from the earth like mushrooms, and they argued that only such a gross distortion of reality could enable his subsequent depiction of children in families as victims of conquest. Jon Parkin has argued that by studying these early responses we can see that Hobbes was not the isolated figure we often imagine, but that he "managed to exercise a profound influence upon the minds of late seventeenth-century English men and women."[52] Indeed, the influence was mutual, and a brief account of these responses can help demonstrate both childhood's importance to the continuing debates over consent and the ways that Hobbes sharpened and refined his depiction of political obligation in conversation with his critics.

John Bramhall (1594–1663) was among the first, most vocal, and most important of Hobbes's critics. The two Royalist exiles met at the Paris residence of William Cavendish, the Marquess of Newcastle, in 1645, two years before the second edition of *De Cive*. Their discussion turned into a written exchange, and the unauthorized publication of Hobbes's side of this correspondence nearly a decade later sparked the most vigorous printed controversy between Hobbes and any of his critics, producing five books of disputation between them.[53] Like many detractors who followed him, Bramhall insisted that Hobbes's "state of meer nature is a drowsie dream of his own feigning, which looketh upon *men as if they were suddenly grown out of the ground like mushroms*."[54]

The gross absurdity of this fiction became clear in Hobbes's attempt to describe the origin of families. "He might as well tell us in plain termes," Bramhall chides, "that all the obligation which a child hath to his parent, is because he did not take him by the heeles and knock out his braines against the walls, so soon as he was born. Though this be intolerable, yet there is something of gratitude in it."[55] This became a standard line of attack. Hobbes's fiction of instant adulthood was "the prettiest *great nothing* that I ever read," wrote arch-Royalist William Lucy (1594–1677) at the Restoration, while the archbishop of Canterbury, Thomas Tenison (1636–1715), described it as a "romance" or "some such cheat upon the World, as Nurses are wont, in sport, to put upon unwary Children, when they tell them, they started up out of the Parsley-bed."[56] John Eachard (1637–97), a Cambridge scholar with Royalist sympathies, wrote a full-blown satire in which he posits a shower of "good, *stout, speaking, understanding men*" from the sky, and no "*Scottish mist* of *Babies*, which would have entangled us again in the *old story* of *children* not being *sociable*."[57] While such a fiction might serve Hobbes's mechanistic theory, all these critics agreed, it left him with an inadequate language to explain the desires that motivate contract.

If men sprang up without relation to one another, no amount of fear would socialize them. This is the work of family as a site of undeniable, and sometimes unreciprocated, altruism. In family life, Bramhall maintained, "we see daily how affection prevails against the dictate of reason."[58] A father, for example, "may love an ungracious Childe, and yet not esteem him good," and while the parent's nurture and love would seem to exceed any rational calculus, it also offered a pattern for the child to emulate.[59] For Hobbes's critics childhood makes inequality a fact of nature, and without the sense of interdependence acquired in infancy, independent men driven by fear would lack the requisite affective machinery to join together in common cause.[60] To understand obligation in all its psychological and theological complexity, Bramhall concludes, we must return to "the primigenious and most natural state of mankind ... in Adam before his fall."[61] Where Hobbes has succumbed to "vain imaginations, and drowsie phantasies," a true account of the social contract must rely on a combination of reason, memory, and history that begins with Adam as the childish creation of a father-king whose authority he internalizes and replicates.[62]

This could simply be dismissed as an obstinate refusal to get Hobbes's point. After all, Hobbes claims he is conducting science, not history, and from this perspective all these criticisms are a little like pointing out that because the planes in Euclidean geometry are strictly imaginary we should reject the whole enterprise. He makes it clear that experience, or "Knowledge of Fact," is for historians; science examines not experience but "*Demonstrations* of Consequence of one Affirmation, to another" (*L* 1.9.148). Hobbes accordingly protested to Bramhall that "I never meant to ground my Answer upon the experience of what *Children, Fools, Madmen*, and *Beasts* do."[63] But in subsequent editions of *De Cive* and later in *Leviathan*, Hobbes strove to encompass his critics' sense that there must be some other process at work besides pure self-interest. Namely, he attempted to "reconstruct his account of natural law," as Parkin notes, "to give some substance to natural obligation."[64]

His approach was, first and foremost, to double down on his critics, countering their evidence of natural affection by using childhood to symbolize mankind's most basic antisocial inclinations. In 1647, two years after his initial debate with Bramhall, Hobbes published the second edition of *De Cive*, with a new preface that highlighted children as part of the primal state of nature rather than eliding them in favor of instant adults: "unless you give children [*infantes*] all they ask for, they are peevish and cry, and even beat their parents, and all this they have from nature. Yet they are free from guilt; neither may we really call them wicked [*mali*], first because they can do no harm, and next because wanting the free use of reason they are exempt from all duties" (*DC*, praefatio, 81). Childish behavior, in this view, correlates perfectly with the abstract original condition Hobbes had sketched in his earlier works. He adds that "a wicked man is almost the same thing as a child grown strong and sturdy, or a man with a childish spirit [*vir animo puerili*]; and malice [*malitia*] is the same thing as a defect of reason at an age when, by nature, governed by discipline and experience of harm, it normally accrues to men" (*DC*, praefatio, 81). Contract, in other words, constitutes maturation, in a subtle reworking of the traditional legal doctrine of *malitia supplet aetatem* (malice supplies the age). Childish, warring parties in the state of nature will seek alliance "as soon as they come to understand this hateful and miserable condition [*simulatque miseriam illam intellexerint*]" (*DC*, praefatio, 81). And just as in the court cases that invoked *malitia supplet aetatem* to punish very young children, this understanding and the legal obligation it brings can now happen long before any conventional age of reason.

Hobbes's argument diminishes the lofty import of choice in the same way he had deflated the high-flown rhetoric of liberty in the *Elements of Law*. As he acerbically wrote to Bramhall, "A *Child* may be so young as to do what it does without all *deliberation*, but that is but till it have the chance to be hurt by doing of somewhat, or till it be of age to understand the rod, for the actions, wherein he hath once had a check, shall be *deliberated* on the second time."[65] While Hobbes has given children a more prominent place in his contract theory than ever, he has decisively eliminated the fraught period of extended childhood and the sense that political coming of age depended on a careful exploration of the powers of reason and conscience. Now all it takes is the lingering smart of the whip to deliberate effectively.

At the same time, he begins to moderate his language in a way that both softens the blow of some of his most shocking pronouncements and extends the mechanism of contract into the affective realm that his critics had cited against him. While the Latin *De Cive* cites the formative "experience of harm" (*damnorum experientia*) in preparing children for political community, for example, the English translation published in 1651 cites "good education and experience," replacing Hobbes's original emphasis on natural, selfish passion with the more typical humanist emphasis on the power of loving, gentle instruction.[66] The shift to "good education" is the kind of interpolation scholars sometimes cite to argue that Hobbes did not have a hand in the translation. But Richard Tuck makes a strong case that Hobbes translated this section of the book at the very minimum, and its new emphasis on positive nurture is undoubtedly reflected elsewhere in Hobbes's works during this time.[67] We find a similar shift, for example, in the first, rather testy, footnote to the revised Latin *De Cive*, making it clear that the experience of harm is not the only force driving men towards society:

> It may seem a wonderful kind of stupidity [*mira stupiditas*], to lay such a stumbling block before the reader in the very threshold of civil doctrine, as to deny man to be born fit for society [*Hominem ad Societatem aptum natum non esse*]. Therefore I must explain more clearly. It is quite true that to man by nature, as man – that is as soon as he is born – perpetual solitude is unendurable; for infants need others to help them live, and when grown, to help them to live well. Therefore I do not deny that men desire to come together, driven by nature [*natura cogente*].(*DC*, praefatio, 81)

Hobbes adds that this natural inclination for fellowship is not the same thing as the formal alliances needed to institute civil societies, but it nevertheless exerts a powerful attractive force. "Many men (perhaps most)," he continues, "remain unfit for society during the whole course of their lives, either through defective mind or defective education [*vel morbo animi vel defectu disciplinae*]" (*DC* 1.2.92). But thanks to the "humane" quality that attracts them to one another, they can be made fit for society "by education [*disciplina*]" (*DC* 1.2.92). In short, alongside his more abstract and theoretical depiction of the mechanisms of consent and obligation, Hobbes begins in his revisions to acknowledge and embrace the idea that a nurturing education, beginning in the home, can engage the child on a complex affective level to produce obligation. This should not come as a total surprise, because Hobbes was serving as a tutor chaperoning his noble charge around the continent when he began working on *De Cive*.[68] But it is only in this revised form, as he responds to his critics, that Hobbes truly becomes identifiable as the kind of writer Deborah Baumgold has described, who is not primarily an "individualistic political thinker" bent on justifying the subjection of abstract everymen, but rather is concerned with analyzing the way political institutions and social roles generate and enforce obligation.[69] After revising his earlier works to address charges that he failed to account for affection, in *Leviathan* he unambiguously gives familial affection binding force, describing it as part of an educational process that weds discipline to contract. In doing so, Hobbes embraces his humanist roots even as he calls for a newly didactic art that will eliminate "poetical fury" from the humanistic educational method.

Nourishing Obligation

When Roger Ascham and the other humanists argued that "love is fitter than feare, and gentlenes better than beating, to bring up a childe rightlie in learninge," their point was not to liberate children with this gentle discipline but to bind these "most slipperie" subjects more securely to the interests of the state.[70] The idea that love could compel, in other words, was a humanist commonplace, and both Ascham and schoolmasters like John Brinsley (1566–c.1624) who followed him agreed that the "milde and loving government" of the humanist classroom was ideally suited to "overcome the most froward nature, and bring all into a cheerefull submission."[71] The challenge for Hobbes was to explain that such nurture operated with the binding force of contract rather than the more ephemeral power typically associated with persuasion.

Leviathan leaves little doubt that this is what Hobbes intends to do. Unlike his earlier works, *Leviathan* unequivocally argues that obligation immediately derives "from the Childs Consent, either expresse, or by other sufficient arguments declared" (*L* 2.20, 253). Hobbes's rationale is the same as in his earlier works, where he had also explained that the mother gained dominion by preserving the child, but in those works he had not explicitly called the child's first acceptance of this preservation "consent," and his equation of manumission and emancipation had implied that very young children were really more like bound slaves than like the unbound slaves who become the models for his notion of "free" citizenship. The child's instant consent in *Leviathan*, however, makes the child's earliest and most abject status the unambiguous product of contract. This is prior even to the "sexual contract" that Pateman describes as the submerged basis of all contract theory, a contract that gives a man political control over a woman and access to her body, thus allowing his subsequent agreements with other men, as the heads of families, in a "fraternal patriarchy."[72] The idea that the child's agreement with his mother precedes the sexual contract may seem counterintuitive, given that a man and woman obviously must have sex to produce a child. But Hobbes pointedly notes that this sometimes happens outside of contract or conquest: in the state of "meer

Nature ... it cannot be known who is the Father, unless it be declared by the Mother" (*L* 2.20.254). The mother first has the child "in her power," and "if she nourish it, it oweth its life to the Mother; and is therefore obliged to obey her" (*L* 2.20.254).

What could a humble and inarticulate child, with fewer rational powers than a beast, offer in exchange for this nourishment? Hobbes's answer is "gratitude," which has a newly legalistic hue in *Leviathan*. Preachers and moralists regularly reiterated that the child's fundamental duty to parents was gratitude, and in his earlier work Hobbes had discussed gratitude in similar terms.[73] In *De Cive*, for example, he explains "free gifts" by claiming that one person may provide a benefit to another because he expects some return out of gratitude. But the violation of this expectation is merely "ingratitude" that specifically does "not violate trust or contract [*violatio non est fidei, siue pactorum violatio*]" (*DC* 3.8.112). Likewise, gratitude seems to operate as a supplement to contract when Hobbes claims in *De Cive* that emancipated children, at this later stage of life, should honor their parents "not only under the title of gratitude but also of contract [*non modo sub titulo gratitudinis, sed etiam Pactionis*]" (*DC* 9.8.167). But in *Leviathan*, as Philip Abbott notes, "Hobbes reduces this notion of gratitude to an exchange just one step removed from contract."[74]

Indeed, it may not even be a step removed. Just a few years earlier, the Presbyterian political theorist Samuel Rutherford (c.1600–61) had suggested that king and people were bound by a mutual covenant precisely by maintaining that the debt of gratitude had legal force: "What fathers do to children, are acts of naturall dutie, and of naturall grace; and yet children owe gratitude to parents, and subjects to good Kings, in a legall sense."[75] The point of Rutherford's argument is that children or subjects may rebel when parents or kings fail to act according to the natural dictates of love and grace. Hobbes jettisons this aspect of the argument while retaining its contractual account of filial obligation:

> Because the first instruction of Children, dependeth on the care of their Parents; it is necessary that they should be obedient to them, whilest they are under their tuition; and not onely so, but that also afterwards (as gratitude requireth,) they acknowledge the benefit of their education by external signes of honour. (*L* 2.30.382)

Peter King has argued that this "misconstrues the nature of the trust and gratitude characteristic of parental love.... Favors may create debts that have to be repaid, but friendship or love arguably do not."[76] But this "misconstrual" seems to be precisely Hobbes's point, and this becomes even clearer in the Latin *Leviathan*, published seventeen years later, where the infant's obligation is described as simple debt: "Matri vitam debet Infans."[77]

According to Schochet, this formulation projects the child's consent "into the future through the fourth law of nature, the law of gratitude,"[78] but Hobbes actually makes it clear that gratitude binds most completely in states of extreme inequality that are instantly in effect:

> To have received from one, to whom we think ourselves equal, greater benefits than there is hope to Requite disposeth to counterfeit love; but really secret hatred; and puts a man into the estate of a desperate debtor, that in declining the sight of his creditor, tacitly wishes him there, where he might never see him more. For benefits oblige; and obligation is thraldom; and unrequitable obligation perpetual thraldom; which is to ones equall, hateful. But to have received benefits from one whom we acknowledge for superior inclines to love. (*L* 1.11.162–63)

In this regard, very young children are the ideal candidates to express gratitude. From the moment children begin to accept parental nourishment, they are bound into a system of profound inequality and absolute obligation. This allows Hobbes to claim without exception that "no Obligation on any man ... ariseth not from some Act of his own" (*L* 2.21.268). The question of the child's rational choice that had bedeviled earlier contract theory has disappeared.

This clears the way for Hobbes to explain the exchange of nourishment and gratitude not as a single, abstract moment, but an ongoing process of education that fits men for society. Nourishment is clearly not merely or even primarily food or material protection: in the Latin *Leviathan* children "owe honour" (*honorem debitum*) to their parents in exchange for their "education and sustenance" (*alimenta & educationem*).[79] The English passage likewise emphasizes the child's gratitude for his "first instruction," "tuition," and "education" (*L* 2.30.382). Most dramatically, although the mother's decision to "nourish, or expose" the child in chapter 20 seems at first glance to take place on blasted heath or battlefield, a marginal note identifies this as dominion acquired by "Education" (*L* 2.20.254).

Accordingly, *Leviathan* is untroubled by the tensions we find in the revised *De Cive*, where Hobbes admits that most men are incapable of the kind of rational contract he had initially described (*DC* 1.2.92). Now these childish subjects simply become the focus of a robust educational process of obligation that Hobbes describes in some detail. Drawing on the familiar image of the child's mind as a blank sheet of paper, Hobbes explains that "the Common-peoples minds, unless they be tainted with dependance on the Potent, or scribbled over with the opinions of their Doctors, are like clean paper, fit to receive whatsoever by Publique Authority shall be imprinted in them" (*L* 2.30.379).[80] The "conduits" of this education, nourishing the commonwealth on all levels of society, are families, pulpits, and the "right teaching of Youth in the Universities" (*L* 2.30.383–84).

In short, in *Leviathan* Hobbes focuses much more on the role of "culture" in making a commonwealth than he had in his previous works. As he explains, "in the first sense the labour bestowed on the Earth, is called Culture; and the education of Children a Culture of their mindes. In the second sense, where mens wills are to be wrought to our purpose, not by Force, but by Compleasance, it signifieth as much as Courting" (*L* 2.31.399). Culture is the labor of making a commonwealth and it is described in precisely the affective terms that humanist educators used when they proposed to win the loving submission of their pupils. It may be possible to justify Hobbesean absolutism via the abstract, rational individualism found in *De Cive* and the *Elements of Law*, but the ideally absolutist state can only really come into being as a product of culture, transmuting the affective realm into contract. This reestablishes a key role for the arts of eloquence that Hobbes described in purely pejorative terms in the *Elements of Law* but which he describes as "power" (in contrast with the "small power" of the sciences) in *Leviathan* (*L* 1.10.151). Hobbes does not only change "his mind about his literary principles as well as his practice between the severely scientific prose of *The Elements* and the highly 'ornamental' style of *Leviathan*," as Skinner has argued.[81] His new emphasis on the culture of commonwealth restores a crucial role for these literary principles in determining obligation.

Hobbes does not detail the reformed curriculum that would properly cultivate his ideal Leviathan state, although clearly it would involve rooting out both the scholastic and republican defenses of political liberty from the universities, where he suggests his own work might be "more profitably taught" (*L*, Review and Conclusion, 728). More broadly, his association of "education, and Discipline" with "judgment, and Fancy" implies a fairly traditional humanistic pedagogical method of alluring the childish mind through poetry and play (*L*, Review and Conclusion, 718). The poet's work, he explained to William Davenant, "is by imitating humane life, in delightfull and measur'd lines, to avert men from vice, and encline them to vertuous and honorable actions."[82] The poet's work, in other words, is to nourish and educate.

Hobbes wrote this in the year of *Leviathan*'s publication, in response to Davenant's preface to *Gondibert*. Davenant dedicated the unfinished poem to Hobbes, who read it in draft, and he clearly felt he was writing a new form of epic that accorded with Hobbes's philosophy. This is in part because Davenant minimizes the martial deeds that had led Hobbes to charge that romantic epics like *Orlando Furioso* fueled the destructive passion of vainglory.[83] By contrast, Davenant has not unleashed fancy or imitated life with all its complexities but has imitated only those aspects of life that are morally profitable. In comparison, he says, Spenser's poetry is like a fever dream.[84] Because he believes drama is the most educational literary form, he has also reproduced its five-act structure, but without the unpredictability of actual performance that, as we saw in Chapter 1, notoriously allowed child actors to stray from the script. Most importantly, in removing such elements from his poem, Davenant claims to have achieved a purely didactic poetry that can instruct without the possibility of error. Poetry's operations are "as resistlesse, secret, easy, and subtle, as the influence of Plannetts," and Davenant's remade heroic poem will have "a force that overmatches the infancy of such mindes as are not enabled by degrees of Education."[85] He admits that "the common Crowd (of whom wee are hopelesse)" may be better disciplined with law than with poesy, but he still hopes that the poetic education of the upper classes will set off a mimetic chain reaction and that even the hopelessly childish mob, led by the "delight of Imitation," will emulate their betters and internalize the lessons of his poem.[86]

In other words, Davenant claims to have eliminated the unpredictable element of the childish mind's encounter with fiction that had made this encounter a site of potential transgression and error from Plato to *Epicoene* (a play he helped bring back to the stage at the Restoration). Whether Davenant achieved this goal is another question, but he certainly managed to produce a poem that is, by most standards, nearly unreadable, especially as it anticipates the jingling pieties of much eighteenth-century children's verse:

> For though Books serve as Diet of the Minde;
> If knowledg, early got, self vallew breeds,
> By false digestion it is turn'd to winde;
> And what should nourish, on the Eater feeds.[87]

Hobbes was eventually embarrassed by his effusive praise of Davenant's widely derided work. But there is no reason to question his advocacy of an art that procures absolute obedience or his endorsement of Davenant's idea that the two men were engaged in a complementary endeavor.[88]

When Hobbes announces on the opening page that "by Art is created that great LEVIATHAN called a COMMON-WEALTH, or STATE, (in latine CIVITAS) which is but an Artificiall Man," he means on one level that states are not made by nature but by men (*L*, Introduction, 81). But his Leviathan state also collapses the distinction between political and artistic representation that Prynne sought to establish, drawing on the concept of the Latin *persona*, "which signifies the *disguise*, or *outward appearance* of a man, counterfeited on the Stage," to describe the way the sovereign represents his people (*L* 2.16.217). Even more importantly, he bases obligation to this sovereign actor not on rational authorization but on the culture of childish minds that he describes in the most diminutive terms – an educational process that purged humanist pedagogy of the "poetical fury" that had long disturbed even its staunchest advocates and that Hobbes in particular thought dangerous when it appeared in heroic poetry and romance, inspiring men to vainglorious acts of rebellion.[89] This is willing subjection, a form of government by consent that eliminates the vagaries of choice. As we shall see in the next section of the book, Milton opposes such a vision at every stage of his career, and this is why he situates his poetry on the threshold between youth and adulthood, where voice and choice emerge.

PART II

Milton and the Children of Liberty

CHAPTER 4

"Perplex't Paths"
Youth and Authority in Milton's Early Work

As witnessed in previous chapters, the transition to a culture of consent saw many attempts to erase complicated, ambiguous childish voices from the political discourse. But John Milton was never one to step lightly away from a *limen*, and the rest of this book explores the threshold between childhood and adulthood as a site of profound power in his poetry and prose. I have cited the legal doctrine of *malitia supplet aetatem* as evidence of the most striking dilemma presented by childhood in this period – the sense that it was impossible to shed childish ignorance without forfeiting childish innocence. If malice supplied the age, to speak as an adult was also to acknowledge one's lack of freedom, demonstrating not only reason but also the bondage of sin and the need for subjugation to law. Milton's work resists this principle at every turn, aspiring instead to seize the ability to speak without seizing the inheritance of sin. This may ultimately be impossible in a fallen world, but for that very reason Milton returns again and again to the moment when voice emerges from infancy.

This is the paradigmatic "Miltonic moment," to use J. Martin Evans's term. As Evans explains, Milton's works tend to "take place between the boundaries that separate one event, or one series of events, from another."[1] Other critics have also noted this quality of "pendency" or betweenness in Milton's work and, like Evans, have in some cases connected it to his famous anxiety over his own slow development.[2] Nevertheless, the roots of this quality in a historically specific conception of childhood have not been acknowledged, even in Milton's 1634 *Mask Presented at Ludlow Castle* (commonly called *Comus*), which is explicitly about three children who get lost in the woods on the way to their father's house. It is the central claim of this chapter, however, that the *Mask*'s true radicalism derives less from the formal innovations, theology, or politics that have been primary scholarly concerns than from its treatment of childhood. Milton's *Mask* suggests that youth's peculiar poetic receptivity – the ability to enter a charming, if dangerous world without being corrupted by it – offers access to a powerful kind of voice. For both its performers and its author the *Mask* itself serves as a testimony to this central pedagogical and poetic idea, and this is both the source of its dramatic interest and the way it points most directly towards Milton's later career.

"Chaste in Body, Pure in Mind"

The claim that the *Mask*'s treatment of childhood is what makes it radical or uniquely Miltonic requires some explanation, because scholars have become accustomed to the idea that Milton's major innovation in the work is writing a "reformed" or "chastened" Puritan masque.[3] There is obviously some truth to this idea. Most masques lack a real sense of trial or dramatic engagement, as in Jonson's *Pleasure Reconciled to Virtue* (1618) or Thomas Carew's *Coelum Britannicum* (1634), in which the Egerton children had performed shortly before appearing in Milton's *Mask*. These works are vehicles for flattery, presenting threats, in the form of antimasques, that are dispelled by the mere glance of a king or queen representing ideal, Neoplatonic virtues.[4] By contrast, in Milton's *Mask*, the evil figure Comus promptly captures the virtuous, aristocratic protagonist and binds her to a chair with troubling "gumms of glutenous heat," where she remains, stuck, after her brothers botch the rescue operation (917). Far from embodying powerful Platonic virtues, they finally need divine assistance to set her free. By the end, they have been through a genuine trial, "hard assays" as the Attendant Spirit puts it, and Milton has replaced what Victoria Kahn calls the "Neoplatonic rhetoric" of earlier masques with a kind of Protestant tightrope walk between works and grace.[5]

It is a mistake, however, to read too much specifically *theological* radicalism into this formal revision, as we can see by turning to the Gospel reading for Michaelmas, the day the *Mask* was first performed.[6] The gospel for the day was Matthew 18.1–10, where Christ instructs his disciples to "become as little children" to "enter into the kingdom of heaven," warning that "whoso shall offend one of these little ones which believe in me, it were better for him that a millstone were hanged about his neck, and that he were drowned in the depth of the sea." Milton's masque may not have been specifically inspired by this liturgical moment, but as Cedric Brown notes, the gospel is clearly relevant to the *Mask*'s action, where children take the leading roles and where they are indeed offended grievously, and we can get a good idea of the *Mask*'s religious and political orthodoxy by seeing how it relates to conventional explications of this scripture.[7]

The gold standard for such a reading is John Boys, the Dean of Canterbury from 1619 until his death in 1625, whose systematic eleven-volume exploration of the church's lectionary was popular enough to require twelve reissues between 1610 and 1616. With Laud in the ascendant throughout the early 1630s, Boys's ardent Calvinistic predestinarianism may have looked a bit less "orthodox" by the time Milton wrote his masque in 1634, but it was also anything but radical. It is, in short, as close as we are likely to come to middle-of-the-road theological thinking in the schismatic world of seventeenth-century England. In his explication of the gospel for Michaelmas, Boys deals with the injunction to "become as little children" by first listing all the ways we *shouldn't* be like children, rehashing much of the conception of childhood familiar from classical and scholastic sources like Bartholomaeus Anglicus. Children are known for "eating dirt and paddling in the mire," and we shouldn't do that.[8] Children are "ignorant," "inconstant," and wholly given over to pleasure and play.[9] The "child plaies with the light of the candle till his fingers be burnt" and "doth esteem an apple more then his fathers inheritance," and those are, unsurprisingly, also things to avoid.[10]

Finally, after listing all the dangers of being like children, Boys gets around to what Christ meant when he told his disciples to emulate them: purity and humility. Children are "chast in body, pure in mind" and "they stand not reasoning what manner of thing it is that their father commands, but instantly they follow his will and word as their rule to work by."[11] Boys pounds in the desirability of passivity and obedience for several more pages, driving home the conservative message that if men heeded Christ's injunction there would be fewer "*state-criticks*" who "speake ill of such as are in authority."[12] Boys's good children follow orders instantly and perfectly: they do not wander astray, or search out answers, or speak. For Boys, as for the Neoplatonists and conservative churchmen described by Leah Marcus, the child is a symbol of "humility and anti-intellectualism," attitudes sharply at odds with "forward-looking ... Puritanism."[13]

Despite its conservative political application, however, Boys's theology does not necessarily preclude human action, and his final word on the relationship between childlike passivity and grace could be a gloss on the action of Milton's *Mask* itself: "the good which a man doth, is both the work of God, and the work of man; of God in being author in giving grace, of man in being actor in using grace."[14] That is essentially the interaction between "hard assays" and grace that we see in the *Mask*. When Barbara Lewalski calls the work "in every respect a reformed masque, a

generic tour de force," for example, she is describing both her claim that
Milton's masque dispenses with elaborate stage machinery (which may
have been impractical for a private entertainment anyway) and the fact
that its principle character is "unable to attain salvation by her own mer-
its" and so must receive help from Sabrina, the "agent for the divine grace
necessary to counter these effects."[15] Since A. S. P. Woodhouse declared in
1942 that the "argument" of the *Mask* was the manifestation of this doctrine of grace, represented by Sabrina, over and against nature, critics have
debated which characters "represent" grace and how specifically it acts in
the world.[16] But in no case, so far as I am aware, have they concluded that
grace in Milton's masque acts in a fundamentally different way than Boys
described its action in the world.

In other words, the way the *Mask* allegorizes a doctrine of works and
grace may be an interesting departure from typical masques, but it is not
necessarily radical or uniquely Miltonic.[17] Gordon Campbell and Thomas
Corns have gone so far, in fact, as to call it "the most complex and thorough expression of Laudian Arminianism and Laudian style within the
Milton oeuvre"![18] What is more radical and Miltonic – in either the poetic
or political sense – is the way the work embraces Boys's notions of grace
and works while rejecting his orthodox quietism. To see how Milton succeeds at embracing Boys's theology while rejecting his quietism, we need
to turn not to the masque's theology but to its children, who negotiate
in dialogue and song Milton's long-standing anxiety about how unripe
youth actualizes adult will and prophetic voice. To be "chast in body, pure
in mind" in Milton's *Mask* means something totally different than it does
for Boys. The *Mask* rejects the idea that children should be seen and not
heard, and especially not heard criticizing the wielders of power. Even
more profoundly, it invites an openness to experience and even indulgence of error that is utterly anathema to Boys's vision. Rather than falling easily into either the camp of backward-looking pro-childishness or
of forward-looking anti-childishness that Marcus describes, Milton's *Mask*
depicts the uneasy transition from childhood to adult responsibility as the
locus of tremendous creative and spiritual power.

Children's Songs

To understand what is at stake in that depiction, we should first take a
brief look at the long-standing anxiety about youth and voice that I am
claiming marked Milton's earlier life and work. Milton was born in 1608,
a short walk from the playhouse where the Children of the Blackfriars

performed *Epicoene* and where his father later became a trustee.[19] By his own account he showed a precocious talent for literature, "for which I had so keen an appetite that from my twelfth year scarcely ever did I leave my studies for my bed before the hour of midnight" (*CPW* 4:612). Yet well into middle age he continued to describe himself as inhabiting an extended, childish spring that made it impossible to write or speak with full adult authority. In *The Reason of Church Government* (1642), written at the age of thirty-four, he was still apologizing for writing "while green yeers are upon my head" (*CPW* 1:806), identifying himself as a youth whose adulthood would in "some few yeers" break forth with an inspired poetic voice (*CPW* 1:820). This is not entirely surprising, considering the seventeenth-century "prolongation of childhood" discussed earlier.[20] But as has been often noted, Milton's obsession with his own belated development, or the "gap between aspiration and accomplishment," seems to have been the source of uncommon apprehension, and this was particularly pronounced in the period just before he composed his *Mask* in 1634.[21]

Milton came down from Cambridge in 1632, moving to his father's house in Hammersmith, where he lived in studious retirement for the next four years.[22] It was probably in December that he wrote Sonnet 7, describing himself as surprised by time and startled by the disjunction between the internal and external evidence of his maturity:

> How soon hath Time the suttle theef of youth,
> Stoln on his wing my three and twentieth yeer!
> My hasting dayes flie on with full career,
> But my late spring no bud or blossom shew'th. (1–4)

As time careens past him, the poet worries that his "semblance might deceive the truth, / That I to manhood am arriv'd so near" (5–6), and this is generally taken to mean that he is more mature on the inside than on the outside. The syntax is ambiguous, however: is his "inward ripeness" (7) simply invisible to the outside world, unlike the visible successes enjoyed by Thomas Randolph (1605–35) or Abraham Cowley (1618–67), who were already being hailed as the most promising poets of his generation?[23] Or is this inward ripeness impossible even for him to discern, although by external, legal standards he knows he should be an adult? Either way, the path to a full adulthood and vocation is perplexing and unclear, and Milton resolves the tensions not by proclaiming his maturity but by determining to stand and wait, as he would do much later in Sonnet 19 (c.1652). "Be it less, or more, or soon or slow," he resolves in Sonnet 7, his payment will be according to God's "strictest measure eev'n"

(9–10). The lines invoke the parable of the vineyard (Matthew 20.1–16), in which Christ proclaims that "the last shall be first, and the first last," and this is obviously comforting, but it still leaves the poet focused on future prospect rather than assured of ripeness.

Not long after he wrote it, Milton included the sonnet in a letter to an older friend who suspected, as Milton put it, "that I have given up my selfe to dreame away my Yeares in the armes of studious retirement like Endymion wth the Moone" (*CPW* 1:319). Endymion is an image of perpetual immaturity: after he falls in love with the moon goddess, she not only inspires him with the "fiery nature of a heavenly Muse," as Michael Drayton tells the story, but also casts him into a deep sleep so she can enjoy him "ever beautifull and yong."[24] Milton only half disavows the association. In an early draft he actually seems to admit that he is motivated by "all the fond hopes that Youth and Vanitie are fledged with," although he later retracts this by inserting a definitive "not" above the line.[25] But he readily admits that he is "something suspicio[us] of my selfe," and faced with such uncertainty about the source of his motivations, he ultimately asserts that so long as he intends to serve God and the truth, even an erroneous, Endymion-like love of learning will "be quickly diverted from the emptie & fantastick chase of shadows & notions to the solid good" (*CPW* 1:320).

Milton describes this chase after shadows in terms often associated with poetic forms, such as romance, that are defined by wandering or "error."[26] As we have seen, the child's tendency to poetical fury made even the most ardent humanist educators leery of exposing children to such poetry, but in Milton's letter the youthful chase after shadows can propel one toward solid goodness even if it starts out in the wrong direction. Youthful wandering, fantastical and empty of agency, may even constitute the necessarily receptive state for discerning God's subtle redirection. Sonnet 7 itself serves as Milton's chief evidence: his letter describes it offhandedly as some of his "nightward thoughts," but tellingly labels it a "stanza," a term implying this is not a circumscribed effort but a part of something larger, a sign of things to come (*CPW* 1:320). He makes a similar gesture in *Ad Patrem*, which he composed around the same time as the *Mask* in order to thank and reassure his father, who may have been growing skeptical about his son's apparently interminable education. "Do not despise divine poetry" (*nec tu vatis opus divinum despice carmen*), Milton implores, because this prophetic form has the potential to confer immortality on both father and son (17). Yet despite all his grand ambitions, he must admit at the poem's conclusion that his verses are "childish songs" (*juvenilia carmina*) or "toys" [*lusus*] (115). The question of how and when he will put these childish things away and begin to speak with the vatic voice is left open.

The *Mask* is, likewise, primarily a vehicle for childish song and performance. Although the protagonist is called "the Lady" (Milton's own nickname at Cambridge), she is introduced less grandly as one of three children lost in the woods. The roles were originally written for and performed by Alice Egerton and her brothers, a girl of fifteen and two boys of decidedly "youthful bloom" (289) at ages eleven and nine. Critics often explain that "though young by modern standards, Lady Alice was at fifteen a marriageable adult,"[27] but this is not quite accurate, for reasons that will by now be familiar. Although she was of marriageable age, she was less than a full adult in the eyes of the law and society and marriageable only with her father's permission. According to the sixteenth-century statute in place at the time, it was illegal for any person to carry away or "by secret Letters, Messages, or otherwise [to] contract Matrimony" with a girl under age sixteen without the knowledge of her father or guardian.[28] Doing so would not only incur a five-year jail sentence for the seducer (if he was over age fourteen), but would also provoke a sort of legal death for the "Woman Child," as any girl between twelve and sixteen is referred to in the statute, who would instantly forfeit her inheritance to her next of kin.[29] Likewise, at fifteen a "woman child's" own "defilement might be by her consent," as the judge and legal writer Matthew Hale put it, so that a rape charge was not automatic in the event of a sexual attack and the woman child herself would need to be scrutinized for signs of willing transgression.[30] In short, the "woman child" between the ages of twelve and sixteen was just old enough to dispossess herself but not old enough to bestow herself, and this is part of a broader legal and cultural tendency to recognize the child's will only when it came into being through acts of malice, crime, or sin ("*malitia supplet aetatem*").[31] A woman child, like her male counterparts, found herself in a kind of double bind: while being "innocent" implied a disabling silence and parental dependence, the discovery of agency and will meant subjection to the harsher regime of law.

This was the uncomfortable status of the child's agency in the overlapping legal and theological discourses of early modern England, and it is the challenge facing the three lost siblings in Milton's *Mask*. They are initially identified not by their own will or actions, but in relation to their father, a "noble Peer of mickle trust, and power" (31). The description of the education given to this peer's "fair offspring" emphasizes their youth and early development: they are "nurs't in Princely lore" (34), a phrase that both implies their early instruction in the courtly arts and recalls traditional injunctions to begin forming noble children by nursing them at their noble mother's breast, or at least to avoid the transmission of negative traits by debauched nursemaids. These are, in other words, babes in the wood, suddenly cut off from the tutelage that has directed their every move. And without that direction, explains the Attendant Spirit, who was played by their real-life tutor Henry Lawes (1596–1662), they are cast into an abyss:

> their way
> Lies through the perplex't paths of this drear Wood,
> The nodding horror of whose shady brows
> Threats the forlorn and wandring Passinger. (36–39)

This depiction of the woods has a particular occasional significance, as Stephen Orgel points out: the masque celebrated the ascension of John Egerton (1579–1649) to the position of Lord President of Wales, a representative of civilized rule at a time when the English generally considered Wales "wild and uncivilized."[32] But the "horror" of the place clearly transcends anything even the untamed Welsh countryside has to offer, and it is not, ultimately, the powerful peer who confronts this horror, but his children: despite all the attention critics have given to the relationship between the masque and Egerton's sociopolitical position, the threat of these perplexed paths is not to law or order, but to "their tender age" (40).[33]

J. C. Maxwell suggests that the description of the wood, with its hopelessly tangled paths, echoes *Aeneid* 9.391–92, and I would add that the allusion to youth in peril is more significant than the verbal similarity.[34] Virgil's lines also describe a youth, Euryalus, who strays into the woods while he is still a boy just showing the first down on his unshaven face ("ora puer prima signans intonsa iuventa").[35] But Virgil's youth, unlike Milton's, does not survive the foray along his perplexed path ("perplexum iter") into the deceptive woods ("fallacis silvae").[36] And this highlights the fact that Milton's three lost children ultimately face a different kind of threat than Virgil's, risking not their lives, but their humanity itself in the forest, where they encounter the scion of Circe and Bacchus, who "Excells his Mother at her mighty Art" (63). If any weary traveler drinks his potion, "their human count'nance, / Th' express resemblance of the gods, is chang'd / Into som brutish form of Woolf, or Bear, / Or Ounce, or Tiger, Hog, or bearded Goat" (68–71). The change is so perfect, in fact so pleasurable, that the victims who wile away their lives in Comus's "sensual stie" never realize that they have forgotten their homes, their families, and the spark of divinity that made them human (77).

Childhood and Circean Transformations

This is rather bad luck for the children of Milton's *Mask*, because youth's vulnerability to such enchantments was a long-established fact. In a few short years Joseph Glanvill (1636–80), of the Royal Society, would even attempt a scientific explanation for why "Witches are most powerful upon Children and timerous Persons," although he did not get further than the common knowledge available to Milton, "*viz.* because their Spirits and Imaginations being weak and passive, are not able to resist the fatal Influence."[37] Comus's "orient liquor in a Crystal Glasse, / To quench the drouth of *Phoebus*" also allures on aesthetic, physical, and emotional levels in a way that is particularly dangerous to youth (65–66). The "intemperate thirst" it quenches may be "fond" (67), but it was also a defining trait of all children, with their hot, moist humoural constitutions, as John Boys highlights when he notes that a child governed by such natural appetites will trade an inheritance for an apple.[38] The Lady seems particularly vulnerable in this regard, as her brothers have set out to fetch her "cooling fruit" (186). This sensual nature is why educators from Vives to Comenius proposed that learning should progress from the sensible to the intellectual, an argument Milton took up himself in *Of Education*: "because our understanding cannot in this body found it selfe but on sensible things, nor arrive so cleerly to the knowledge of God and things invisible, as by orderly conning over the visible and inferior creature, the same method is necessarily to be follow'd in all discreet teaching" (*CPW* 2:368–69).

Comus offers liquor, not learning, but through his mother Circe he has a well-established ancestry in the humanistic pedagogical discourse. In *De Pueris*, for example, Erasmus describes abusive, incompetent schoolmasters as Circe figures capable of turning children into beasts. He argues that Circe's ability to encase "human souls within bestial bodies" (*animus humanus in corpore bestiae*) is not merely a fiction, as witnessed by Augustine's belief that men could be transformed into werewolves.[39] He then turns the tables on parents who allow schoolmasters to instill "beastly" qualities like anger and drunkenness in their children: "If there was a Thessalian witch who had the power and desire to change your son into a swine or a wolf," he then asks, "would you think that any punishment could be too severe for her?"[40] Beating and harsh treatment, Erasmus argues repeatedly, are treatments fit for beasts and can only produce beastly behavior.

It was this insight that prompted the program of gentle discipline discussed in this book's opening chapters. To cultivate a virtuous and robust adult voice, the teacher should engage the child's naturally mimetic instincts, employing the alluring arts of poetry and drama to teach children "in the most loving in gentle manner," as the Puritan schoolmaster John Brinsley (1566–c.1624) put it, "as it were in playing."[41] But we have also seen the anxiety that accompanied this program – the sense that the child, especially in what Roger Ascham calls the "most slipperie time" of youth, is simply too easily caught up in fantastic flights of poesy.[42] This is why Ascham recommends extreme caution in this period to ensure that the young person does not "glutte himself with vainity, or walter in filthiness like a Swyne," because then, even without beating, "quicklie shall he becum a dull Asse, to understand either learnyng or honestie: and yet shall he be as sutle as a Foxe, in breedyng of mischief, in bringyng in misorder," like "all those that serve in *Circes* Court."[43]

As he confronts the tendency of childish charges to roll in a sensual sty, Ascham shifts dramatically away from the depiction of learning as sweet and pleasurable to emphasize that learning, like the Circean antidote moly, is difficult to swallow:

> The true medicine against the inchantmentes of *Circes*, the vanitie of licencious pleasure, the inticementes of all sinne, is, in *Homere*, the herbe *Moly*, with the blacke roote, and white flooer, sower at the first, but sweete in the end: which *Hesiodus* termeth the study of virtue.[44]

As Erica Fudge explains, the line between human and beast was not a firm one during the early modern period, and in this delicate balancing act between nurturing and repressing the child's instincts, the child always threatens to slip back across the line into a merely animal life.[45] In the pedagogical tradition stretching from Erasmus to Locke, the human was not just born but had to be made.

Milton shows how complicated that construction could be in *Elegia Prima*, which in this regard is another important precursor of the *Mask*. In the elegy – a verse letter to Charles Diodati – he embraces the delights of theatrical play to distinguish his tender sensibilities from those of his "unfeeling" (*duri*) Cambridge tutor (15). This passage has been the center of much debate over whether Milton had actually come into conflict with his tutor and been disciplined, or even whipped and rusticated.[46] But as he recoils from the "threats" (*minas*) of a harsh pedagogue and discovers true learning in the embrace of literature and drama that "ravish [him] completely" (*totum rapiunt*), Milton could just as well be reenacting one of the many Erasmian anecdotes in which the tender student is stunted by a harsh disciplinarian but blossoms in the embrace of gentle discipline.

At its very end, however, the elegy takes a puzzling turn. Circe enters the poem in the final six lines, in a version of the metaphor more akin to Ascham than Erasmus, and the youth renounces his apparently ideal education as he resolves to return to the "barren fields" (*nuda arva*) of Cambridge, fleeing the enchanted city "to escape the infamous halls of deceptive Circe, with the aid of divine moly" [*vitare procul malefidae infamia Circes / Atria, divini Molyos usus ope*] (85–88). The lines imply Milton has been enjoying his education a little too much and transforming, perhaps without fully realizing it, into something less than human. The youth's very positive sensitivity – whether to the beauty that strikes him "senseless" (*stupui*), the books that master him, or the drama that moves him to tears – also puts him at some undefined risk (53). It will take divine aid to escape: the aid of the plant moly, which will reappear in Milton's *Mask*. But what kind of escape is this? The deceptive halls of Circe, Milton's own wanderings through a labyrinthine program of independent study, will merely be replaced by the halls of Cambridge, which Milton derides in the third *Prolusion* for being dominated by other deceptions, such as the scholastics' "useless and barren controversies," a "workshop of tricks and fallacies" (*CPW* 1:244).

The Circean temptations may have threatened the youth's humanity, but they also put him in touch with divinity in a way that the barren university curriculum did not. In other words, it is specifically his wandering through the Circean halls of poesy that makes him eligible for divine moly, that allows him to know it even exists, even if the herb's rather unsatisfactory effect in *Elegia Prima* is to transport him from danger to dullness. In the *Mask*, Milton ultimately embraces the conclusion he could not quite reach in *Elegia Prima*: escape is not a salvation from this wandering but a result of it.

In fact, by the time he wrote his *Apology Against a Pamphlet* eight years later, Milton had embraced this idea as part of his own poetic trajectory, describing how his "younger feet wander'd" into realms of erotic and romantic poetry, but "that even those books which to many others have bin the fuell of wantonnesse and loose living, I cannot thinke how unless by divine indulgence prov'd to me so many incitements ... to the love and stedfast observation of that vertue which abhorres the society of Bordello's" (*CPW* 1:891). Likewise, for the children of the *Mask*, the Circean allurement of the shadowy poetic world helps create the will and develop a voice of distinctive power.

Learning to Sing: Echo and Translation

The figure for such a voice, from early poems like *Il Penseroso* and *Lycidas* to late works like *Paradise Lost*, is Orpheus, whose beautiful songs are able to move rocks and trees and suspend even the torments of hell.[47] Despite this tremendous power or because of it, Orpheus is torn apart by the Thracian women, and Milton invokes him as both an aspirational and cautionary figure. Orpheus is often depicted as a youth ("iuventus"),[48] and in *Ad Patrem* the Orphic voice emerges just at the horizon of parental authority, as the youthful singer attempts to claim a voice that is distinctly different from the father's. "What good is finely tuned vocal music," he asks his musician father, "if it lacks sense, or words, or measured speech? Such strains befit a woodland choir, not Orpheus."[49] Music without the contribution of poetry is little better than parroting birdsong, and the son's speech aspires to an authority that even his father's does not hold. This seems like a strange bit of one-upmanship, or even malice, in a poem that is intended as a compliment, but it may also be understood as a genuine inquiry into the origins of Orphic voice. It cannot merely mimic parental authority, or any other authority, but must push beyond such boundaries to create its own authority, answerable only to the divine. The Orphic voice is where poetry and prophecy meet, where the poet must transform the raw material of youth into world-shaking speech.

Orpheus appears in both familiar and surprising iterations in the *Mask*. In the first scene, for example, the Attendant Spirit adopts the guise of a shepherd with the ability to "still the wilde winds when they roar, / And hush the waving Woods" (87–88), and J. Andrew Hubbell claims that this sets up a "typological relationship" between Orpheus and the Attendant Spirit.[50] That may be, but the association of Orpheus with various pastoral figures was also fairly conventional.[51] More uniquely Miltonic, and ultimately more meaningful, is the association of the mythic bard with the Lady – a lost, childish figure with no poetic vocation, but one who develops a powerful voice in the course of the masque.

The Attendant Spirit makes the analogy between the Lady and Orpheus when she first wanders onto the stage, lost and alone, and sings a song that he says "might create a soul / Under the ribs of Death" (561–62). This act of vocal creation, which changes Death himself into something vital, recalls Orpheus's triumph in Hades, where his beautiful song procures the release of his wife, Eurydice, by moving Pluto to tears. Likewise, even Comus agrees that the Lady's song exhibits something more than human power, and the would-be ravisher himself claims to experience "ravishment" at the sound (249). Her song really is unlike anything else in the masque: on the most basic level it is more structurally complex than other songs in the work, incorporating a greater number of verse forms, including the masque's only Alexandrine, "And give resounding grace to all Heav'ns Harmonies" (243). But while the song is the first and most overt association of the Lady's vocal power with Orpheus, it is not an isolated one. The trope runs throughout, and when Comus later holds the Lady captive, it underpins her claim that her words defending chastity could exert a tangible effect:

> dumb things would be mov'd to sympathize,
> And the brute Earth would lend her nerves and shake,
> Till all thy magick structures rear'd so high
> Were shatter'd into heaps o're thy false head. (796–99)

Whether she *actually* has that power is a question for debate, one we will return to. But regardless, it is intriguing and surprising that she can claim this power and even convince others of her abilities when her only experiences thus far are loss, darkness, and captivity. After all, while the Lady's chastity and innocence, as well as her humble reliance on grace, fit precisely into the dominant concept of childhood that underpins John Boys's Michaelmas commentary, her ability to speak with authority does not: one key way we should emulate children, according to Boys, is to "studie to be quiet."[52] If we are offended, we "may complain to the Church our Mother," who alone has the authority to speak for us and seek redress for our wrongs.[53] Such reserve was even more expected of the woman child than of her male counterpart. While humanist prodigies like the Lady's brothers were expected to perfect the arts of eloquence, even the most enlightened educational handbooks for young women tended to view female literacy as a tool for cultivating decidedly quiet virtues.[54] The woman child's goal was "conversation" rather than oratory, and while she might be an exemplary student of virtue, she was hardly expected to become its public advocate.[55]

The youth's superior receptivity to grace, then, is only one part of the story. The other part – the explanation of how the Lady develops her voice – must be found in her encounters with shadow and danger and in youth's characteristic receptivity to the poetic forms they take in this masque. And here it is worth looking in some detail at her song, how it works, and where it comes from, because it gives us the first clear evidence that, as Comus puts it, "somthing holy lodges in that brest" (246). In fact, it is worth quoting it in full:

> Sweet Echo, sweetest Nymph that liv'st unseen
>> Within thy airy shell
> By slow Meander's margent green,
> And in the violet-imbroider'd vale
>> Where the love-lorn Nightingale
> Nightly to thee her sad Song mourneth well.
> Canst thou not tell me of a gentle Pair
>> That likest thy Narcissus are?
>>> O if thou have
>> Hid them in som flowry Cave,
>>> Tell me but where
> Sweet Queen of Parly, Daughter of the Sphear,
> So maist thou be translated to the skies,
> And give resounding grace to all Heav'ns Harmonies. (230–43)

The oddities of this song have often been noted. The Lady's choice of mythological allusions, for example, does not immediately inspire confidence. As William Shullenberger puts it, Echo is "cursed by the goddess [Juno], dispossessed of an originating, self-generating voice, wasted by a love she cannot express," and she ultimately dies, "withering into a voice of pure reflexivity."[56] The Lady also does not do her brothers any favors by associating them with Echo's love, Narcissus, who famously succumbs to his own "pure reflexivity," pining away with an inexpressible love for his own image. If they are, cleverly, the beautiful images of one another, they are also both *merely* images, a pair of mirrors reflecting one another in a kind of infinite regress. This is, for Milton's contemporary George Sandys (1578–1644) in his gloss on Ovid's version of the episode, the consummate image of "youth, that is, the soul of a rash and ignorant man, [who] beholds not his owne face, nor considers of his proper essence or virtue, but pursues his shadow in the fountaine."[57] If the imagery is forbidding, then, it may also be quite appropriate to the plight of three lost children attempting to exercise personal agency for perhaps the first time.

But that still does not explain how the Lady achieves this haunting voice with its ravishing power. A key to that question may lie in another oddity noted by Orgel: the "baffling" lack of an answering echo.[58] We might expect such an answer to the Lady's plaint, given that it was typical of the familiar genre of seventeenth-century echo songs and poems. A song in Jonson's masque *Pan's Anniversary*, for example, invokes Echo this way:

> Eccho, the truest Oracle on ground,
> Though nothing but a sound.

(Echo: Though nothing but a sound.)
Belov'd of Pan, the Valleyes Queene
(Echo: The Valleyes Queene)
And often heard, though never seene,
(Echo: Though never seene). (7:220–26)

Sometimes the echo even provided productive instruction, as in Herbert's poem "Heaven" where Echo responds to the query "what is the supreme delight?" by answering "Light."[59] But neither Milton's text nor Lawes's setting of the song includes any echo – no comforting return of "resounding grace to all Heav'ns Harmonies."[60] According to Orgel, the lack of an answering echo emphasizes "the fact that the Lady has *only* herself to rely on," that she is in fact surrounded by multiple versions of the self, or solipsism.[61] By the same token, Comus and the Attendant Spirit are versions of one another, Sabrina is a version of the Lady, and "freedom is the mirror image of bondage."[62] There is something to this, although freedom is never quite as simple as a "mirror image" of anything in Milton. The intermixture of freedom and bondage, good and evil, is almost always more complex than the neat opposition and separation that a mirror image implies, because, as he later notes of sin and virtue in *Areopagitica*, "the matter of them both is the same" (*CPW* 2:527).

And so among the various mirrorings and echoes that Orgel and others have cited in the Lady's song and in the masque's mythic structures, we could add that her song is itself an echo of Comus's own auditory presence, but with a unique productive power.[63] It has often been noted that Comus, with his superior "command of metaphor and poetic language," gives us some of the most evocative poetry in the masque.[64] Certainly, even more than his mother, he locates himself in a world of poetry and allusion that is much like the shadowy realm of ideas that evidently enchanted the young Milton. His opening recitative is a bravura display of poetic ability, building to a dance that Milton describes in his manuscript as a "wild, rude, & wanton antick."[65] As Comus shifts from stately, seductive imagery in iambic pentameter to a quickening, Puckish tetrameter, to his characteristic seven-syllable-lines (the appropriately "headless" form of catalectic tetrameter), we see that he hardly needs his liquor to be utterly charming:

> The Sounds, and Seas with all their finny drove
> Now to the Moon in wavering Morrice move,
> And on the Tawny Sands and Shelves,
> Trip the pert Fairies and the dapper Elves;
> By dimpled Brook, and Fountain Brim,
> The Wood-Nymphs deckt with Daisies trim,

Their merry wakes and pastimes keep:
What hath night to do with sleep? (115–22)

Marcus, among others, insightfully demonstrates that these "merry wakes
and pastimes" have political implications as a critique of Caroline court
culture.[66] But to argue that the primary effect of lines like these is critique,
or that the reader or audience is expected to respond to them *primarily*
by placing them on the "opposite pole" from virtue, as Stanley Fish does,
is surely a bit perverse.[67] For Fish, the *Mask* is "terribly static" because
Milton's characters are always already either redeemed or damned – the
protagonist never learns or develops, but just maintains a single-minded
obedience to God while he or she is battered from without by the forces
of darkness.[68]

Certainly Milton leaves us little doubt that Comus and his crew are not
nice: the passage about merry wakes and pastimes later invokes the orgiastic fertility goddess Cotytto and the witch Hecate, and the "wanton antic"
that they dance would seem to speak for itself.[69] But just as the "antic" is
disorder shaped to pleasing artistic effect, Comus's images of the "finny
drove," and all nature, moving in harmony with the moon are also profoundly beautiful, a version of the animating power of chastity (through
the allusion to Diana) that the Lady will later make her own. In the grip
of such a vision, it is easy to see how one might dream away one's years
"like Endymion wth the Moone," to borrow a phrase from Milton's letter
to his friend (*CPW* 1:319).

This poetry directly prompts the Lady's song. She stumbles onto the
stage by following the sound: "this way the noise was, if mine ear be true,
/ My best guide now, me thought it was the sound / Of Riot, and ill
manag'd Merriment" (171–72). She says she would be "loath" to meet the
insolent "Wassailers" who made the noise, but still she seeks it out (176).
Why? She is pressed by necessity, she says, looking for directions and nothing more. But she also says the sound is "rife, and perfet in my list'ning
ear" (203). This line was not included in the initial performance, if we
take the so-called Bridgewater Manuscript as representative of that performance.[70] But Milton retains it in his personal notebook and in all subsequent publications, and it complicates her experience profoundly and in a
way that may not have been totally appealing to the girl's family when they
gathered to watch their daughter take her star turn. Without this line, her
song could be seen as an expression of pure innocence and personal integrity – she hears some noise, walks on stage, and sings, clearly unmoved by
the sound of "ill manag'd Merriment" (172). But with it, Comus seems to
have penetrated her physically and mentally, much the way Satan, "squat

like a toad" by Eve's ear, will move the "organs" of her fancy in *Paradise Lost* (4.800–02). The Lady's ear is not a resisting organ, but a listening one, and Comus's sounds are powerful, full ("rife") and perhaps even pleasant, but certainly complete ("perfet") within it (203). The effect is pronounced, and Milton drives it home in other lines that did not appear in the initial performance: "a thousand fantasies," she says, "Begin to throng into my memorie / Of calling shapes, and beckning shadows dire, / And airy tongues, that syllable mens names / On Sands, and Shoars, and desert Wildernesses" (205–09). Comus has, of course, just been singing of "Tawny sounds and Shelves" (117), and his words are thronging through her. It is only when she has entered this realm of fantasy, when she has become rapt by it like Mulcaster fears his students will become rapt by poetical fury, that she claims to see Chastity "visibly" and begins to sing (216). Fish's notion of a static experience may have been somewhat true of the *Mask*'s first performance, but as Milton revised and republished the work, he made it clear that the Lady's encounter with Comus changes her and that her voice emerges from the experience.

In the performance version and Lawes's setting, though not in the later printed texts, the Lady ends her song with the vision of Echo holding "a Counterpointe to all heav'ns harmonies."[71] But her route to this heavenly image is through holding a counterpoint to Comus's harmonies. The art of counterpoint, as it developed in the Renaissance, typically involved two voices or melodies moving according to distinct rhythms yet forming a harmonic whole, and in both its imagistic and metrical echoes the Lady's song counterpoints Comus's recitative in this way.[72] Her imagery – a sweet nymph, flowery caves and valleys, the margin or brim of a languid stream – all harmonizes with Comus's own vision of pert fairies, dimpled brooks, and flower-bedecked nymphs. She also echoes his verse forms and his ability, which is unique in the masque until now, to use these shifting forms, through the medium of her voice, to enrapture her audience.

But here she also goes beyond echo. For where the pace of Comus's verse quickens as he builds to a crescendo of orgiastic dance, hers spreads out and slows down, shifting in the final lines of her song into iambic pentameter and the Baroque Alexandrine – the work's longest line – that resounds with the harmonies of heaven. Comus notes the calming effect, "at every fall smoothing the Raven doune / Of darkness till it smil'd," and says it is unlike anything he's ever heard (251–52). As it reforms its materials, the song reenacts something of the process of humanist education, but in Milton's version the reservations and qualifications are gone and a powerful personal voice emerges from materials of decidedly questionable morality. This is related to the idea that what "purifies us is triall, and triall is by what is contrary" – Milton's famous pronouncement from *Areopagitica* that is often used to describe how this masque differs from others in the genre (*CPW* 2:515). But it is not quite the same thing as the outright clash between good and evil that this is sometimes made to imply, because even though Comus is clearly the bad guy and clearly to be shunned, he is not *just* "what is contrary."[73] Something in the Lady responds to him. And just as she hopes to see the damned Echo "translated to the skies," her song and words throughout the rest of the masque attempt to translate her response to Comus into something heavenly (242).

As Shullenberger suggests, in her song "the Lady begins to figure out who she is by reading her own situation in relation to classical stories," and soon finds herself "at that threshold between the imaginary and symbolic orders where the imagination, if it anchors itself patiently in chastity, discovers its power to transfigure violence against the person into inviolable voice."[74] But this kind of reading is not automatic. It is enabled by the Lady's passionate response to something less purposive, to an experience of being lost in the realm of riot and shadowy dreams that Milton fundamentally associates with youth. As it calms the night and ravishes her would-be ravisher, her song is a precursor to her development of an independent Orphic voice (which may never quite be "inviolable"). And it is also still enough of an echo to raise the question of whether Comus is in fact ravished by his own version of narcissism. The immediate impression it leaves on him, after all, is "home-felt delight" (262) – a Miltonic coinage that editors often gloss as "heartfelt" or "intimate," with a possible allusion to the Egerton family's domestic virtues.[75] More obviously, it seems to mean that the Lady's song resonates with something that was already in Comus's heart, where it hits home with surprising force. For her part, the only response the Lady receives to her echo song comes from Comus, who welcomes her with his own echo of Ferdinand's greeting of the "wonderful child" Miranda in the *Tempest*: "Hail forren wonder" (265).[76] As the intertexts mount, who echoes whom? Is it really possible to talk about resistance, will, or individual voice when the actual experience is shadows on top of shadows, echoes responding to echoes?

The Voice That Outstrips the Will

This kind of experience may be inevitable for a "Lady" who is really still in the liminal, childhood space between having a voice and will of her own and not having one. The Lady's gender is a factor, but it is far from the only one, and the failure to connect her predicament to the broader problems of consent figured by children has been a shortcoming in many otherwise insightful discussions of the Lady's gendered subjectivity. These include the attempts to relate the *Mask* to the case of the fourteen-year-old rape victim Margery Evans, which was carefully investigated by John Egerton, or the rape of Alice Egerton's thirteen-year-old cousin, who was a victim in the sensational Castlehaven sex scandal.[77] In both cases, a powerful man preyed on a woman child, but gaps in the law made it difficult for her to claim justice.[78] The legal system could readily accept that the "defilement" of a child this age "might be by her own consent," thus exonerating her attackers, but these cases show that the system often failed to recognize the child's will, and thus credit her resistance, when this would convict her assailant.[79] There are uncanny similarities between these cases and Milton's *Mask*, which also depicts a woman child menaced by an imbruting force.

But for that very reason scholars connecting them tend to overlook the central experience of the *Mask*, which is neither about the Earl of Bridgewater's superior legal judgment nor even, really, about "sex," so much as about three children's encounters with allurement and shadow and their attempts to exercise their will in the world. What makes both the Lady's situation and these legal cases problematic, from an interpretive point of view, is the grey area surrounding consent and childhood and the corresponding breakdown of any authoritative frames of reference that make violation absolutely a crime or resistance absolutely a possibility. The cases, in other words, do not necessarily look like Milton's *Mask* because of influence or because of Milton's proto-feministic impulses, but because they lay bare a major intellectual problem of the era that the masque's writer had experienced firsthand in his own path towards a poetic vocation.

After all, Lady Alice, who is delivered from Comus and handed to her father because no other fate is imaginable, is not the only one in the *Mask* with no legal will of her own. Her brothers are in precisely the same position. And while their transition into married life, outside the masque, would obviously take a different form from their sister's, their halting transition from dependency to adult agency would not necessarily differ from her experiences in the masque. Nor, for that matter, would the transition to adult agency differ tremendously for the *Mask*'s twenty-five-year-old author, who was beyond the age of consent but still living in his father's house.

In the *Mask*, as in *Ad Patrem*, as in the law, the youth forges a path to adult agency only over very treacherous ground. The *Mask*, like *Ad Patrem*, pays homage to a father. But both works really are more interested in the dramas of the will that take place without or even against the father, the moments when an individual must choose freedom or subjection, voice or silence, even if the governing paradigm would seem to deny them the option of choice. If the Lady's song echoes her dreamy, poetic, danger- ous surroundings and their local Lord Comus, this is not really "trans- gressive" – a favorite critical term to describe any moment when Comus's power seems less-than-neatly contained.[80] It reflects, instead, the childish capacity to enter and respond to a world of shadowy poetic allurement without falling prey to its darker impulses. To captivate the child and allow for the educative process of error and redirection, "divine philos- ophy" must indeed be "charming," as the Younger Brother rather comi- cally chirps in response to his sibling's enthusiastic description of unchaste souls that become contaminated by sin and take refuge in charnel houses full of dead and degraded bodies (476). In this sense, in his ability to incite and enflame his listeners, the *Mask*'s principle charmer is no worse a tutor than the Attendant Spirit.

Indeed, what is fascinating about the Elder Brother's defense of chastity is that it is painfully, embarrassingly wrong, despite its own eloquence and charm. Like the Lady's echo song, his ability to speak powerfully seems to outstrip his ability to speak purposively. With wonderful confidence he proclaims his sister's secret weapon:

> 'Tis chastity, my brother, chastity:
> She that has that, is clad in compleat steel,
> And like a quiver'd Nymph with Arrows keen
> May trace huge Forests, and unharbour'd Heaths,
> Infamous Hills, and sandy perilous wildes,
> Where through the sacred rayes of Chastity,
> No savage fierce, Bandite, or mountaneer
> Will dare to soyl her Virgin purity,
> Yea there, where very desolation dwels,
> By grots, and caverns shag'd with horrid shades,
> She may pass on with unblench't majesty.... (420–30)

Yet Comus *has* "dared" soil her virgin purity, has captured her and led her deep into the woods. Shortly the brothers will find that rather than saun- tering majestically past danger, she has been glued to a chair with "gums of glutenous heat" (916) – a very physical predicament that contrasts dra- matically with the Elder Brother's picture of a chastity that can translate flesh itself "to the souls essence, / Till all be made immortal" (462–63). Ultimately, of course, the Lady's virtue emerges from her trial unharmed, but this requires a major, if subtle, revision to the Elder Brother's depiction of a chaste maiden striding like Britomart through the fire into Busyrane's castle.

If his seemingly triumphant speech leads him down the garden path, then what is the point of this schoolboy debate? For one thing, in its own echoes, allusions, and oppositions, it generates some pretty impressive poetry: the boy might not be Orpheus yet, but the language here works about as hard and productively as it does anywhere in the masque. In the brief passage from lines 410 to 429, for instance, Milton offers the Oxford English Dictionary's first recorded usage of two words, "unharbour'd," and "unblench't," and a unique usage of "arbitrate" to mean "to judge of."[81] It is truly generative language, but this "original" voice does not yet manifest an original and independent will so much as it shows the will in vitro, enfolded in the literary echoes that give the passage its shape. "Unharbour'd heaths," for example, is sandwiched between borrowings from Horace and Shakespeare, respectively: "trace huge Forests," according to John Carey, echoes a passage from *Midsummer Night's Dream*, while "Infamous Hills" recalls a passage from Horace's *Odes*.[82] And these are not the only borrowings: Carey also attributes "compleat steel" and "mountaneer" to Shakespeare, while those caverns "shag'd" with shades are a Spenserianism.[83] As the Elder Brother continues his somewhat wild-eyed evocation of chastity's miraculous powers, he serially invokes Fletcher's *Faithful Shepherdess*, Shakespeare's *Hamlet*, Homer, Spenser, and Plato, and provides the OED's first recorded usages for at least two more words, "Imbodies" and "imbrutes."[84] Of course, the allusive fabric of Milton's work is so rich and ubiquitous that the scholarly presses have been busy with it for decades, so this kind of structure is perhaps not unique. But that is precisely the point – the young boy, like his sister, learns to mobilize his voice through a process much like the one employed by the young poet.

While the debate between the brothers orients them within the same educational process as their sister, her developing ability to speak truth to power provides the *Mask*'s real excitement. They show potential, but she most obviously realizes that potential as she develops from a lost girl, invoking a voiceless nymph, into a firebrand. The change is apparent from the moment she opens her mouth in Comus's palace, responding to his threat to chain her nerves in alabaster or leave her "Root-bound" like Daphne: "Fool do not boast, / Thou canst not touch the freedom of my minde / With all thy charms" (663–65). This seems to be a case where malice supplies the age, but it is a righteous anger, a zeal that speaks with authority even as it continues to claim the "credulous innocence" of child-hood (697). As Milton would explain years later in *The Christian Doctrine* (*De Doctrina Christiana*), zeal does not just happen – it is not *only* inspi-ration – but just such an angry response to external stimuli that provokes a "feeling of indignation [*indignatio*] against things which tend to the vio-lation or contempt of religion" (*C* 17:152, *CPW* 6:697). Milton inserted the Lady's proud, disdainful retort in revision – originally in the Trinity Manuscript, Comus rattled on for upward of twenty lines while she sat mute – and that revision nicely enacts her will coming into its own, trans-muting the stuff of charming echoes into self-actuating voice.

Comus continues to tempt her with "all the pleasures / That fancy can beget on youthfull thoughts" (669), but now it is *his* understanding that is barren and limited. He offers a rich, if tired, idea of cavalier excess, and is shocked when she returns it to him in radically altered form, as a vision of abundance for all. Indulge your "dainty limms" (680), he says, echo-ing exponents of carpe diem from Horace to Samuel Daniel and Thomas Carew even as he improves on their poetry. Nature is made for enjoyment, indeed demands it:

> Wherefore did Nature powre her bounties forth,
> With such a full and unwithdrawing hand,
> Covering the earth with odours, fruits, and flocks,
> Thronging the Seas with spawn innumberable,
> But all to please, and sate the curious taste?
> And set to work millions of spinning Worms,
> That in their green shops weave the smooth-hair'd silk
> To deck her Sons, and that no corner might
> Be vacant of her plenty, in her own loyns
> She hutch't th' all-worshipt ore, and precious gems
> To store her children with. (710–20)

Time is fleeting, and nature's bounty, which is expressed in the Lady's vir-ginity, must be consumed, exploited. For if beauty is left unconsumed, "like a neglected rose / It withers on the stalk with languish't head" (743–44). That description of the rose, along with the rest of Comus's "List Lady be not coy" speech, is not in the Bridgewater manuscript, but the addition really does not enrich Comus's arguments so much as show how threadbare they are (and this barrenness, contrasted with his lush imagery, supplies one of the poem's supreme ironies). Years before, in Sonnet 130, Shakespeare had put paid to the already-hackneyed rose-as-female-beauty image, proclaiming that he saw "no such roses" in his mistress's cheeks, and when Herrick and other Cavaliers employed the trope, they nearly always did it with a wink and nudge.[85] Comus is either too unsophisticated to employ the like irony (which seems unlikely) or he thinks the Lady is too childish to need it.

But of course he is wrong. She is not about to trade her whole inheritance for an apple, as children are wont to do. She rightly understands that his proffered vision of nature here is shallow and tawdry, the argument, in later days, of a Texas oil man hell-bent on squeezing every last drop from the earth. This is worth noting, by the way, in response to the idea that the *Mask* is "essentially static."[86] The view espoused by Comus here is a debasement of his earlier view of nature's harmony, and he looks smaller for it, just as Satan gradually, dynamically, looks smaller throughout *Paradise Lost*. It is hard, ultimately, not to think of this self-described spirit of "purer fire" as a child gone wrong himself, like those "of a more delicious and airie spirit" that Milton describes in *Of Education*: trapped by a barren education, they retire "to the enjoyments of ease and luxury, living out their daies in feast and jollity" (*CPW* 2:376). And even this, Milton claims, is not the worst fate imaginable: they could become lawyers (*CPW* 2:376). Comus has decayed into late-stage libertinism, but he once produced visions of greater things.

The Lady, in contrast, continues to echo his earlier view of natural harmony, but with an inspired sense of its connection to divine justice. "Imposter," she snaps, and she utterly demolishes his idea that nature's "children should be riotous / With her abundance" (762–63). There is no better way to capture the newfound authority in her voice than to quote at length:

> If every just man that now pines with want
> Had but a moderate and beseeming share
> Of that which lewdly pamper'd Luxury
> Now heaps upon som few with vast excess,
> Natures full blessings would be well dispenc't
> In unsuperfluous eeven proportion,
> And she no whit encomber'd with her store,
> And then the giver would be better thank'd,
> His praise due paid, for swinish gluttony
> Ne're looks to Heav'n amidst his gorgeous feast,
> But with besotted base ingratitude
> Cramms, and blasphemes his feeder. (768–79)

By the end, her disdainful alliteration practically leaves her spitting her words at her besotted, base target. This vehemence comes with the best authority: Plato, Aristotle, the Gospels, Calvin, and any number of other Protestant writers urged moderation in the desire for wealth, but as Cedric Brown notes, the fierceness of her critique of riches remains "unique in the masque of the period."[87] No wonder, given that masques including this one were paid for and commissioned by rich people, were made possible by their vast excess.

That does not imply anything indecorous in the passage. Presuming that the girl's father is part of the solution rather than the problem, the lines offer a fine compliment to him as one of the benevolent elite, who facilitates the dispensation of wealth. All the same, this is obviously a place where the sacred vehemence of the young Lady's words transcends her situation, where she is not just a powerless captive speaking to her captor, but a voice of righteousness in the wider world. This is a critique not just of unregulated consumption but of the vastly different power relations that deprive everyone, at some point in their lives, of the ability to do anything but pine, like Echo, with want.

Milton clearly wanted to cultivate this effect of the voice unleashed, as he added a full twenty-seven powerful new lines to the Lady's speech between the performance and the 1637 printing. These lines, 779–806, make the Lady's claim to Orphic speech overt. "Enjoy your deer Wit, and gay Rhetorick / That hath so well been taught her dazling fence," she says, because she now has something better than the probationary fencing exercises of wit and rhetoric – she has inspiration (789–90). Really riffing now, she rhymes that "Thou are not fit to hear thyself convinced," but gives him a taste of her powers anyway:

> Yet should I try, the uncontrouled worth
> Of this pure cause would kindle my rap't spirits
> To such a flame of sacred vehemence,
> That dumb things would be mov'd to sympathize,
> And the brute Earth would lend her nerves and shake,
> Till all thy magick structures rear'd so high,
> Were shatter'd into heaps o're thy false head. (792–99)

In the first performance, the audience could presumably tell that the Lady spoke with a new zeal and persuasive force, but she did not identify this as the "flame of sacred vehemence" as such. Nor did she imply that she had tapped into hermetic networks of sympathy, a kind of magic that promised limitless power to those who cracked the natural world's codes and learned how to speak the pure, Adamic language.[88]

Perhaps most importantly, in the first performance Comus did not confirm these impressions by noting that "she fables not, I feel that I do fear /

Her words set off by som superior power" (801–02). Instead, he responded in this early incarnation of the masque only by noting the childishness of her speech: "Come, noe more / this is meere morrall babble."[89] By the time Milton finished revising, Comus was still trying to dismiss her words as babble, the incessant, unwilled, parroting talk of children, but this attempt was more clearly demarcated not only as wrongheaded but craven and duplicitous. He does not just fear her words; he *feels* that he fears them. He does not just push the crystal glass to her lips because he is tired of arguing, but because he is desperate to shut her up. Over time, Milton's revisions consistently enhanced this effect of childish simplicity giving way to authoritative speech. In an early draft, for example, the Lady gasps, "O my simplicity," when Comus tempts her, where she would later command, "Hence with thy brew'd inchantments."[90] In the first version she protests her childish incapability, whereas in the later version she asserts her verbal command.

At the same time, the various revised editions of Milton's masque show his own authorship coming into being. Ann Baynes Coiro has discussed the way the *Mask*'s first printed edition, in 1637, reflects its collaborative and occasional production, significantly lacking any authorial attribution to Milton but prominently featuring the names of the aristocratic performers and, on the title page, the name, rank, and position of their father.[91] Coiro does not note that each publication, however, continued to strip away the layers. In 1645, the title page retained the name of the Earl of Bridgewater, and the prefatory material included Lawes's dedication to viscount Viscount Brackley as well as the names of all the aristocratic performers, but the title page now gave top billing to the "AUTHOR," John Milton.[92] By the 1673 edition of Milton's poems, no names of Milton's patrons, or any of the other prefatory material, remained.[93]

Of course, in the end, to speak of authority or agency as if the Lady achieved those things absolutely is to miss the point. Milton never lets us know for certain that the Lady has achieved the Orphic voice. She threatens to move dumb things to sympathize, but it could be a bluff or the kind of childish sentiment her Elder Brother attached to chastity. Comus feels *something*, but attempts to force her anyway. And there really is no way of knowing whether he could have succeeded because "the Brothers rush in with Swords drawn, wrest his Glass out of his hand, and break it against the ground" (814). That, of course, is as much a failure as a success, because the Attendant Spirit immediately points out that they let the enchanter escape with his potent wand and left their sister captive. So the boys' education too leaves their capability a little wanting. They receive the magic herb Haemony, which offers an antidote to Circean enchantments through the transfer of knowledge, just like Ascham's description of education-as-moly. But ultimately it does not work "'Gainst all inchantments" as their tutor claimed (640).

Just as Milton cultivated the sense that the Lady gained an efficacious voice in his revision of her debate with Comus, he carefully retained the ambiguity surrounding the children's accomplishment in the final scenes. In the performance, at least, the brothers appear to have participated in Sabrina's invocation, but in his printed and manuscript versions Milton definitively gave this job to the Attendant Spirit alone; in performance the Elder Brother joined his sister and suggested continuing their journey, but in his final versions Milton has the Attendant Spirit make this suggestion, which coming from an adult is really a command. The theological upshot, as noted earlier, is that human action can only do so much and that heaven must ultimately lend us grace to complete the equation. What it means in practical, dramatic terms is that in the final scenes supernatural adults free the captive while the children watch silently.

In the final scene the Lady does not assume the role of a prophet, or an Orpheus, but a marriageable daughter in her father's house, and this happens not just because she is a girl but for the same reason her brothers fail to liberate her: they have to fail, they are children. It is a frustrating conclusion in some ways, but a very true one. To achieve adult will, in art as in law, is a halting, tortuous process, one that requires making impossible decisions, stepping outside the paradigm only to fall back within it. Although heaven has "timely tri'd their youth, / Their faith, their patience, and their truth," the children are in the end still negotiating exercises set by someone else, still dancing a measured round under the watchful eye of their powerful father (970–71). If that final dance reveals the limits of childhood, it also shows the potential of art. It is, as Blair Hoxby argues, "a triumph of personal conscience" expressed by the "well-tutored movements of the continent body."[94] Retracing in "victorious dance" (970) the ground that had only moments before represented the tangled paths of error, the children demonstrate the possibility of achieving virtuosity within bounds, of mastering the self in a process of growing up that is never quite complete.

The fully realized depiction of this idea makes the *Mask* a fitting capstone to Milton's 1645 *Poems*, a volume that Milton characterized in *Ad Joannem Rousium*, a verse letter to the Oxford University Librarian as a product of his own youthful "wandering" [*vagus*] (7). The *Mask* is the last English work in the volume, at the end of a series of English poems that testify, on the one hand, to the author's precocity, and on the other to his as-yet-unrealized potential. The most obvious example is the first poem in the collection, "On the Morning of Christ's Nativity." Dated 1629, the year of Milton's twenty-first birthday, the poem famously both celebrates the birth of the savior and "marks Milton's coming of age as a Christian writer."[95] But characteristically, it ends not as the poet triumphantly joins his "voice unto the Angel Quire" (27), but as he falls silent until some later date: "Time is our tedious Song should here have ending" (239). The poem is followed by more juvenilia, including the incomplete "The Passion," which breaks off with a note indicating that "the Subject the Author finding to be above the yeers he had, when he wrote it, and nothing satisfi'd with what was begun, left it unfinished" (57–59). Such gestures prompt Louis Martz's argument that the "dominant theme" of the entire volume is the precocious young author's "growth toward maturity," and I would only add that this growth is never complete.[96] Like the sonnet copied into Milton's "Letter to a Friend," these works bear witness to a power they have not fully realized, and like the *Mask*, they admit childhood's limitations without embracing the quiescence normally associated with this state by John Boys and others. Perhaps the Orphic voice must always be prevenient, existing prior to the will, even enabling the will, like the prevenient grace that enables salvation. That possibility, as much as the theological idea that evil is always with us, is why Comus needs to be left loose at the *Mask*'s conclusion. For those who wish to speak with a voice that can shake the earth, the wandering in his woods, the entanglement in his charms, never really ends.

CHAPTER 5

"Children of Reviving Libertie"
The Radical Politics of Milton's Pedagogy

In his *Mask* and other early works, Milton turns humanist education's potential for error into a productive resource, dramatizing the role of poetical fury in forming authoritative voice. This was also the most unique aspect of the pedagogical theory that informed all his subsequent work and that he put into practice in his home, where he educated his sister's sons and a few other young children. In contrast not only to obvious opponents, like the arch-absolutist Hobbes and the authoritarian Prynne, but also to many reformers in his own increasingly radical circles, Milton insisted on plunging the student into an unadulterated reading experience that would make the individual conscience a battleground for the trial of virtue. This pedagogy preserved and expanded choice, and it was essential to securing the "three varieties of liberty" – ecclesiastical, domestic, and civil – that Milton made it his life's work to advocate (*CPW* 4:624).

Understanding the role of this pedagogy and its assumptions about childhood in Milton's work will help address two persistent critical concerns. The first is the debate over whether Milton, for all his apparent radicalism, was really a political elitist and religious authoritarian, devoted to a theology that subsumed individual choice and agency in a corporate, absolutist identity. Stanley Fish most famously and powerfully champions this view, arguing that Milton's works dissuade us from learning any lesson except absolute obedience to the divine. "Conflict, ambivalence, and open-endedness," Fish maintains, "are not constitutive features of the poetry but products of a systematic misreading of it," and even in *Areopagitica*, Milton's celebrated defense of an unlicensed press, he "does not unambiguously value freedom at all."[1] To hear Barbara Lewalski and most other Miltonists describe him, on the other hand, Milton is the spokesperson for all our better liberal impulses, and he intended his works "to be educative, supposing that they could help produce discerning, virtuous, liberty-loving human beings and citizens."[2] How can these two brilliant scholars be discussing the same writer? The question matters in part because it opens onto a second and still larger critical discussion over whether the humanist tradition that reached its apogee with Milton ultimately enhanced human freedom or whether, as Richard Halpern has argued, the whole project of forging individual styles and voices "merely restructures the social authority that it seems to reject."[3]

Should we understand Milton as the ultimate exemplar of this disciplinary tendency, an elitist and petty bourgeois poet par excellence? Or is he the finest proponent of what Rebecca Bushnell has identified as a liberating *"functional ambivalence:* where one tendency of early modern humanist pedagogy always allowed for the realization of an opposite one"?[4] In what follows, I hope to show that Milton's pedagogy actually goes beyond "ambivalence" to advocate genuinely radical liberty, but that his use of childhood to conceptualize this liberty ultimately makes his efforts consistent with Fish's argument. Absolute obedience to the divine will is indeed the final value in Milton's universe, as Fish suggests. But as Fish would surely acknowledge, Milton does not suppose this (re)union with the divine can happen until the apocalypse, as Paul explains in 1 Corinthians 13.9: "We know in part, and we prophecy in part. But when that which is perfect is come, then that which is in part, shall be abolished." Paul compares this development with the moment we become men and "put away childish things," but until then the voices of the prophet, the "tongues of men and angels," are finally childish performances, acts of becoming that navigate the *saeculum,* or the period of time between Christ's ascension into heaven and his return to judge the quick and the dead. This principle is central to Milton's pedagogy and the political tracts he wrote during the Civil War and Interregnum, where it provides his answer to the questions we have followed throughout this book: what is the difference between speaking and making a noise, and is it possible for the people to speak without giving their voices away? Unlike Hobbes and Prynne, who elide the troublesome grey area between infancy and adulthood in ways that intentionally restrict freedom and silence unruly voices, the "childish" period of development for Milton is a secular time and space (the *saeculum*) where choice must always be free and liberty must always be in the making.

"Enflam'd with the Study of Learning"

To see just how profoundly this sets Milton's pedagogy apart from that of his contemporaries, and to begin to understand the political and poetic implications, it will be useful to begin by comparing it with the work of

Jan Amos Comenius (1592–1670), a refugee from Ferdinand II's persecu-
tion of Protestants in Bohemia. At first glance, Comenius would seem to
be a natural educational ally. Comenius and Milton shared an association with Samuel Hartlib (c.1600–62), a German émigré at the center of
a variety of schemes for English educational reform and scientific inquiry,
to whom Milton dedicated his 1644 tract, *Of Education*.[5] Hartlib made a
special project of promoting Comenius's ideas: he translated and distrib-
uted Comenian texts in England, sponsored Comenius's trip to England
in 1641–42, and attempted to establish him there permanently as the head
of a universal college.[6] Milton must have known Comenius's work, and as
James G. Turner notes, "Milton's programme closely matches Comenius'
belief that the key to pedagogy was the apprehension of the concrete,
material world, sequenced according to the natural development of the
child and leading to the spontaneous, unforced 'flow' of wisdom."[7]

Comenius was a devotee of Bacon and attempted to replicate his
empirical approach in the classroom, producing the first comprehensive
educational "method" in the modern, scientific sense of the word. Starting
with the child's earliest infancy, he explained that the student should be
stimulated with physical objects like rocks, wood, maps, and globes, and
would gradually build from this foundation in concrete particulars to
become the master of a vast body of knowledge.[8] His grand achievement
of this goal in print is the *Orbis Pictus* ("the world in pictures"), which
employs hundreds of illustrations, matched to their names in Latin and
the vernacular, to progress from the names of animals and simple material
objects to more complex moral concepts. Milton explains his own theory
to Hartlib in terms that would seem to situate it as part of the same project: "because our understanding cannot in this body found it selfe but on
sensible things, nor arrive so cleerly to the knowledge of God and things
invisible, as by orderly conning over the visible and inferior creature, the
same method is necessarily to be follow'd in all discreet teaching" (*CPW*
2:368–69).

Even more striking, both Comenius and Milton proclaim that they are
employing this method to facilitate a return to Eden. Milton famously
announces that "the end of learning is to repair the ruins of our first
parents" (*CPW* 2:366–7), a project that points the way directly toward
the pedagogical mission of his great poems on "man's first disobedience"
(*Paradise Lost* 1.1) and "Recover'd Paradise to all mankind" (*Paradise
Regained* 1.3). Comenius makes his own objective of recovering Paradise
equally explicit, prefacing the *Orbis Pictus* with Genesis 2.19–20, "The
Lord God brought unto *Adam* every Beast of the Field, and every Fowl

of the air, to see what he would call them. And *Adam* gave names to all."⁹ The child given this book will reenact this scene of prelapsarian naming, which had been a part of God's own pedagogy, much as it will later be in *Paradise Lost*. "Even before the fall," Comenius writes in his pedagogical masterwork *Didactica Magna*, "a school was opened for man in Paradise, through which he might proceed by degrees ... for although he lacked neither physical mobility, nor the power of speech, nor reason, he totally lacked the knowledge of things derived from experience."¹⁰ Joanna Picciotto has described at length the way Adam's innocent labor became a model for scientific inquiry and "paradisal Restoration became coextensive with knowledge production" during the seventeenth century.¹¹ For Comenius as for Milton, the application of New Scientific methods to educational labor offered not a discovery but a recovery, and the ground of this recovery was the child's consciousness.

Yet for all these affinities, Milton unceremoniously dismisses Comenius's two best-known works in the first paragraph of the educational tract he wrote at Hartlib's urging: "to search what many modern *Janua's* and *Didactics* more than ever I shall read, have projected, my inclination leads me not" (*CPW* 2:364). This is a remarkable gesture, especially given that it seems transparently disingenuous – a prodigiously well-read schoolmaster like Milton, as Lewalski notes, was surely not ignorant of Comenius's widely used and discussed works, particularly considering his own connections to Hartlib.¹² Milton's declaration that he simply cannot be bothered to look into these books smacks of the same contempt he deploys in his other polemics against his declared enemies. It was clearly important enough for him to distinguish his program from Comenius's to risk this seeming breach of decorum with the Bohemian exile's chief English benefactor, and the grounds of the disagreement are central to Milton's social and poetic vision.

Comenius's entire program of sensuous education is premised on the idea that it offers the best hope for engaging unpredictable childish minds, "flickering Wits," as he describes them in Charles Hoole's translation of the *Orbis Pictus*, that "wry themselves hither and thither."¹³ That target is telling: for all his emphasis on what we would now call "play-based education," Comenius is obsessed with eliminating the kind of uncertainty that those "flickering" wits imply, and in this regard his project is better understood as a reformation of humanism than a rejection of it.¹⁴ His emphasis on play, gentle discipline, and the child's impressionable mind and mimetic nature is identical to his humanist forebears, as is his idea that learning cannot be forced on the child, as this nourishment must be "assimilated through its innermost parts."[15] What distinguishes him from them and puts him at an opposite pole from Milton is his attempt to eliminate the poetical fury that, as we have seen, had long troubled both humanists and their critics. To make the child's education the site of paradisal restoration, it would be necessary to "banish desire from discourse," as Robert Stillman has put it, repairing the breach between words and things that came into being with the fall, and this makes poetry and imaginative writing particularly problematic.[16]

Children's minds are empty vessels, Comenius explains, easily filled with "strange fire" (*alieno igne*), and for this reason he banishes "jesting Plautus, lascivious Catullus, impure Ovid, impious Lucian, and obscene Martial" from his classroom.[17] It is not merely their moral content, but the very nature of poetic language – the gap between truth and fiction – that Comenius abhors, because it is the ground where the child reenacts Adam's fall. Indeed, Comenius maintains that Satan embodied in the serpent was the first to use such deceptive poetic language. It is like "poison" (*venenum*) that has been "mixed in a most excellent food or drink."[18] And this venomous drink "intoxicates the minds of the indiscreet [*incautas mentes*] and sends them to sleep, and, while they sleep, plies them with monstrous opinions, dangerous opinions, and loathsome desires."[19] Unlike Milton's Lady, who has a tantalizing drink held to her lips, Comenius's students will be spared such temptations, and once they are eliminated from his system, he believes he can produce an extremely efficient pedagogical machine. The transformation of the humanist model, sans poetical fury, is especially clear in the way Comenius adapts the traditional idea of the child as a blank page to bring it into the age of the printing press. The image is so familiar, yet so new, that the passage deserves to be quoted at length:

> There will be as much difference between the customary system and the new as we see between the old art of multiplying books, by the pen, and the new method, by the printing press; that is, the art of printing, though difficult, costly and complicated, can reproduce books with greater speed, accuracy, and elegance than was formerly possible; in the same way, my new method will produce a greater number of scholars, though its difficulties may be somewhat frightening at first, and they will be better educated, and take more pleasure in this training.... Knowledge, then, can be impressed on the mind in the same way that its external form can be printed on paper. In fact, we might adapt the term of "Typography" and call the new method of teaching "Didachography."[20]

Comenius spends the entire penultimate chapter of *Didactica Magna* exploring this analogy. He describes different kinds of wits as different kinds of paper, textbooks as "type," and the teacher's voice as the ink that is carefully mixed and modulated to leave the deepest, most distinct impression. In this "didachography" the emphasis is still inward, unlike discipline by the rod, but it is automated by a new system of uniformity, with hundreds of boys simultaneously working from the same, standardized textbook, experiencing the same sensory stimulation, and subjected to the same discipline of "perpetual watchfulness" (*Attentio perpetua*) that Jeremy Bentham would much later envision for prisoners in his Panopticon.[21] As Comenius sees it, his method will use soft discipline to enable the boys to overcome or "subdue their selves" (*superandis seipsis*).[22] If ever there were an example of the kind of self-abnegation Fish sees everywhere in Milton's poetry, or of humanist discipline working in the way Catherine Belsey has described it, with the "autonomous subject ... subjected to and subjected by ... ruthless mechanisms of power," this is surely it.[23]

But despite Milton's claims to method, his pedagogy is nothing like this. It is not really didactic in the sense that we usually mean the term to imply a kind of prescriptive learning. Rather, it is "not so much a Teaching as an Intangling," as he famously describes Christ's educational techniques in *Tetrachordon* (*CPW* 2:642).[24] Milton pointedly reinstates the drama and poetry that Comenius stripped out of the humanistic curriculum, embracing the idea that his efforts will kindle an "infinite desire" for learning in children (*CPW* 2:377). Indeed, Milton considerably expands the field of offerings beyond the typical humanist plan, recommending "some choise comedies Greek, Latin, or *Italian*," as well as "Those *tragedies* also that treate of houshold matters, as *Trachiniae, Alcestis* and the like" (*CPW* 2:397–98). The inclusion of Italian comedy, to cite just one example, would have scandalized a figure like Ascham, who devotes a chapter to "the inchantmentes of *Circes*, brought out of *Italie*."[25] Still more striking is Milton's inclusion of the "the two egregious poets, *Lucretius* and *Manilius*," as his nephew Edward Philips described them in a recollection of his uncle's educational program.[26] Lucretius in particular was egregious, his poem *De Rerum Natura* a dangerous vessel for an Epicurean materialist philosophy that replaced divine intervention in the universe with simple chance.[27] But although Milton mentions that these materials should be selected with "wariness, and good antidote," he displays little of the worry about the child's exposure to negative influences that unsettles even classical purists like Vives and Erasmus (*CPW* 2:373).

These authors warily recommend that instructors excerpt texts to avoid dangerous material and they invoke the principle of negative example to argue that teachers can sometimes use unsavory characters, like the bawds

and tricky slaves in Roman comedy, to expose the loathsomeness of vice.
Milton merely announces, with utmost confidence, that his program will
leave children "enflam'd with the study of learning, and the admiration of
virtue" (*CPW* 2:385). Rather than generating anxiety, immersing children
in these morally dubious materials generates the ability to choose wisely
and thus constitutes virtue. It leaves them "furnished ... with that act of
reason which in *Ethics* is called *Proairesis*: that they may with some judgment contemplate upon moral good and evil" (*CPW* 2:385). Rarely used
in English, *proairesis* is another word for choice, or a decision based on
reason. Nigel Smith notes that it shares a root with "heresy" (*hairesis*),
and he has argued that Milton's use of it here is part of a "forceful plea to
return to the original meaning of 'heresy' in Greek philosophy: 'choice.'"[28]
As Milton explains in *Of Civil Power* (1659), "heresie by what it signifies
in that language is no word of evil note," indicating only the freedom to
follow "any opinion good or bad, in religion, or any other learning," even
though this may "seem erroneous" to others (*CPW* 7:247). In other words,
the very aspects of the child's unpredictable encounter with literary and
dramatic play that troubled Comenius are precisely what recommend it to
Milton, as it preserves the trial and choice necessary to fit "a man to perform justly, skillfully and magnanimously all the offices both private and
publike of peace and war" (*CPW* 2:378–79).

This leads to one of the most unusual aspects of Milton's pedagogy, the
fact that "subjects normally taught to young children – rhetoric, logic, and
original composition – were to be left until the very end."[29] Milton's students wait a very long time before they speak on their own, because there
is little value in words "wrung from poor striplings, like blood out of the
nose, or the plucking of untimely fruit" (*CPW* 2:373). Instead, they learn
just enough grammar to enter a sustained, extensive period of reading.
But while this may sound more relaxed than the traditional method, just
the opposite is true, as Milton's pupils move through the curriculum at
breakneck speed, acquiring Latin and Greek, via Aristotle, Theophrastus,
Seneca, Pliny, and others, while "at the same time, some other hour of the
day" learning arithmetic (*CPW* 2:386). And this is just a warm up:

> Having thus past the principles of *Arithmetic, Geometry, Astronomy*, and
> *Geography* with a general compact of Physicks, thcy may descend in
> *Mathematicks* to the instrumental science of *Trigonometry*, and from
> thence to Fortification, *Architecture*, Enginry, or navigation. And in natural
> Philosophy they may proceed leisurly from the History of *Meteors*, miner-
> als, plants and living creatures as farre as Anatomy.(*CPW* 2:391–92)

"Leisurly" indeed. They pick up Italian "at any odde hour" and learn Hebrew, Aramaic, and Syriac before Milton has a chance to explain where, exactly, this fits into his program (*CPW* 2:397). On top of all this, Milton's charges are fencing, drilling, traveling dynamos, masters of the Greek, Roman, and Common Law, agricultural scientists ready to reclaim England's bogs and wastes. Not until they have mastered all this and more are they ready to read poetry and then, finally, to speak for themselves: "not till now will be the right season of forming them to be able writers and composers in every excellent matter, when they shall be thus fraught with an universall insight into things" (*CPW* 2:406).

Even by the ambitious standards of men like Mulcaster, Ascham, and John Brinsley, Milton's plan is frenzied, and it is no wonder that John Dury (1596–1680), who was no slouch when it came to ambitious schemes for educational reform, told Hartlib that it "hath many requisits wch I doubt will hardly be obtained in a tyme of Peace."[30] Chief among those requisites, surely, is finding either children or teachers, in times of peace or war, capable of covering so much ground so quickly. Milton himself admits (or boasts?) that such a teacher "will require sinews almost equall to those which Homer gave Ulysses" (*CPW* 2:415). The image helps makes sense of all the hustle and bustle, the pressure to learn combined with the sense of perpetual unripeness that is familiar from Milton's descriptions of himself: education is not some preparation for later heroic work; it *is* that work. Milton's pedagogy shifts the ground of heroic battle from the obviously adult realm of civic or military conflict to the childish realm of becoming. Ultimately then, the cultivation of *proairesis* is not nearly so systematic as his description of it as a "method" implies, because truth cannot simply be printed onto children's minds. As Milton explained in *Areopagitica* the same year that he wrote *Of Education*, "Truth ... when she gets a free and willing hand, opens her self faster, then the pace of method" (*CPW* 2:521). Indeed, we begin to see in *Areopagitica* how Milton's pedagogical vision extends far beyond the period of formal education to define principles of liberty for the nation at large.

"Not to Captivat under a Perpetuall Childhood of Prescription"

Milton's case against censorship in *Areopagitica* is a pedagogical one, and although it echoes and responds to contemporary debates over natural law and custom, it also illustrates the originality of his claim for freedom as the central condition of human development.[31] Most strikingly, in a famous passage Milton rejects the traditional humanist emphasis on the child's purity and replaces it with a visceral sense of original sin:

> Assuredly we bring not innocence into the world, we bring impurity much rather: that which purifies us is triall, and triall is by what is contrary. That virtue therefore which is but a youngling in the contemplation of evill, and knows not the utmost that vice promises to her followers, and rejects it, is but a blank vertue, not a pure; her whiteness is but an excremental whiteness. (*CPW* 2:515–16)

"Excremental whiteness" is the closest Milton comes to traditional images of the child's mind as blank, white paper that may be inscribed or imprinted at will – an image common both to humanists like Erasmus and to reformers like Comenius. At the same time, his point is precisely the opposite of Puritans like John Stockwood or Richard Baxter, who emphasize the child's original depravity to call for stricter parental discipline. "Banish all objects of lust," Milton writes, "shut up all youth into the severest discipline that can be exercis'd in any hermitage, ye cannot make them chaste, that came not thither so" (*CPW* 2:527). It is a remarkable, even bizarre argument: personal virtue is not born but made, and it is made through exposure to vice. As Philip Donnelley notes, this "process of helping readers to know truth and to cultivate virtue through encounters with vice" does not make virtue itself dependent on vice because it does not posit "that strife is the ground or *telos* of being, specifically because he presumes the ontic goodness of creation's origin and end."[32] This (barely) avoids blasphemous theological implications, but it remains totally heterodox and unique as an educational assumption, suggesting that corrupted man can restore his Edenic state only by replaying, again and again, the scene of original sin where Adam chose an apple above his inheritance.[33] Returning to this childish moment of choice is the necessary condition of repairing the ruins of our first parents.

In this way, Milton claims a role for perplexed paths at the center of his social pedagogy, where voice emerges from a seductive encounter with error that echoes the Lady's discovery of her voice in the *Mask*. In Milton's much earlier works, produced during his own student days, the quest for truth tended to take the form of a Spenserian Romance, complete with paper monsters and cardboard castles. As in the first book of the *Faerie Queene*, Error in Milton's fourth *Prolusion*, for example, is a "one-eyed and nearsighted" monster, and in the fifth of these academic exercises, "invincible Truth" (*invicta Veritas*) must face down the "claws of Error" with martial bravura (*CPW* 1:250, 264; *C* 12:174, 202). But rather than encountering error vomiting up schismatic books and pamphlets in

Areopagitica, as we find her in the *Faerie Queene*, Milton here shifts to the more subtle temptations of Spenser's second book where, as Milton tells it, Guyon is brought "through the cave of Mammon, and the bowr of earthly blisse that he might see and know, and yet abstain" (*CPW* 2:516). Now it is Truth herself who at "first appearance to our eyes blear'd and dimm'd with prejudice and custom, is more unsightly and unplausible then many errors" (*CPW* 2:565). Rather than unmasking error, as Spenser does again and again in the *Faerie Queen*, Milton offers to unmask truth through error. Spenser had suggested that it was the goal of literature to "fashion a gentleman" in "vertuous and gentle discipline," but Milton's work increasingly suggests that it is impossible to do this without allowing a free reading experience, shorn of prescriptive labels.[34]

At first glance, the idea that such a gentleman needed to be fashioned at all would seem to run counter to Milton's citation of the Pauline principle that "to the pure all things are pure" (*CPW* 2:512). The principle, from Titus 1.15, was popular with some radical antinomian groups like the Ranters, who took it to mean that virtue and holiness were states of grace that could not be earned, and it might seem to confirm Fish's suspicion that *Areopagitica* actually closes off any possibility for the educational development of virtue.[35] Likewise, Milton dismisses concerns that bad books can corrupt truly virtuous men, because "to all men, such books are not temptations," but merely "usefull drugs" to inoculate them against vice (*CPW* 2:521). But it turns out that Milton means something very specific by "all men": it refers not to a state of age but to a state of achievement. This is why Milton follows his statement about imperturbable virtuous men by adding that "The rest, as children and childish men, who have not the art to qualifie and prepare these working mineralls, well may be exhorted to forbear, but hinder'd forcibly they cannot be by all the licencing that Sainted Inquisition could ever yet contrive" (*CPW* 2:521). This initially looks like a call for didacticism of the kind we find in Hobbes, Prynne, or Comenius; virtuous men are safe and sound, and they should exhort children and childish men to avoid dangerous reading matter. But midway through the sentence, Milton makes a characteristic hairpin turn, retrospectively casting such exhortation as the futile Papist cloistering of virtue and forcing of conscience: "hinder'd forcibly they cannot be" (*CPW* 2:521). Without the freedom to fall in this childish period, no one becomes the kind of man who can avoid all temptation. And this raises the question: does anyone ever become that kind of man?

Milton leaves the answer deliberately open. He pursues a double rhetorical strategy, insisting that truly virtuous men need not fear temptation even as he maintains that everyone else needs temptation to become virtuous. But if true and absolute virtue remains an ideal, the need for development clearly remains our present condition: "he who thinks we are to pitch our tent here, and have attain'd the utmost prospect of reformation, that the mortall glass wherein we contemplate, can shew us, till we come to the *beatific* vision, that man by this very opinion declares, that he is yet farre short of the Truth" (*CPW* 2:549). Milton's reference here is to 1 Corinthians 13.11–12, where Paul compares our present vision of truth, "through a glass, darkly," to our "childish" condition, insisting that we will continue to speak and understand as children until "that which is perfect is come." This reclamation of Pauline childishness for radical purposes was actually not unique and should be added to Nigel Smith's discussion of the way *Areopagitica* "internalizes various positions from across the Parliamentarian and Puritan spectrum."[36] Countering depictions of themselves as unruly children, some of the seventeenth century's most daring radicals defended their license to speak, learn, and discover by embracing the idea that "I account it a part of my condition here, not to see all at once," as the prophetic Civil War firebrand John Saltmarsh (d. 1647) announced in a pamphlet published within a few months of *Areopagitica*. "I can freely joyn with any in censuring any unregenerate part in me," he continued, "as I esteem much of my Carnal reason to be. *When I was a childe, I spake as a childe;* neither *have I any fruit* now (as the Apostle sayes) *of some of those things.*"[37]

Milton's development of this epistemological principle into a theory of political liberty, however, is uniquely sustained. It goes back to Adam, which is to say it goes to the very origins of human freedom and the sin that compromised that freedom: "It was from out the rinde of one apple tasted, that the knowledge of good and evill as two twins cleaving together leapt forth into the World. And perhaps this is that doom which *Adam* fell into of knowing good and evill, that is to say of knowing good by evill" (*CPW* 2:514). This means that we always risk blinding ourselves to the truth if we attempt to create the kind of sanitized experience that Comenius offered in his pedagogy. Moreover, we lose the constitutive experience of virtue. This is why, even before evil leapt into the world with the first bite of the apple, God set before Adam "a provoking object, ever almost in his eyes" (*CPW* 2:527). Hence, Milton opposes the censorship even of books like Aretino's ("that notorious ribald of *Arezzo*") that were deemed obscene and pornographic both on the ground that such censorship is impractical and because it restricts this essential freedom to choose (*CPW* 2:518). God created "passions within us, pleasures round about us," because "these rightly temper'd are the very ingredients of vertu" (*CPW* 2.527).

They cannot be tempered from without, by an overweening schoolmaster or a licenser, because "God uses not to captivat under a perpetuall childhood of prescription, but trusts him with the gift of reason to be his own chooser" (*CPW* 2:514). Again, Milton's brief here is not against perpetual childhood, but against the idea of God as a schoolmaster who relies on "prescription," like the schoolmasters described in *Of Education* who leave their charges so infantilized that "tyrannous aphorismes appear to them the highest points of wisdom; instilling their barren hearts with a conscientious slavery" (*CPW* 2:375–76). When Milton asks, in *Areopagitica*, "what advantage is it to be a man, over a boy at school, if we have only escaped the ferula to come under the fescue of an Imprimature," we should recognize not only a distinction between adult freedom and infantile slavery, but between good and bad pedagogy (*CPW* 2:514). This is a consummately humanist rejection of the "painful" discipline advocated by Puritan moralists like Jonson's Censure, as explored in Chapter 2. In Milton's own system, childhood is precisely where we receive the gift of *proairesis*, of choice, and it is through this gift that we are always working toward truth, which Milton famously describes by invoking the image of Osiris with his limbs hacked apart and scattered to the winds. It is our task to search for those fragments of truth, to gather them up, but "We have not yet found them all, Lords and Commons, nor ever shall doe, till her Masters second coming" (*CPW* 2:549). All attempts to articulate truth in the meanwhile are childish performances, yet this does not negate their power or the necessity of their freedom. On the contrary, childishness is the condition of their power and freedom.

This revaluation of childish subjectivity can be understood both as part of the broader rethinking of patriarchal political theory discussed in the first section of this book and as a manifestation of what C. John Sommerville describes as the "future orientation" of radical groups – the sense among dissenters that the careful education of their children was key to securing continuing social and religious reformation.[38] As discussed earlier, Milton had contributed to the former through his insistence that if Charles wanted to claim a fatherly role in the commonwealth, he must be held to the standards of domestic, affective justice. Here he continues to use childhood to conceptualize an authority that would secure rather than restrict liberty. At the same time, his future orientation responds to the very real sense in which the English Civil War was daily confirming the revolutionary potential of youth. From the early 1640s, when London's apprentice community first metastasized dissent in vocal protests against the bishops, to the development of Quakerism, which in its early days was very much a youth movement, complete with "quaking boy" preachers and the defiant refusal to doff hats to parents and other elders, England's youth seemed to show promise of continuing reformation.[39] For Milton, these are the signs of a nation "as an Eagle muing her mighty youth," and he scoffs at those who would allow their fear of "sects and schisms" to lead them to "suppresse all this flowry crop of knowledge and new light sprung up" (*CPW* 2:558).

Of course, as some have noted with a sense of rich irony, Milton would seem to violate his own apparent principles of toleration when he adds, "I mean not tolerated Popery, and open superstition, which as it extirpats all religions and civill supremacies, so it self should be extirpat" (*CPW* 2:565).[40] But those who highlight Milton's hypocrisy or the limits of freedom in *Areopagitica* rarely give much attention to the second part of the sentence, which continues: "provided first that all charitable and compassionat means be us'd to win and regain the weak and the misled" (*CPW* 2:565). This language comes straight out of Milton's *Of Education*, where the free experience of reading functions to "win them early to the love of vertue and true labour" (*CPW* 2:383). If the rhetorical demands of his pamphlet and political realities of his moment necessitate his indulgence of a few moments of knee-jerk anti-Catholicism, Milton's commitment to forging virtue nevertheless continues to take precedence over any practical, immediate plans for extirpation, which remain deferred to some undefined future moment. Milton remains the author who dined at the Jesuit college in Rome during his European tour only a few years earlier and the one who continued to recommend such travels into Circe's den for his own students. Moreover, he brings this same insistence on freedom and development to the central problem facing the commonwealth in the years immediately following the publication of *Areopagitica* – if government was to be based on the consent of the people, then who were the people, and how could their consent be recognized?

"To Make the People Fittest to Chuse"

This question grew louder as thousands of pamphlets poured from the presses after censorship lapsed in 1640–41, jostling over the state's most basic terminology.[41] As Sir Robert Filmer complained, "Among the many printed books and several discourses touching the right of kings and the liberty of the people, I cannot find that as yet the first and chief point is agreed upon or indeed so much as once disputed. The word 'king' and the word 'people' are familiar, one would think every simple man could tell what they signified. But upon examination it will be found that the learnedest cannot agree of their meaning."[42] Such confusion was perhaps inevitable from the moment that parliamentary forces took to the field to fight against the king in the name of "King and Parliament," and it was only heightened in the events that followed. The "Rump" Parliament, after being purged by military force to a bare minority, finally claimed in 1649 that "the Commons … being chosen by and representing, the People, have the supreme Power in this Nation," but it required a fundamental redefinition of terms for that claim to be anything but a laughable fiction.[43] Of the 470 MPs qualified to sit in Parliament in 1648, men who had of course been elected by a minority of the English populace in the first place, only about 100 were left after the purge to cast votes on this defining resolution and the related one to set up a court to try King Charles as a traitor.[44] Clearly, whether "the people" meant the economically independent "freeborn Englishmen" historically comprehended by the term in Parliament, or even some radically contracted definition, most of England's population had little say in their representation.

Nor does Milton always write as if they should have a say, depicting them, for example, in Sonnet 12 as a bestial rabble who "bawle for freedom in their senceless mood, / And still revolt when truth would set them free. / Licence they mean when they cry libertie" (9–11). These people are not speaking, they are just making a noise, and Milton's resistance to hearing their bawling as speech reflects a serious dilemma for someone with his political opinions: after the king's defeat, it quickly became clear that expanding the suffrage as groups like the Levelers were demanding would actually result in a quick return of monarchy. There was a genuine danger, as Milton put it in *The Readie and Easie Way to Establish a Free Commonwealth*, that the "most voices" would "enslave the less number that would be free" (*CPW* 7:455). In fact, by the time Milton's first edition of this tract came off the press in February 1660, General Monk had escorted secluded members to the Parliament, where they quickly began reversing the revolution and clearing the way for a full election that would return monarchy to England. Almost suicidally undeterred, Milton then forged ahead with a second, expanded edition of the tract that would not see print until April 1660, when it was all too clear that the revolution was in ruins.[45] Nevertheless, as Sharon Achinstein shows, throughout the prose tracts of this period Milton remained "surprisingly committed to a single goal, that of making his public fit to achieve self-governance through training in virtue."[46]

He did this, as Achinstein suggests, by positing an idealized vision of the people, or "making up the public" as he went along.[47] But he also did it through taking a pedagogical role that often makes him sound as if he is the only adult in the room, and in this regard, those who accuse him of elitism are undoubtedly correct. As we have seen, children were often described as slippery, prodigal, or full of "uncertain motion, both in soule and body," and Milton finds the mass of people of revolutionary England childish in exactly this way.[48] They are "exorbitant and excessive in all their motions," as he puts it in *Eikonoklastes*, and therefore easily "stupifi'd and bewitch'd" by Royalist fictions (*CPW* 3:343, 347).[49] And in the *Readie and Easie Way*, this perpetual unripeness inspires a lament: "Shall we never grow old anough to be wise to make seasonable use of gravest autorities, experiences, examples?" (*CPW* 7:448).

On the surface, there seems little difference between this and the Royalist propaganda that regularly chastised the rebels for their "childishness" or reminded them that the people were merely the wayward children of the king.[50] The distinction (and it makes all the difference) is that even when Milton depicts the people as childish he insists that they have the capacity for growth and change. This means that where Hobbes had utterly conflated the idea of the slave and the child, Milton distinguishes them firmly, contrasting those who may "grow" with those who are content merely to "clink our shackles, lockt on by pretended law of subjection, more intolerable and hopeless to be ever shaken off, then those which are knockt on by illegal injurie and violence" (*CPW* 7:448). Here Milton embraces the contemporary neo-Roman theory of servitude that Quentin Skinner has described, in which writers like Henry Parker argued that "the very existence of prerogative powers reduces us to a level below that of free subjects"; the ability of someone to impinge arbitrarily on your will, whether they do so or not, makes you a slave.[51] But Milton's reclamation of childhood means he embraces this theory with a difference, because it emphasizes that even if our choices are constrained – we are never all equal, nor do we have a perfect clarity of vision in this vale of tears – we can exercise the nascent right to choose among conflicting opinions. This is in fact necessary to prove ours is not merely "a ridiculous and painted freedom, fit to coz'n babies," as Milton suggests in the *Tenure of Kings and Magistrates* (*CPW* 3:236). This is Miltonic pedagogy as political practice, and it makes his social vision progressive (literally) in a way that is not often the case even among the most vigorous defenders of parliamentary liberty. Parker, for example, could casually dismiss opponents that wanted a greater voice in their governance as "women, boys, Mechanics, and the most sordid sediment of Plebians."[52]

Milton's difference in this regard may not be immediately apparent, and it has contributed to the view of him as a somewhat "confused elitist."[53] In the first few pages of his *Second Defense of the People of England* (*Pro Populo Anglicano Defensio Secunda*), for example, Milton actually divides the populace into three key groups: the "citizens" (*civium virtus*) who have performed valorous deeds to deliver the nation from its servitude and establish republican principles (*C* 8:2; *CPW* 4:548); the "multitude" or mob (*multi, vulgi*) who oppose this project (*C* 8:2; *CPW* 4:549); and the "people of England" (*populi Anglicani*) whose cause Milton proclaims to defend but who are largely an imaginary entity (*C* 8:4; *CPW* 4:549). As Hugh Jenkins puts it, the people are "a work in progress," and in fact all these categories are defined by moral achievement, education, and political orientation rather than by socioeconomic status or birth.[54] Milton makes this clear when he describes his eminent scholarly opponent Salmasius "one, above the rest" (*unus prae caeteris*) of the *vulgus*, but still essentially a spokesperson for the mob from which he comes (*C* 8:2; *CPW* 4:549). As things stand, Milton talks dismissively of giving ploughboys and herdsmen the vote, but he also makes it clear that his opposition is not to the idea that they should govern themselves, but that they should do so "suddenly" (*extemplo*) before they discover "what law is, what reason, what right or justice" (*C* 8:246; *CPW* 4:682). To contract in such circumstances would be to bind their voices before truly learning to speak, like Hobbes's mushroom men or his neonate victims of conquest. The "citizens," in other words, may be a vanguard, but they are not different in kind from those whom they lead and who demonstrate their own, heroic potential. Milton's leaders are always an elite, formed through a process of sifting and winnowing, but the goal of that process is to refine and reform as much as to skim, and the reformation never stops until that which is perfect has come.

This is most pronounced when Milton describes Cromwell as the *pater patriae*. Critics have long recognized that this may function either as sincere praise or subtle rebuke, considering that the Roman Senate gave the title "father of his country" to Cicero, the defender of republicanism, before later giving it to Caesar when he began his imperial, anti-republican rule.[55] As Su Fang Ng notes, Milton reminds Cromwell that "republican fatherhood is most true when it remembers it is about being a son."[56] He does this in part by emphasizing that the nation's liberty has merely been "entrusted" (*concreditum*) with Cromwell "by how dear a mother [*parente*], your native land" (*C* 8:224; *CPW* 4:673). But even more pronounced than this shift from paternal to filial rule is the way the *Second Defense* rhetorically enacts the abdication or fading away of the *pater patriae* as Milton describes the people's ongoing development. He first addresses Cromwell as the father of his country. Next, he proposes that the Lord Protector invite an elite few to share his rule in fraternal harmony, explicitly singling out several men who are products of an ideal liberal education; Overton, for example, is linked to Milton himself by the "likeness of our tastes and sweetness of disposition," while Montague and Lawrence are "cultivated in the liberal arts" (*C* 8:232–34; *CPW* 4:676). He then makes a plea "that you might take more thought for the education and morality of the young [*juventutis*] than has yet been done" (*C* 8:236; *CPW* 4:679), and as he builds to his final crescendo he shifts away from either paternal or filial models to a model of wardship:

> He who has no command of himself, who either through poverty of intellect [*inopiam mentis*] or madness cannot properly administer his own affairs, should not be his own master, but like a ward [*pupillus*] be given over to the power of another. Much less should he be put in charge of the affairs of other men, or of the state. Therefore, you who wish to remain free, either be wise at the outset, or recover your senses as soon as possible. If to be a slave is hard, and you do not wish it, learn to obey right reason, to master yourselves [*vestrum esse compotes*].(*C* 8:250; *CPW* 4:684)

This language of self-mastery is pedagogical, following the rhetoric of Edenic recovery and self-discovery that we have seen from both Milton and Comenius. Driving this aspect of his argument home, Milton repeats the wardship metaphor a few lines later, this time pairing it with the kind of heroic tutelage he described in *Of Education* and emphasizing that wardship, "*pupillus*," is also a state of "pupilage." The nation in wardship, he says, needs "a potent tutor, an overseer, a faithful and courageous superintendent of your affairs" [*tutore potius aliquo rerumque vestrarum fideli ac forti curatore tanquam pupilla gens, tum quidem indigeatis*] (*C* 8:250; *CPW* 4:684). Whether he has in mind Cromwell or himself, Milton capitalizes not only on the pejorative connotations of wardship but also on its potential. Utterly subverting the royalist argument that the rebels are unruly children, Milton explores the possibility that this state, like the period of childhood tutelage in his *Mask* or *Of Education*, offers the chance to cultivate a truly powerful voice. According to *Glanvill*, the twelfth-century treatise often described as the first textbook of English common law, "guardians must restore inheritances to heirs in good condition and free of debts."[57] Milton accordingly both reminds the people that they must be fit to receive this inheritance and reminds Cromwell that he will be required to "restore to us our liberty safe, and augmented" (*C* 8:229; *CPW* 4:674). This is utterly opposed to the kind of static, authoritative representational system being proposed by writers as diverse as Thomas Hobbes and William Prynne at exactly the same time – the kind of system that imagined a definitive and absolute transfer of power from governed to governor. It is a very similar dynamic, as I argue in the following chapters, to the one in *Paradise Lost* that prompts William Empson to claim that Milton's God is "an emergent or evolutionary deity" and one who would ultimately "abdicate."[58] The progression from father, to brother, to youthful people engaged in the heroic work of learning is matched by a corresponding shift in the imagined audience of Milton's address. While he begins by praising and exhorting the *pater patriae*, he finishes by addressing "you, citizens" (*vos, o cives*), the "people" he had originally set out to defend (*C* 8:238; *CPW* 4:680).

Jenkins sees the New Model Army as the primary vehicle for this journey toward enlightenment. But from the *Reason of Church Government* in 1641 to the *Readie and Easie Way* in 1660, Milton clearly ascribes this role to a liberal and literary education. Taking the pedagogy of play to an entirely new level in *The Reason of Church Government*, Milton even suggests that the government establish a state-sponsored theatre to "civilize, adorn and make discreet our minds" (*CPW* 1:819), working in tandem with newly established academies to "win most upon the people to receiv at once both recreation, & instruction" (*CPW* 1:820). In fact, the *Second Defense* explicitly notes that the nation must shift away from a military model to these pedagogical recreations, warning that "If, after putting an end to war, you neglect the arts of peace … what you think liberty will prove to be your slavery" (*C* 8:241; *CPW* 4:680). We might translate "the arts of peace," or "*pacis studia*," as "the studies of peace," and Milton continues to elaborate the way these studies would proceed in *The Readie and Easie Way*, where he insists that children throughout the country must be instructed "not in grammar only, but in all liberal arts and exercises" (*CPW* 7:460). This distinction between the simple rules of grammar and the deeper assimilation of learning is key, as Milton claims his educational plan will succeed in "communicating the natural heat of government and culture more distributively to all extreme parts" of the land (*CPW* 7:460). It is the same imagery of assimilation that Comenius was fond of invoking, but Milton makes it a matter of *Realpolitik*, creating a people who have internalized the "natural heat" of government.

This educational reform facilitates a new model of political representation that is not unlike the search for truth in *Areopagitica*. Through the
continual exercise of choice, Milton explains in the *Readie and Easie Way*,
the commonwealth will always be moving toward a government that more
perfectly embodies the best qualities of its people:

> Another way will be, to wel-qualifie and refine elections: not committing
> all to the noise and shouting of a rude multitude, but permitting only
> those of them who are rightly qualifi'd, to nominate as many as they will;
> and out of that number others of a better breeding, to chuse a less number
> more judiciously, till after a third or fourth sifting and refining of exact-
> est choice, they only be left chosen who are the due number, and seem
> by most voices the worthiest. To make the people fittest to chuse, and the
> chosen fittest to govern, will be to mend our corrupt and faulty education.
> (*CPW* 7:442–43)

Ingenuously, Milton seems to have met his goal of preventing the majority of the less fit from enslaving the minority of the more fit while still
being able to claim that this government represents the "most voices." The
Grand Council he proposes is gradually refined through a series of ever
more informed choices and can genuinely claim some popular mandate.
The people meanwhile are simultaneously made "fittest to chuse" both
through this electoral system, where they practice free choice, and through
an education that develops the capacity for *proairesis*. This is radical education, the kind the twentieth century would label "critical pedagogy" or
the "pedagogy of the oppressed."[59]

By the time he wrote the *Readie and Easie Way*, Milton knew the
scheme had no chance for actual implementation, but its pedagogical
values inform his revolutionary prose, which becomes his true vehicle for
this reformed education. In these works, he emerges as a heroic instructor
"who could rightly counsel, encourage, and inspire" (*monere recta, hortari,
incitare*), as he describes himself at the conclusion of the *Second Defense* (*C*
8:254; *CPW* 4:685). The language echoes the inspiring and enflaming pedagogy in *Of Education*, which called for an instructor with "sinews almost
equall to those which Homer gave Ulysses" (*CPW* 2:415). Throughout the
revolutionary prose we see Milton stretching those sinews in ways that
look forward to his great epic.

Unlike the Comenian pedagogue, whose personality is totally absorbed
into an anonymous educational machine, the Miltonic instructor in these
tracts engages in a singular struggle, a form of self-study that requires him
to "turn the inside outwards," as he explains by way of a preface to the
autobiographical discussion of his own education in *An Apology Against a*

Pamphlet (*CPW* 1.889). Stephen Fallon notes that Milton's autobiographical set-pieces forgo the Pauline or Augustinian models favored by many contemporary Puritan writers, where the author searches out his own sinful nature and displays it in order to speak from a position of humility and virtuous authority.[60] Instead, Milton favors the model of ethical proof from ancient and classical rhetoric. As Aristotle wrote, "character is almost, so to speak, the controlling factor in persuasion," so the effective orator must persuade his audience of his own goodness, a persuasion that typically refers to a life of virtuous achievements and displays pride in "personal abilities and accomplishments."[61] But in at least one way Milton mediates between classical and Augustinian models rather than simply choosing one over the other: while he does not acknowledge his sin as such, he does dwell to an unusual degree on his youthful development rather than his adult deeds. As he does so, he entwines his own educational trajectory with his defenses of an English people who are clearly less-than-enflamed with a sense of their own liberty, offering his own experience as a difficult but inspiring path to authoritative voice.

In the *Apology*, for example, he recalls that from his earliest youth he was spurred by "self-esteem either of what I was, or *what I might be*" (*CPW* 1:890, my emphasis). The movement onward and upward is key, as in his later announcement in the *First Defense* that "from my youth upward [*ineunte adolescentia*] I had been fired [*incensus*] with a zeal which kept urging me, if not to do great deeds myself, at least to celebrate them" (*C* 7:8; *CPW* 4:305). This forward trajectory is essential to Milton's ability "to operate as a double agent," as Turner describes it, inhabiting the depths of a shadowy libertine world without falling irredeemably into them.[62] Thus even as he insists on his purity and providential gifts, Milton also describes his education in libertine literature in a way that emphasizes the importance of a free encounter with all that vice can offer, explaining that "the fuell of wantonnesse and loose living ... by divine indulgence prov'd to me so many incitements as you have heard, to the love and stedfast observation of ... virtue" (*CPW* 1:891). Such details provide an important qualification to Fish's argument that in Milton we find "no instancing of books whose publication is causally related to a virtuous result."[63] When Milton calls *Areopagitica* a "certaine testimony" (*CPW* 2.487), we must understand the persona that Milton develops in his prose tracts as the evidence that a liberated reading experience cultivates virtue from more humble beginnings. By the 1650s, Milton had taken a phrase from 2 Corinthians 12.9–10 as his personal motto, "my strength is made perfect in weakness." The phrase, which Milton inscribed into several autograph albums and referred to in the *Second Defense*, is usually taken as a reference to Milton's blindness, but it also makes his achievements a model for his audience. Divine indulgence coupled with studious observation, a "ceaseless round of study and reading," converts vulnerability into strength (*CPW* 1:891).

This makes perfect sense of the "uncharacteristically frank admissions of weakness" that Fallon has diagnosed, for example, at various points in Milton's *Defense of Himself* (*Pro Se Defensio*).[64] These admissions become a way of defending and even valorizing an English people that, as his polemical opponent Alexander More insightfully notes, Milton had made "a mere appendage" of himself.[65] "You are that mushroom [*fungus*], who, when only just out of your boyhood, went to Geneva, and all at once [*subito*] popped up as a professor of Greek," Milton taunts More, whereas "I always preferred to grow slowly [*lente crescere*], and by imperceptible advances" (*C* 9:281; *CPW* 4:819). It is easy to mistake a quick, imaginary liberty for true freedom, but as Milton illuminates More's notorious life, he makes it clear that the result is actually license and bondage to sin. The cultivation of virtue and true freedom takes time, and Milton's own extended "pastime in the shade," battling imaginary tyrants in the realm of poesy, has prepared him for his later work "when the Republic stood in need" (*C* 9:225; *CPW* 4:795).

As Milton transforms from the tentative figure who speaks "while green yeers are upon my head" into the very voice of freedom, his experience of poetic fury becomes a model for the development of national virtue (1:806). Just as he was "fired" (*incensus*) to celebrate great deeds from his earliest youth (*C* 7:8 *CPW* 4:1:305), he stresses the corresponding need for his own style to "incite, and in a manner, charme the multitude into the love of that which is really good as to imbrace it ever after, not of custome and awe, which most men do, but of choice and purpose, with true and constant delight" (*CPW* 1:746). By way of contrast, he regularly denigrates his chief opponent Salmasius as a "grammarian," with the obvious implication that he is the kind of harsh, incompetent schoolmaster who cultivates slavish habits rather than true freedom: "you may be absolved from all other restraints, you Kings, if you will but do homage to Salmasius the grammarian [*Grammatico*], and make your scepters bend beneath his ferrule" (*C* 8:96; *CPW* 4:601). Salmasius gathers and reads excerpts rather than digesting complete works, and he is addicted to "anthologies, and dictionaries, and glossaries," all the sorts of tools that even humanists recommended to tame the reading experience and limit the capacity for error, and as a result he has never "tasted the least drop of real learning" [*doctrinae solidioris ne guttulum quidem hausisse te ostendis*]

(*C* 7:66, *CPW* 4:338). Indeed, even if he turns himself "inside out," he is "a grammarian and nothing but a grammarian" [*nihil nisi grammaticus*] (*C* 7.68, *CPW* 4:339). Milton lambasts More in the same tones, as "the most pernicious tutor [*praeceptor*] of youth" and a "professor of babbling" [*Battologiae professor*] (*C* 9:226, 140). The implication is that where their arguments rely on hidebound didacticism and can only reinforce servile habits, Milton's depend on passionate engagement and offer the possibility that a still-imperfect people can mature and change.

We see this pedagogy in action as Milton turns his defenses into a literary feast. Salmasius becomes a Eunuch out of Terence (*C* 7:14; *CPW* 4:309), then with a couplet from Ovid he becomes the fountain Salmacis that unsexes unwary bathers (*C* 7:20; *CPW* 4:312), and soon he is described as a braggart soldier from Terence (*C* 7:22; *CPW* 4:313). With his "mushroom growing newly tumescent" (*fungo recens tuberante*), More participates in escapades that could come straight from Aretino, laying "Claudia on her back among the mushrooms, and the garden vegetables, and gardening tools" (*C* 9:280; *CPW* 4:819).[66] The authors Milton draws on here would be prohibited by Comenius and his style would scandalize that earnest Bohemian. Indeed, Pierre du Moulin, the author of *Regii Sanguinis Clamor* (*Cry of the King's Blood*), criticized Milton for offering moral advice, like a "schoolmaster" (*praeceptore*), even as he used language that reeked of "prodigal entertainments" [*nepotum festivitatibus*] (*C* 9:176, 174; *CPW* 4:772, 771). But rather than shrinking from the charge, Milton embraces the claim that he has used "salty" (*sales*) language as part of his uncloistered instructional program (*C* 9:174; *CPW* 4:771).[67] Just as in *Areopagitica*, the witty account of such matters will not impair "the modesty of any modest person, but nothing else seems more effectually to produce shame, where there was none before, in the shameless culprit" (*CPW* 4:774; *C* 9:182).

Milton has rubbed this salacious salt into his opponents' wounds not only to chasten them, but also because he recognizes Cicero's principle that language has the greatest effect on the people when it is "seasoned with wit and gaiety" [*lepore & festivitate conditior*] (*C* 9:176; *CPW* 4:771).[68] Indeed, in both the *Second Defense* and *Defense of Himself*, Milton very much sets out in the role he practiced in his sixth *Prolusion*, the playfully raunchy Cambridge salting that took as its organizing principle the humanist dictum that "play is not prejudicial to studies" [*exercitationes nonnunquam Ludicras Philosophiae studiis non obesse*] (*C* 12:204; *CPW* 1:226). This is revolutionary pedagogy as literary performance. Just as Milton described the process by which dramatic play and literary eloquence "captured" him, when he wrote the *Elegia Prima* to Charles Diodati, he envisions his own eloquence in the *Second Defense* enrapturing and captivating an entire world: "I shall outstrip all the orators of every age in the grandeur of my subject and my theme ... some in silence approve, others openly cast their votes, some make haste to applaud, others, conquered at last by the truth, acknowledge themselves my captives" (*CPW* 4:554–55; *C* 8:13).

In short, when Milton asked in the *Readie and Easie Way* whether his country would ever grow old enough to learn from wise examples, he was invested in the question in more ways than one. Not only had he already spent a career offering those examples, but he had identified himself with the country's dilemma of green youth screwing up the nerve to speak, of studying to develop greatness, making ready even when the moment seemed, to some, to have passed. And although he posed this question on the cusp of the Restoration, it need not be heard as a simple cry of despair or a relegation of the people to a perpetual and hopeless infancy. "I trust I shall have spoken perswasion," he concludes, "to som perhaps whom God may raise of these stones to become children of reviving libertie" (*CPW* 7:463). The allusion is to John the Baptist in Matthew 3.7–9, crying out against the Pharisees in the wilderness that they must "flee from the wrath to come." But in the context of Milton's long engagement with questions of education and liberty, this warning also reaffirms the power of the poet-prophet's voice. The children of "reviving liberty" may not have arisen – the "people" Milton has been defending may still not exist – but a heroic tutor, enflamed with an inspired poetical fury, may yet speak them into being.

CHAPTER 6

"Youthful Beauty"
Infancy and Adulthood among the Angels of Paradise Lost

Milton's children of reviving liberty did not rise up in time to prevent the Restoration, which was welcomed instead by a revival of Jonson's *Epicoene* and its concluding affirmation of sanctioned play's ability to silence unruly childish voices. Shorn of its Jacobean political and satirical context, it was an ideal play to usher in an age of prescriptive didacticism. John Dryden (1631–1700), who had been reading his Hobbes, captured the spirit of that age soon afterward as he began promoting a form of rhyming dramatic poesy that "Bounds and Circumscribes the fancy," safely restraining a poetical fury "so wild and lawless, that like an high-ranging spaniel, it must have clogs tied to it."[1] But in the year Dryden became poet laureate, Milton published *Paradise Lost*, and in this work he made it clear that the heroic pedagogical struggle to secure liberty, described in the previous chapter, would now take place on the most elemental level of his poetics. *Paradise Lost*, he explained in a defiant preface to the second edition, is "an example set, the first in *English*, of ancient liberty recover'd to Heroic Poem from the troublesom and modern bondage of Rimeing" (Note on the Verse, 15–16). The following two chapters show that this commitment to a poetics of liberty ensured Milton's continuing development of the questions of childhood and voice we have been exploring thus far.

The current chapter argues that Milton registers those questions where we might least expect them – among his ranks of fallen and unfallen angels. The assumption that angels are ageless is curiously imbedded in Milton criticism, despite Milton's regular depictions of them exhibiting qualities like "youthful beautie" (4.845). This description of the youthful Zephon, explains Joad Raymond, "is a synecdoche, as angels are sempiternal and do not age."[2] Likewise, when Satan disguises himself as a "stripling Cherube ... / not of the prime" (3.636–37), Alastair Fowler claims that these markers of childishness in an ageless being can be "sufficiently explained by cherubic iconography," while Satan's naïve questions and pretended educational quest would not arouse suspicion because "Cherubs excelled in knowledge, and would naturally ask many questions."[3] Roy Flannagan confidently annotates a "stripling Cherube ... not of the prime" (3.636–37) as "not of the first rank," although he makes no notation when the archangel Michael's "starrie Helme unbuckl'd shew'd him prime / In Manhood where Youth ended" (11.245–46).[4]

These are all cases of protesting too much, although it is easy to understand why. Neither scholastic nor reformed sources provide precedent for aging angels, and to propose such a thing is to risk sounding ludicrous, as well as to invite unseemly questions about angelic birth or to take too literally what Henry Vaughan described as "angel infancy."[5] But as Raymond and Feisal Mohamed have shown, angels were the objects of intense theological and proto-scientific speculation throughout the seventeenth century. To delve into questions of angelic substance or perception was to engage with some of the era's most pressing concerns about the relation between flesh and spirit and the hierarchies that organize both the natural world and human society.[6] Once Milton makes it clear that his angels eat and have sex, the idea that they age actually seems pretty tame. His frequent reminders that angels live in differential stages of childish development, however, represent a profound revision to familiar concepts of freedom and sin. In *Areopagitica*, childish things very specifically mark our fallen perspective, the dark glass through which we see; we cannot put them away and speak with the perfection of full adults until that which is perfect is come. But by emphasizing the maturation of even unfallen angels in *Paradise Lost*, Milton extends this condition beyond our vale of tears. Humanity's childish nature becomes not something that separates us from our original purity, but something that unifies us to a process of development that began before the fall and that will end only when "God shall be All in All" (3.341).

"Birth Mature"

To begin making that case, it is useful to examine the poem's most vigorous argument that angels do not grow and change – that they are not childish and never have been. Milton gives this argument to Satan, who taunts the loyal angel Abdiel with it. "Who saw / When this creation was? remember'st thou / Thy making?" (5.856–58), Satan asks, and as Regina Schwartz suggests, his "question haunts a poem persistently engaged in inquiring into origins."[7] Indeed, Satan attempts to elide those origins with a narrative of self-creation that sounds uncannily like Hobbes's description of a state of nature where men spring from the ground "instantly" (*iamiam*)[8] like mushrooms:

> We know no time when we were not as now;
> Know none before us, self-begot, self-rais'd
> By our own quick'ning power, when fatal course
> Had circl'd his full Orbe, the birth mature
> Of this our native Heav'n, Ethereal Sons. (5.860–63)

Others have noted *Paradise Lost*'s persistent association of Satan with Hobbesian materialism and political theory; in what may be an explicit allusion, the poem's first glimpse of Satan compares him to "that Sea-beast / *Leviathan*" (1.200–01).[9] But Satan's account of instant adulthood may have the most important bearing on the poem's political and poetic orientation. Chapter 3 showed that the Hobbesian "mushroom man," sprung up from the ground in full adulthood, became a kind of shorthand for an extreme version of contract theory in which social relations are drained of all affect and based on force and self-interest. Satan's assertion of angelic agelessness provides the false ontological grounding for such a theory in Milton's poem.

Critical response to Satan's "theory that he sprouted from the soil like a vegetable," as C. S. Lewis characterizes it, divides into familiar camps.[10] Those inclined to accept or praise Milton's poem as an expression of essentially orthodox "mere Christianity," like Lewis and Stanley Fish, reject the claim to be "self-raised" as a simple lie, its assertion of individual agency an original sin.[11] The problem with this, as John Rogers explains, is that Satan's account of self-birth "articulates a physiological process that resembles, in too many respects to ignore, the dynamics of autonomous self-organization that is Miltonic creation."[12] For critics like Rogers, who emphasize Milton's heterodox and "liberal" tendencies, the result is a productive ambiguity, although the atomistic liberalism that emerges from the poem is nevertheless "vaguely repressive."[13]

The emphasis in both camps on Satan's claim to be "self-raised," however, overlooks his more obvious and important mendacity that this was a "birth mature" (5.862). Adam's rhetorical question, "who himself beginning knew?" (8.251), confirms the difficulty of imagining one's own creation, but his account of walking and talking in the garden with God demonstrates that remembering parental nurture is an entirely different matter. It is this nurture and his own process of childish development that Satan forcibly elides. The problem here, in other words, is not the "quick'ning power" that Rogers rightly suggests Milton elsewhere endorses, but the idea of an automatic adulthood that he everywhere rejects.

This is why Satan's disguise as "stripling Cherube" works and why it is also an ironically fitting display of his "Hypocrisie," which "neither Man nor Angel can discern" (3.636, 683). Satan's performance of childhood relies not only on feigning an appearance where "Youth smil'd Celestial, and to every Limb / Sutable grace diffus'd" (3.638–39), but also on simulating an "unspeakable desire to see, and know / All these his wondrous works" (3.662–63). Milton vows to cultivate exactly this sort of "infinite desire" in *Of Education* by catering to his pupils' childish appetite for sensible particulars (*CPW* 2:377). In other words, Satan acts his age – or rather he enacts a developmental stage that all angels have experienced but that he has explicitly forsaken. Milton in fact goes to some lengths to mark Satan's decline into sin as a process of accelerated aging, so that when he first speaks to his rebel host in hell, we see that "his face / Deep scars of Thunder had intrencht, and care / Sat on his faded cheek" (1.600–02). The war in heaven demonstrates that angel bodies are self-healing, popping back into shape no matter how they are crushed or hewn, so these scars are not the result of an external blow. The Son's thunder is "infix'd," Raphael later explains, leaving the rebel host "draind" of their "wonted vigour" (6.837–38, 851), a loss of vital heat and moisture that would be familiar from seventeenth-century explanations of human aging.[14]

Again, this obviously risks an unseemly literalism. For William Empson, the whole episode "makes another puzzle about the biology of the angels ... because we can accept a unique birth of Sin followed by incestuous Death, arranged by God, but we can't imagine all these angels without a picture of their habitual mode of life."[15] The contradiction "feels bad," and Empson gets out of it by explaining that the stripling "counts as young because he has recently been promoted to the position."[16] But once we have admitted this much – that angels can be promoted for good behavior – we are a short step to the more intriguing possibility that angels in Milton's heaven mature and grow. This does not mean that they are constantly being born or that when they "embrace" they procreate (8.626). But it should remind us that for Milton, the theory of accommodation, where divine things are conveyed to human understanding, is more than a metaphor. "We ought not to imagine that God would have said anything or caused anything to be written about himself unless he intended that it should be part of our conception of him," Milton wrote in *Christian Doctrine*:

> If it is said that God, after working for six days, *rested and was refreshed*, Exod. xxxi.17, and if he *feared his enemy's displeasure*, Deut xxxii.27, let

us believe that it is not beneath God to feel what grief he does feel, to be refreshed by what refreshes him, and to fear what he does fear.(*CPW* 6:134–35)

If his angels or his Son appear youthful, we should also let them reveal whatever childishness they reveal.

This may be an important moment to reiterate a point from my Introduction, which will perhaps already be apparent: the "childish" state I am describing is often identified in my sources as "wardship" or "youth," and this is particularly true of Milton's poem, where "youthful" is the nearly universal marker of a liminal developmental stage that nevertheless clearly falls short of full adulthood. We do not need to imagine angel babies, or think that Milton imagined them, but we should recognize that when the Spirit, at the beginning of time, sat "brooding on the vast Abyss / And mad'st it pregnant," this started rather than completed a process of universal development (1.21–22).

The unfallen angels are like the English nation "muing her mighty youth" in *Areopagitica* (*CPW* 2:558), engaged in a continual process of renewal. This is the only way to understand scenes like the one we find at the gates of Paradise, where Gabriel sits while "About him exercis'd Heroic Games / Th' unarmed Youth of Heav'n" (4.551–52). This playful but vigorous education clearly fits Milton's pedagogical program, where "in sport, but with much exactnesse, and dayly muster," young students practice "embattailing, marching, encamping, fortifying, beseiging, and battering" (*CPW* 2:411). "Games" and "sport" are key terms in both accounts, making it clear that in heaven, as in the *Second Defense*, Milton's model is not primarily the army but the ludic classroom.[17] In *Of Education*, Milton promises to teach his students "even playing" and insists time spent "in recreating" is also time spent "in profit and delight" (*CPW* 2:386, 409). Likewise, even God's command that the angels "Inhabit laxe" while he creates the earth has a pedagogical valence (7.162). To "inhabit lax" is to go and play, choosing your pleasure. As shown in Chapter 4, Milton insists on the value of such free experience in his *Mask*, where the Lady finds herself open to the dreamy world of night and shadows while her brothers engage in a charming but erroneous debate about chastity. To inhabit lax may be, as Milton admits in his "Letter to a Friend," to appear to "dreame away my Yeares in the armes of studious retirement like Endymion wth the Moone," but it also fosters the capacity of free choice necessary to perform the will of heaven (*CPW* 1:319). As the angels variously join in song, witness the creation, or guard the gates of hell against escaping devils, they all "play / In presence of th' Almightie Father," as Milton describes his own muse's recreation, and this play has genuine pedagogical value (7.10–11).

Accordingly, Raphael is on an "excursion" to guard the gates of hell on the day of creation, but clearly there is no practical reason for his field trip:

> Not that they durst without his leave attempt,
> But us he sends upon his high behests
> For state, as Sovran King, and to enure
> Our prompt obedience. (8.237–40)

Again, Empson finds this distasteful, because it is pointless: "they knew, and they knew God knew that they knew, that this tiresome chore was completely useless."[18] On the other end of the ideological spectrum, Fish endorses the very stasis that makes Empson recoil. Defining "to enure" as "to apply the use of" obedience, Fish insists that the whole point is that there is no point to any individual action, as Milton's poem downgrades positive choice in favor of simple devotion.[19] But "to inure" more readily means "to bring (a person, etc) by use, habit, or continual exercise to a certain condition or state of mind."[20] *Of Education* proposes that inuring students in this way is not a passive but an active process that leaves them "furnisht ... more distinctly with that act of reason which in *Ethics* is call'd *Proairesis*" (*CPW* 2:396). From his *Mask* to his epic, Milton privileges the childish period between infancy and adulthood as the space of free play where this development occurs. As the angels become inured – as they inure themselves – they change and grow, just as surely as Raphael suggests Adam and Eve might be "Improv'd by tract of time, and wingd ascend / Ethereal" (5.496–99).[21] Earning their wings would be a promotion, and in heaven promotions apparently happen all the time.

"This Day I Have Begot"

This bothers Satan, who would like to think of himself as inhabiting a much more rigid place in the hierarchy and who never tires of rehearsing the degrees of "Princes, Potentates" (1.315), "Powers and Dominions, Deities of Heaven" (2.11), and "Empyreal Thrones" (2.430). He does not want to inhabit lax, nor does he want his legions to do so, admonishing them to "intermit no watch / Against a wakeful Foe" while he investigates the new earth (2.463–64). He is always wakeful, and always waking people up, unsettling Eve's sleep or asking Beelzebub, "what sleep can close thy eyelids?" (5.673). He chafes at the Father's announcement of the Son's reign, to which his own proposal of self-begetting echoes and responds, because it implies an instability or fluidity in a system that he wants to be static and secure. This announcement changes everything, however, because it shows that everything can change:

> This day I have begot whom I declare
> My onely Son, and on this holy Hill
> Him have anointed, whom ye now behold
> At my right hand; your Head I him appoint. (5.603–06)

Scholars have long debated why the Son's begetting takes place at this particular moment, whether it is a newly earned, meritocratic position, as William B. Hunter argues, or whether it demonstrates God's "arbitrary and unmotivated" will and serves to test the angels, as Christopher Kendrick suggests.[22] What is certain is that *this* day is different from the one before it and the one after. The universe before the fall was typically described as timeless, or at least governed by a kind of "sacred time" that had little in common with the postlapsarian teleology of days passing into weeks and years.[23] But Milton goes out of his way to alter this account. Raphael explains that the Son's begetting happened "on a day," adding that "Time, though in Eternitie, appli'd / To motion, measures all things" (5.579–81). Even before the sun has been created, Milton's heaven has morning and night, and it is possible to chart the poem's thirty-three days with remarkable precision.[24] In short, the angels live in time and have personal, developmental histories, and this is what Satan strives to forget.

Such forgetting has major political consequences, both within Milton's poem and in the world to which it speaks. As Raymond has shown, most medieval and early modern writers who gave the matter any thought, if pressed, would admit that angels existed in time, but this was not the quality they emphasized. Instead, the focus in both Protestant and Catholic accounts of angels was typically their incorruptibility and eternal, ageless existence.[25] This aspect of angelology crossed over into politics in the idea of the *character angelicus*, which was central to the concept of the king's two bodies. As John Fortescue (1397–1479) explained in his foundational text *The Governance of England*, the king's political body was a likeness of the "holy sprites and angels, that mey not sinne, wex old, be seke, or hurte [t]ham self."[26] As king, the monarch does not have the capacity to sin, err, or age. His will is absolute and immutable, even if his physical body is enfeebled by infancy or decrepitude. Paul Raffield notes that by the seventeenth century, great legal theorists like Sir Edward Coke and Matthew Hale had ensured that the "*character angelicus*, hitherto associated exclusively with kingship, was invoked in the service of common law."[27] This "quality of immutability" gave lawyers and parliamentarians their own claim to sovereign power, and as we saw in Chapter 2, this power could be asserted vigorously during the Civil War years to silence childish voices.[28] Satan's fantasy that the angels are an immutable "birth mature" is perfectly suited to either Hobbes's absolutism or Prynne's legalism. Throw out the *character angelicus*, however, and you throw out this absolutist political worldview with it.

Milton made it clear that he detested principles "congeal'd into a stony rigor" and laws "impos'd even against the venerable & secret power of natures impression" (*CPW* 2:238). This is why he flicked away Prynne's criticisms of his divorce tracts as "the gout and dropsy of a big margent, litter'd and overlaid with crude and huddl'd quotations"; if a text is the vital essence of a man, as Milton argued in *Areopagitica*, Prynne's "old and stale" textual encrustations left that spirit bound to a diseased body (*CPW* 2:723–24). By contrast, nature's impression, the felt experience of living and feeling, almost always trumps other forms of authority in Milton's work, and it is a phrase well suited to the angels of *Paradise Lost*. They are "agents with freewill, responsibility, and leisure time," as Raymond explains, physical beings (of an extremely refined substance) moving through space and time.[29] And thus, while Raymond protests that angels are "sempiternal," it is easy to understand how a clinical psychologist like Richard Fulmer could argue that "the developmental period through which the characters of the poem are struggling is Young Adulthood," with Satan a classic manifestation of the Oedipal complex (and God prone to thoughtless authoritarian parenting, "perhaps because of his own lack of experience as a child").[30] Once Milton makes it clear that his angels live and play in time, exercising, traveling in small groups and alone to new worlds, learning facts and having experiences that their peers do not necessarily share, such an interpretation becomes available.

The most credible framework for understanding the development of Milton's angels is not psychoanalysis, however, but Milton's own pedagogy and political theory, which premised social change on education. In this context, childishness marked not weakness but possibility, and Satan's denial of his begetting demonstrates his rejection of such a system in favor of "stony rigor" (*CPW* 2:238). Without the ability to recognize within another's exaltation his own potential, Satan cannot help but think "himself impair'd" when he sees the Son "Honour'd by his great Father, and proclaimd / *Messiah* King annointed" (5.665, 563–64). This sense of impairment comes despite the fact that the Son's exaltation actually results in an *improvement* in Satan's own status, as Abdiel explains:

> nor by his Reign obscur'd,
> But more illustrious made, since he the Head
> One of our number thus reduc't becomes,
> His Laws our Laws, all honour to him done
> Returns our own. (5.841–45)

In front of his rebel cohort, Satan denies this idea vehemently. It is this, in fact, that prompts him to make his claim that the angels sprung up like mushrooms, "By our own quick'ning power" (5.861). But later, alone, he admits that it was his inability to reconcile growth with gratitude that drove him over the edge:

> lifted up so high
> I sdeind subjection, and thought one step higher
> Would set me highest, and in a moment quit
> The debt immense of endless gratitude. (4.49–52)

Satan cannot experience change but as a threat, and so he is ironically doomed to deterioration where he could have had elevation, degenerating from a proud and disdainful monarch to a groveling serpent, abject and speechless.[31] The one option he is not given is staying the same.

With remarkable precision, the whole sordid affair demonstrates the failure of the Hobbesian psychology of contract. As shown in Chapter 3, Hobbes invoked the law of gratitude to help explain the obligation of children to parents. Even if they can provide no material benefits and lack the rational capabilities to signify consent in other ways, children can express gratitude for parental nurture and parents can receive this gratitude as honor. Hobbes went to some lengths to construe this as a mechanism of debt and exchange, emphasizing that gratitude binds most completely in situations of gross inequality, because "to have received from one, to whom we think ourselves equal, greater benefits than there is hope to Requite disposeth to counterfeit love; but really secret hatred; and puts a man into the estate of a desperate debtor" (*L* 1.11.162–63). To be an effective basis of filial obligation then, gratitude and honor must be exchanged in a system that lacks growth or where the perception of inequality remains insurmountable.

Satan is just such a desperate debtor as Hobbes describes. Alone in the garden, he laments the inability of escaping "The debt immense of endless gratitude, / So burthensome, still paying, still to ow; / Forgetful what from him I receivd" (4.52–54). In this rare moment of candor, Satan identifies his own forgetfulness, his elision of the Father's nurturing care, as the root cause of his sin. Now, in retrospect, he understands what he had willfully forgotten, "that a grateful mind / By owing owes not but still pays, at once / Indebted and discharged" (4.55–57). He even understands that he has never, really, come close to achieving equality with the Father and never would, no matter how great he might grow. But understanding is not enough. Satan tries to puzzle out a rational model of where, exactly, his exchange of gratitude with God failed, but this reasoning ultimately reaches a dead end:

> O had his powerful Destiny ordained
> Me some inferior Angel, I had stood
> Then happie; no unbounded hope had rais'd
> Ambition. Yet why not? som other Power
> As great might have aspir'd, and me though mean
> Drawn to his part; but other Powers as great
> Fell not, but stand unshak'n, from within
> Or from without, to all temptations arm'd. (4.58–65)

According to the OED, which cites the Smectymnuus tracts written by Milton's allies for its source, "inferior" could mean not just "lower," but "lower in the stream of time."[32] Whether Satan yearns for an actual later birth – an infancy that escapes the ambiguities of adolescence – or whether he yearns for a lower "rank" that manifests even more clearly the gulf between himself and God, the failure of the Hobbesian model is basically the same.

Without some deeper affective experience, its model of exchange leaves something lacking "within." Satan's Hobbesian thinking is unable to accommodate growth or maturation and it leaves him stunted and servile, as Gabriel recalls when he asks "who more than thou / Once fawn'd, and cring'd, and servilly ador'd / Heav'ns awful Monarch?" (4.958–60).[33] Satan is a great company man, and he does not mind abasing himself as long as the rules and rewards are set and his own position is assured. His first reaction on meeting angelic guards in Paradise is to pull rank: "Know you not mee? Ye knew me once no mate / For you, there sitting where ye durst not soare" (4.828–29). But the Satanic contract is prone to fall apart in the face of change or growing equality, and this is a major problem in a universe where all things are growing toward perfection, as Raphael explains:

> one Almightie is, from whom
> All things proceed, and up to him return,

> If not depraved from good, created all
> Such to perfection, one first matter all,
> Endued with various forms, various degrees
> Of substance, and in things that live, of life. (5.469–74)

Satan's amnesiac account of his own development attempts to turn this vitalistic universe into an authoritarian one, privileging the various degrees of substance over the process of refinement that makes all things "up to spirit work" (5.478).

"Yielded with Full Consent"

Such authoritarianism is a familiar feature of forms of representation that make a strong claim for "consent" while limiting the power to choose (variously advocated by Hobbes and Prynne in both their monarchical and republican incarnations). Accordingly, generations of readers seeking political allegory in *Paradise Lost* have noticed that Satan is oddly suitable as a figure of either Charles or Cromwell, while his legions might be taken as embodiments of Cavalier excess or parliamentary overreach.[34] As Sharon Achinstein shows, the opening books of Milton's poem are in fact deeply responsive to the sheaves of Royalist propaganda that depicted Republican leaders as a "Parliament of Hell," doing Satan's bidding or enthralled to a Satanic Cromwell. The grand assembly in Milton's poem oscillates between parliamentary and monarchical models. Satan proposes a "Full Counsel" (1.660), and we soon find a "Synod of Gods" (2.391) in vigorous debate. But he presides over the whole affair from "High on a Throne of Royal State, which far / Outshon the wealth of *Ormus* and of *Ind*" (2.1–2), and it finally serves as a rubber stamp for the plan he concocts. "The kind of tyranny Satan projects," notes Achinstein, "is like any other kind of tyranny, including that of Charles I and even that of the parliamentary leaders."[35]

What has not been noted is the very specific manner in which this tyranny substitutes assent for consent, a sleight of hand significant in light of the developments this book has been chronicling. We have witnessed the new authority vested during this era in government based not on birth but on choice, or as Mark Kishlansky has characterized it, the process through which "consent" replaced "assent" in matters of political obligation.[36] But as Satan addresses his Parliament of Hell, he moves in the opposite direction. He initially proclaims that in hell "We shall be free" and identifies the fallen host as "faithful friends" and "copartners" (1.259, 264, 265).

After this initial nod to principles of equality and mutuality, however, the justification for his rule becomes tangled:

> Mee though just right, and the fixt Laws of Heav'n
> Did first create your Leader, next, free choice,
> With what besides, in Counsel or in Fight,
> Hath been achievd of merit, yet this loss
> Thus farr at least recover'd, hath much more
> Establisht in a safe unenvied Throne
> Yielded with full consent. (2.18–24)

It takes six lines of hedging to get from the pronoun "Mee" to the verb "Establisht," which then rushes Satan into his "safe unenvied Throne" before anyone has a chance to ask the obvious questions. What are these "fixt laws of Heav'n" and do they apply in hell? And what exactly has "been achievd of merit?" The performance is a "perfect pattern of rhetorical composition, hardly to be equaled in English," notes Lord Monboddo, one of Milton's earliest and most astute commentators: "instead of saying plainly, and naturally, 'That the loss they had sustained had established himself much more firmly than ever in his throne,' he has contrived to express it in the most perplexed way."[37] The rebel host seems never to have had the power to bestow this throne on anyone, but suddenly it has been "yielded with full consent." Their shout of approval finally carries all the weight of the "childish" voices in *Coriolanus*, discussed in Chapter 2, who contemplate denying their votes to the Roman war hero before realizing that those voices have already been compelled: "We have power in ourselves to do it, but it is a power that we have no power to do."[38]

If this effectively degrades the value of consent, Milton soon removes even the pretense that the demons exercise the "free choice" Satan attributes to them. After Beelzebub proposes the plan ("first devis'd / By *Satan*") to conquer the newly created world, the fallen angels participate in history's first electoral referendum: "with full assent / They vote" (2.379–80, 388–89). "Assent" marks this as something less than consent, and it is probably not accidental that the voters here do not actually *say* anything. They appear totally silent, infantilized in the strict sense of the word, and when they eventually do register their approval audibly, they are most decidedly not speaking, but "making a noise," to return once more to Jacques Rancière's characterization of political disempowerment.[39] "Of their session ended they bid cry / With Trumpets regal sound the great result" and "all the host of Hell / With deafning shout, return'd them loud acclaim" (2.514–15, 519–20). The irony is that by accepting Satan's myth of instant adulthood, the fallen angels lose the very freedom of choice that Milton associates with the education of children. As in *Areopagitica*, "God uses not to captivat under a perpetuall childhood of prescription, but trusts him with the gift of reason to be his own chooser" (*CPW* 2:514). But when they reject the possibility of their own childish development, the rebel angels lose the ability, or the desire, to discern between prescription and freedom. This truly does make their prescription perpetual, no matter how free they believe they are to hatch empires in hell.

Their abortive exercise of consent leads directly to Satan's encounter with Sin and Death at the gates of hell, an episode that demonstrates just how completely Satan's notion of his own "birth mature" has perverted the natural filial bonds that hold heavenly society together. Just as he has denied his own birth and nurture, so Satan expresses complete surprise when Sin identifies him as her father and the parent of her monstrous child, Death:

> [T]hou call'st
> Me Father, and that Fantasm call'st my Son?
> I know thee not, nor ever saw till now
> Sight more detestable then him and thee. (2.742–45)

Allegorically, this demonstrates Satan's lack of repentance and blindness to his own sin, but the sudden injection of allegory into the poem has long troubled readers, and Louis Schwartz suggests that "few ... have paid enough attention to the episode's pathos, the way it seems to be inviting us, to some extent, to pay attention to Sin as a subject."[40] Schwartz shows that the very aspects of this scene that have repelled some critics – particularly the mix of allegorical and naturalistic elements that seem to give Sin being as a gestating, suffering, material, and maternal agent – contribute to the way it "ties birth to the negative side of the poem's dynamic of fall and redemption while at the same time suggesting how, via trial, it can lead us to the positive side."[41] Schwartz's sensitive reading focuses on the poem's theological register, particularly in the way painful birth serves both as punishment for human sin and path to human redemption. But Sin's monstrous paternal misconception also makes her a fascinating figure for the kind of political subjectivity bred by Satanic authoritarian representation.

When Sin springs from Satan's head "at th' Assembly" in heaven where the rebel angels conspire to revolt (2.749), Satan quickly becomes "enamour'd" of her ability to reflect his own "perfect image" and impregnates her (2.765, 764). As Su Fang Ng says, "there may be a mocking reference to Royalist family metaphors here: incest is what we get when we conflate the two Royalist metaphors of the lover and the spouse."[42] Indeed, when Charles claims to be the *pater patriae* in *Eikon Basilike*, Milton happily casts him as an incestuous abomination, given that the Parliament was also

> his Mother, which, to civil being, created both him and the Royalty he wore. And if it hath bin anciently interpreted the presaging signe of a future Tyrant, but to dream of copulation with his Mother, what can it be less than actual Tyranny to affirme waking, that the Parlament, which is his Mother, can neither conceive or bring forth *any autoritative Act* without his Masculine coition. (*CPW* 3:467)

Milton is adept at appropriating Royalist metaphors, literalizing them, and pushing them to their logical conclusions.[43] But Satan's encounter with Sin and Death cannot be reduced to simple Royalist parody.

Just as the earlier scenes drew from Royalist depictions of the "Parliament of Hell," this one engages the Royalist propaganda discussed in Chapter 3 that cast Milton himself and his fellow Regicides as "monsterous Children, who are borne with teeth in their mouthes, bite off the nipple, and starve themselves for lack of sustenance."[44] Like those accounts, Milton's voracious Death may also owe something to medieval Romances such as *Sir Gowther*, where the eponymous protagonist is sired by a demon and sucks nine nursemaids to death before biting off his mother's nipple.[45] But the state of war Milton depicts between parent and child also has a distinctly Hobbesian resonance:

> this odious offspring whom thou seest
> Thine own Begotten, breaking violent way
> Tore through my entrails, that with fear and pain
> Distorted, all my nether shape thus grew
> Tranform'd: but he my inbred enemie
> Forth issu'd, brandishing his fatal Dart
> Made to destroy: I fled, and cry'd out *Death*. (2.781–87)

It is as if Milton has combined Hobbes's two paradigmatic scenarios of original contract – the men who spring up from the ground, fully formed, into a state of war (*DC* 8.1.160), and the mother "in whose power it is to save or destroy" her child in order to prevent living in "danger or subjection" to that child at a later date (*EL* 2.4.3.132). As Barbara Lewalski notes, Satan's decision to forgo gruesome battle with his son is likewise a calculated plan to avoid a battle he cannot win; after Sin describes Death's awesome power, Satan shifts comically from bombast and insult to flattery:

"the subtle Fiend his lore / Soon learned, now milder, and thus answered smooth" (2.815–16).[46] "The passion to be reckoned upon, is Fear," says Hobbes, whether of "The Power of Spirits Invisible," or "the Power of those men they shall therein Offend" (*L* 1.14.200), and Satan's promise to provide sustenance to his phantasmagoric children is in this regard premised on a classic Hobbesian contract.

Among the many parodies and travesties of the *Aeneid* in *Paradise Lost*, this may be the most profound. The *Aeneid* is a tale of filial and paternal love, as Aeneas not only braves the depths of hell to seek his father's counsel but also risks life and limb to secure his own son's future.[47] He is as future-oriented as any good Puritan, and throughout the *Aeneid* there is no fate more cruel than the death of sons: this is literally the "unspeakable" (*infandum*), as Pallas's father explains.[48] By contrast, Satan's children are mere afterthoughts of his own imperial plans (literally: Sin surprises everyone when she bursts from Satan's head after he announces his rebellion).

With each incestuous generation, Sin's children, if they can even be called that, become further distanced from the capacity for meaningful speech or being. Stephen Fallon suggests that "by Milton's time allegory was an ideal vehicle for presenting deficient ontology as well as deficient epistemology," and Sin and Death accordingly represent a privation of being in the poem's vitalist materialist universe.[49] If they are subjects, in other words, they are the "phenomenologically thin subject[s] of modern contract theory" that Victoria Kahn has described – the kinds of subjects that can create, or be created by, Hobbesian patriarchy.[50] Death hovers even more uneasily between material substance and nonentity than his mother, a "shape, / If shape it might be called that shape had none" (2.666–67). And his maternal rape begets beasts that have only the ability to make noise without real voice:

> These yelling Monsters that with ceaseless cry
> Surround me, as thou sawst, hourly conceiv'd
> And hourly born, with sorrow infinite
> To me, for when they list into the womb
> That bred them they return, and howle and gnaw
> My Bowels, thir repast. (2.795–800)

Such horrors are not just the result of monarchical rule but of any system that makes consent a matter of force and makes contracts instruments of prescription rather than of liberty. If the account of Sin's monstrous birth(s) echoes Milton's attacks on Charles, it just as closely resonates with his use of childbearing imagery to describe "the vigorous birth of our republic" (*fortiter parta, de nostra republica*) in the *Second Defense* (*C* 8:226; *CPW*

4:673). The sense of birth in "parta" is clearly central to Milton's rhetoric as he darkly warns Cromwell, the new *pater patriae*, that he must exercise caution lest this nation's liberty is "*aborta*," a miscarriage or abortive issue (*C* 8:226; *CPW* 4:673). To ensure the nation brings forth its promised liberty, Milton warns Cromwell that he must not allow her to be "violated by yourself" [*violatam per te*] (*C* 8:226; *CPW* 4:673). Milton also concludes by warning the people themselves that they must also banish avarice and ambition from their minds and families or else "intolerable tyrants will be hatched daily in your own bowels" [*tyranni ex ipsis praecordiis vestris intolerandi pululabunt*] (*C* 8:240; *CPW* 4:681). To prevent this fate, which so closely anticipates Sin's daily birth of the monsters that gnaw her bowels, Milton argues not that the people must remain loyal and devout but that they must recognize their incomplete education and learn the ways of liberty.

By contrast, Sin hails Satan as a victor who "hast atchiev'd our libertie" (10.368), as if this is something that can merely be passed from father to child, inherited via birth rather than inured through the long cultivation of "that act of reason which in *Ethics* is call'd *Proairesis*," or choice (*CPW* 2:396). Sin and Death appropriately commemorate this newfound liberty by building a bridge that violates every principle of Milton's vitalistic universe:

> The aggregated Soyle
> *Death* with his Mace petrific, cold and dry,
> As with a Trident smote, and fix't as firm
> As *Delos* floating once; the rest his look
> Bound with *Gorgonian* rigor not to move. (10.293–97)

This "pontifical" bridge (10.313), punningly embodying the stultifying rigor of the Papal hierarchy, is the only kind of structure that can be reared from Hobbesian art.[51] As John Rumrich notes, the indeterminate first matter of chaos, the raw stuff that serves both nature's womb and grave, revolts against this unnatural artifice, noisily assailing the bridge.[52] The structure has been "made all fast, too fast," locked into place "with Pinns of Adamant / And Chains" (10. 319–20). Although it connects earth and hell, it is a bridge to nowhere because it arrests the principle of liberty on which all growth in *Paradise Lost* is premised.

By way of contrast, God's creation is "hanging in a golden Chain" (2.1051), but rather than binding matter down, the chain supports a "pendant world" (2.1052) suspended in a free space of play (literally: "play" is "free or unimpeded movement, esp. from or about a fixed point," a definition that accurately describes the motion of a pendant).⁵³ The difference could not be more profound, especially as God's creation facilitates a childish state of free development that Satan's twisted paternity everywhere denies. As Patricia Parker argues, such pendency is a fundamental component of Milton's poetics, which is built on "undecided" moments of suspension that offer a free "interpretative space, a kind of dilation of possibility."⁵⁴ Milton indicates as much when he claims his poem is an example of "ancient liberty recover'd to Heroic Poem," and *Paradise Lost* shows unfallen angels and humans participating in this dilation of possibility throughout the poem (Note on the Verse, 15–16). The next chapter explains the way this makes the childish period between youth and adulthood crucial to human freedom both before and after the fall. But to conclude here, we might briefly return to its expression among the ranks of Milton's youthful, unfallen angels and to the Son himself, who perfectly embodies "Filial obedience" (3.269).

When the Son jokes around with his father in heaven, Empson cracks that "the youth is eager to win his spurs," and while this account of the childish and perhaps "simple-minded" Son is facetious it also bears serious consideration in Milton's dynamic universe.⁵⁵ When we encounter him in his human incarnation in *Paradise Regained*, the Son is after all in "youth's full flowr" (1.67), and in *Paradise Lost* too he is emphatically not an example of Satanic "birth mature" (5.862). Instead, God pointedly declares him "By merit more then Birthright Son of God" (3.309).⁵⁶ To say such a thing was to impress Milton's Arian heresy deeply on the poem – his belief, confirmed in *The Christian Doctrine*, that the Father was prior and superior to the Son.⁵⁷ The Son must earn his position, in short, and the language Milton uses to describe his achievement resonates clearly with contemporary debates over childhood and consent. Unlike the noisy rebels who imagine themselves fully adult but who bind themselves into subjection with their infantile yelps, vaunts, and cries, the Son's "meek aspect / Silent yet spake, and breath'd immortal love / To mortal men" (3.266–68). The Son embraces meekness and silence, the classic signs of childishness, and comes to embody not perpetual bondage but freedom from it. It is from this position of filial obedience that he becomes the Word itself: "Inhabit laxe, ye Powers of Heav'n, / And thou my Word, begotten Son, by thee / This I perform, speak thou, and be it don" (7.162–64). As the final chapter shows, this is a pattern offered to all mankind.

CHAPTER 7

Children of Paradise

As with Milton's angels, most critics have refused to think that his Adam and Eve are childish in any meaningful way. In Thomas Corns's lively account, for example, Milton is unable to draw on "the development of the human infant" to depict his first humans because children are "not perceived as wholly rational"; by contrast, Corns suggests that we might picture Milton's Adam as "a deeply traumatized genius" with amnesia.[1] Scott Maisano basically sees Adam and Eve as robots that "come into the world as full-grown adults with fully-developed vocabularies and a pre-programmed propensity for self-reflection."[2] Even Margaret Thickstun, who is one of the few people to admit that Milton's angels grow and change (although they "grow as adults"), emphasizes that Adam and Eve are always already "adult human beings."[3] Such sentiments, however, echo Satan's claim to be the product of a "birth mature" (5.862), explored in the previous chapter, and I hope to show here that they misrepresent the universe of *Paradise Lost* in a similar way.

Perhaps most prominently, the failure to recognize Adam and Eve's childishness reinforces the idea that Eve is somehow deficient and that "nowhere are the designs of orthodoxy more vividly displayed than in [the] passage in which Eve herself utters the words which consign her authority to Adam, and through him to Milton's God, and thence to Milton's poem, and through the poem to the ancient patriarchal tradition."[4] In fact, Eve's awareness of her childishness is the source of her freedom and a prerequisite for achieving human redemption after the fall. In the case of both Adam and Eve, the revaluation of such childishness is one of the poem's chief innovations, linking fallen and unfallen humanity in a way that makes it possible to "repair the ruins of our first parents," as Milton aspires to do in *Of Education* (*CPW* 2:366–67). In the creation of Adam and Eve and in the repeated scenes of their education, Milton draws on familiar concepts of childhood to present a model of universal development that is totally unlike Satan's stunted authoritarianism. The poem's reticulated structure repeatedly presents their nascent moments of consciousness and learning, leveraging notions of childhood and familial nurture to elucidate forms of obligation without subjection and to facilitate the experience of error without sin.

"This Is *Adam*"

Any writer discussing Adam and Eve had to choose from a range of characteristics: were they perfect adults, ageless spiritual beings, innocent children, wayward youths, or the exemplars of parental authority? Each choice had ramifications for concepts of freedom and sin both before and after the fall. Just as the *character angelicus* was used throughout the period to conceptualize the immutable authority of the sovereign or the law, as argued in the previous chapter, Eden was the starting point for discussing the origins and history of this authority, the benchmark for deciding whether any given political settlement was a fulfillment or corruption of God's natural order. Before turning to Milton's own depiction of Adam and Eve, it will be useful then to consider the field of possibilities he had to navigate.

Sir Robert Filmer, for example, constructed the entire fabric of his patriarchal theory from the single fact of Adam's creation as an adult king: "Adam was a king from his creation, and in the state of innocency he had been governor of his children."[5] Accordingly, while Filmer admired Hobbes's extreme absolutism he was bewildered by the attempt to justify it without reference to Eden: "We must not deny the truth of the history of creation," Filmer snapped, arguing that Hobbes's "right of nature" was just as much an imagination as his mushroom society.[6] Based on such sentiments, Su Fang Ng identifies Eden as the "central myth of patriarchalism," which is true, although it was also the de facto starting place for establishing alternative forms of authority to traditional patriarchalism.[7] Hugo Grotius, for example, begins his account of natural and positive law with an analysis of the laws handed down to Adam.[8]

It is no surprise, then, that Adam's dominion figures prominently among the favorite *Witty Apophthegms* collected by the arch-Royalist Thomas Bayly and published after the Restoration: "Monarchicall Government by Secular Kings and Priests is the only Ordinance of God," read one notable maxim by King James, "and the Republick only a depraved institution of man for depraved ends, as appears manifestly by the whole current of Scripture, even from *Adam*."[9] Equally witty, thought Bayly, was Charles's confidant Edward Somerset (d. 1667), who brushed aside volumes of tedious constitutional law by noting that "*Adam* was the first, that ever had fulness of power granted unto him, *viz.* when God gave him power to subdue the earth, and to have dominion over every living creature."[10] Neither saying really succeeds as an aphorism, but both do manage to distill a single political principle from a complex mythology. Although Adam in each of these accounts is newly created, he is also a king and a father. He has very little to learn but much to teach.

This authoritarian Adam sorted well with Augustine's influential depiction of our first parents as wholly rational, dispassionate beings. As best as Augustine can reckon, before the fall, Adam and Eve could even procreate without emotional agitation; Adam could have controlled his erections "by will only," like making a fist, and Eve could have responded in kind.[11] They never had the chance to employ this mechanism because they sinned and were exiled first, but Augustine finds it important to establish that unruly passions, which so clearly characterize youth and childhood in his own *Confessions*, result from the fall.[12] By contrast, our first parents were thoroughly adult, characterized by "harmonious alertness of mind and body and an effortless observance of God's command."[13]

As William Poole notes, however, Augustine's exaltation of Adam and Eve's adult intellect and capabilities was something of an innovation, deriving from his fierce anti-Pelagian focus on original sin.[14] Competing with the depictions of our regal and mature first parents, the idea that Adam and Eve were childish was both current in the seventeenth century and grounded in a long theological tradition. The second-century theologian Irenaeus, for example, wrote that in Eden, "man was a child, not yet having his understanding perfected; wherefore he was easily led astray by the deceiver."[15] Although this childishness seems to precipitate the fall, Irenaeus also makes it a cornerstone of his theology. Adam's childlike innocence becomes a quality for emulation, prefiguring Christ's injunction to "become as little children" in Matthew 18.3.

Likewise, Clement of Alexandria (c.150–215), whom Milton cited with approval in *Areopagitica* but rebuked in *Of Reformation*, anticipated the English doctrine of *malitia supplet aetatem* when he claimed Edenic man "was as a child seduced by lusts, and grew old in disobedience."[16] And Theophilus of Antioch (c.130–80), who seems to have introduced the idea of the trinity to Christian theology, understood Adam's creation in similar terms:

> Adam, being yet an infant in age, was on this account as yet unable to receive knowledge worthily. For now, also, when a child is born it is not at once able to eat bread, but is nourished first with milk, and then, with the

increment of years, it advances to solid food. Thus, too, would it have been with Adam; for not as one who grudged him, as some suppose, did God command him not to eat of knowledge. But He wished also to make proof of him, whether he was submissive to His commandment. And at the same time He wished man, infant as he was, to remain for some time longer simple and sincere .... Besides, it is unseemly that children in infancy be wise beyond their years.[17]

The passage illustrates the sense in which descriptions of a childish Adam often hover between metaphor and literalism. At first, Theophilus distinguishes between Adam being an "infant in age" and a truly preverbal neonate, but he immediately begins collapsing the distinction, listing the various ways that Adam went through genuine and necessary developmental stages, like an infant progressing from liquid to solid foods. His final remark, likewise, seems to rely on the sense that there is something uncanny about extreme precociousness in a genuinely diminutive child. Theophilus's account clearly attempts to imply Adam's incompleteness, or insufficiency, without committing to the idea that he was actually toddling around Paradise, but it is finally the "infancy" of this physically grown man that provides a space for testing and trial, a pedagogical path to adulthood.

Such ideas crop up with surprising frequency in the seventeenth century, across a spectrum of theological writing that ranges from the fiery heretical visions of Jacob Boehme (1575–1624) to the felicitous meditations of Thomas Traherne (c. 1637–74). Boehme regularly mentions Adam's "child-like" traits in his rambling and widely read exposition of Genesis, the *Mysterium Magnum*.[18] Apparently drawing on the traditional association of children with mimesis, Boehme sees this childlike mind as a fecund source of imaginative power that essentially produces the created world around it. Had he remained unfallen, man (who was a hermaphroditic creature in Boehme's scheme) "should have walked naked upon the Earth ... in a childe-like minde; he should have eaten, and drunk in a *magicall* manner."[19] In this same sense, "*Eve* is the right magicall childe" of the hermaphroditical Adam, a manifestation of Adam's own creative power, his "Paradisicall Rose-Garden in peculiar Love, wherein he loved himselfe."[20] In Boehme's strange and oft-confused vision, the development of adult desire and sexuality is equated with the fall itself, as the magical children Adam and Eve succumb to desires and lusts that transform them from celestial to carnal creatures. As Boehme describes the fall into degraded carnality and encourages readers to seek an Edenic return, Christ's words in Matthew 18.3 become a refrain: "unlesse that ye be converted, and become as children, ye cannot see the Kingdome of God."[21]

Thomas Traherne, a professed admirer of Irenaeus, is both more optimistic and more literal about the resemblance of the child's consciousness to Adam's.[22] Throughout the *Centuries of Meditations*, which circulated only in manuscript during Traherne's lifetime, he describes the child as "a little Adam," whose untainted perceptions give us both a window into Edenic life and a pathway to regain this prelapsarian vision.[23] And in his manuscript *Commentaries of Heaven* (British Library MS Add. 63054), he makes it clear that he considers Adam himself as a childish youth, "an Heir, yet in Minority. Apt to be Tempted, Able to Stand, & Capable of falling."[24] For Traherne, Adam's childishness takes a familiarly mimetic form, making it possible to apprehend and experience the world from a wholly unmitigated perspective:

> When Adam first awaked out of his Dust, & Saw so Glorious a Brightness on evry side, His Soul being a pure & clear mirror representing the Beauties of the Universe in their Divinity, his first Divertisemt was a Rapture & Extasie inspired by his Sence of the Magnificence of the World. For the first Object making the first Impression of his Soul being Right, he did rightly apprehend & resent [i.e., "experience"[25]] the same.[26]

Adam was, Traherne reiterates, "Ravished" with beauty, just like all children who have not yet learned the false values that adults attach to worldly possessions.[27] On the blank page and infant consciousness, Traherne found the opportunity to rewrite the story of Eden without the fall: "An Empty Book is like an Infants Soul, in which any Thing may be Written."[28]

Although Traherne is generally considered a politically and religiously orthodox thinker (perhaps more than is warranted), he was joined in this effort by radicals like the Digger Gerrard Winstanley.[29] Joanna Picciotto has shown that Adam was a powerful figure of innocent perception for radicals like Winstanley, but the importance of childhood to reconstituting such innocent perception remains unremarked.[30] For the communistic Winstanley as for Traherne, the child's pure perception provides the fertile ground on which to raise a new society: "Look upon a childe that is new borne, or till he grows up to some few yeares, he is innocent, harmlesse, humble, patient, gentle, easie to be entreated, not envious; this is *Adam*."[31] As Winstanley notes of this Adamic infancy elsewhere, "there is a time in the entering of the understanding age, wherein every branch of man-kinde is put to his choice."[32] Not only was every child born in the state of Adam, but every child offered the possibility of choosing differently, coming of age without malice and creating a just and free society.

Although Milton probably encountered some of these descriptions of Adam and Eve, and more like them, in his vast reading, the point here is not to argue for direct influence. Rather, it is simply to note that neither the depiction of Adam and Eve as strapping, lordly adults nor as mystical children would have been a foregone conclusion for an author contemplating a work on the fall of man. Both choices brought distinct poetic possibilities and political valences, and Milton's poem navigates them carefully.

"Here Had New Begun My Wandering"

Considering Milton's political inclinations, we may in fact be somewhat surprised by our first glimpse of his Adam and Eve, who "seemd Lords of all" and who are also "not equal, as thir sex not equal seemd" (4.290). Even if we allow, as many have argued, that we are at this point looking over Satan's shoulder and seeing our first parents refracted by his own hierarchical and monarchical thinking, it still becomes immediately clear that these are not children in any conventional sense and that they do not represent some primal equality available to every Adamic child.[33] In addition to their lordly bearing, James G. Turner has shown that Milton goes out of his way to present them as fully sexualized humans, inhabiting a world dripping with a very adult sensuality – literally "Satiate with genial moisture" in Book 7's highly erotic creation account (7.282).[34] Adam has "manly" hair (4.302), which seems to mean it looks a bit like Milton's own shoulder-length locks, and Eve praises his "manly grace" (4.490). But as we have seen throughout this book, it was not at all uncommon for young people to be viewed as sexually capable adults or to exhibit other manly qualities while other aspects of their lives were downgraded to the status of children. This was the condition of youth, the childish period when self-regulation became possible and limits gave way to liberties.

Milton makes it clear that he has situated Adam and Eve in this liminal period. Before Satan provides us with a view of the regal Adam, the Son describes this creature not as the Father's newest, or latest, but his "youngest Son" (3.151). That this implies actual youth and not just birth order becomes sadly apparent when Michael warns the fallen Adam in Book 11 that if he avoids disfiguring illness he must still "outlive / Thy youth, thy strength, thy beauty" (11.538–39). Physiologically, Adam's blood retains the "Aire of youth, / Hopeful and cheerful" (11.542–43), like the Lady whose "fresh blood grows lively" in the *Mask* (670). With horror, Adam discovers that age will leave it "cold and dry" (11.544).

Soon after Satan observes the couple's noble bearing and Adam's "Absolute rule" (4.301), we in fact see them engaged in much less imposing "youthful dalliance as beseems / Fair couple" (4.338–39). As "dalliance" implies, Paradise at this point is a pleasure garden, totally given over to play:

> About them frisking playd
> All Beasts of th' Earth, since wilde, and of all chase
> In Wood or Wilderness, Forest or Den;
> Sporting the Lion rampd, and in his paw
> Dandl'd the Kid; Bears, Tygers, Ounces, Pards
> Gambold before them, th' unweildy Elephant
> To make them mirth us'd all his might, and wreathd
> His Lithe Proboscis. (4.340–47)

This is during a break from their labor, and the fact of their paradisal work has been the subject of useful critical attention for the way it weds the impulses to *labor* and *amor* that epic so often places in opposition (as Dido and Aeneas learn) and for the way it models a kind of innocent empiricism.[35] It is also said that "tending the garden helps Adam and Eve build a genuine sense of self-worth."[36] But while all these discussions of labor point in the right direction, this latter especially threatens to make Edenic work sound more useful and purposive than it really is – like a trade school or the Comenian campus where children would be given small versions of adult tools so that their play could be directed to productive purposes. By contrast, we are told that the ultimate point of Adam and Eve's work is to make "ease / More easie, wholsom thirst and appetite / More grateful" (4.329–30). This is as far from Comenius's educational model as it is from the authoritarian culture of the mind that Hobbes recommends because it does not presume a particular outcome beyond the affective one. Adam and Eve's labor produces only gratitude, which is not owed as a debt but expressed through the very enjoyment of freedom and ease.

   This is our first encounter with God's pedagogy in the poem, and we may already begin to see that it works far differently than the hectoring, "imperious" mode of correction that Stanley Fish sees as the poem's own educational model.[37] God is no "schoolmaister of perishable rites," as Milton says in *The Reason of Church Government*, "but a most indulgent father governing his Church as a family of sons in their discreet age" (*CPW* 1:837). Beginning with this early treatise, Milton had dealt carefully with the dynamics of God's paternity, fully aware that conservatives found in this über-father a model of authority and obedience that they could press into the service of the established religious or political order. The sons who serve as model members of the Church in this tract are past the age of discretion, which was generally fourteen, but they are still governed with the "sweetest and mildest manner of paternal discipline" (*CPW* 1:837) suiting even the youngest children, much like the students in *Of Education*, who are also "between twelve, and one-and-twenty" (*CPW* 2:379). Newly born into the world, Milton's Adam and Eve resemble these sons, neither lords of all they see nor babbling babes. The glory that makes them seem "Lords of all" derives not from mature self-possession, but rather is "in true filial freedom plac't; / Whence true autoritie in men" (4.294–95). Such freedom stands opposed to the rule-bound grammatical instruction that Milton denigrates in his defenses of the English people, but it accords perfectly with the course he recommends for the "Children of reviving libertie" (*CPW* 7:463). Milton's God proclaims his creatures sufficient to stand but then spends the balance of the epic educating them.

It is worth lingering for a moment on Adam as a subject of this education before turning to the childish qualities that have caused some critics to view Eve as deficient, because it is much easier to mistake his extreme precocity for instant maturity. Critics have often noted that Adam is faster on his feet than Eve, and John Leonard observes that his spontaneous speech bypasses typical childish babble: "Adam speaks with the wonder of a child, but not with 'childish tripps,' or 'sinews weak' that Milton elsewhere described as the hallmarks of 'infant lipps'."[38] For that reason it is easy to overlook the signs of his immaturity, but Leonard captures very well Adam's habitation of the intermediary zone between adult proficiency and childish wonder, a state that again recalls the precocious children of the *Mask*. Unlike so many Adams of the authoritarian tradition, this Adam's regal bearing is hard won. Even at his most lordly, the poem never lets us forget that he has a lot to learn.

He awakes into existence drenched in "Balmie sweat" and lies staring at the heavens with "wondring Eyes" for some time even after that sweat has dried (8.255, 257). During this time, his mind is a *tabula rasa*, blank as the sky he stares into, but soon his wondering eyes become wandering eyes as he springs up and begins to survey "Hill, Dale, and shadie Woods, and sunnie Plaines, / And liquid Lapse of murmuring Streams" (8.262–63). Enraptured by the experience, he next begins to peruse himself "Limb by Limb" (8.267), before indulging his capacity for motion without restraint (play), walking and running "with supple joints, as lively vigour led" (8.269). This is one moment when Milton's imagination seems to have been in sympathy with Comenius, who had suggested that instructors might reenact Adamic education by giving his *Orbis Pictus* ("The World in Pictures") "into the hands of children to delight themselves withall as they please."[39] Adam's delighted exploration, however, soon leads to erroneous wandering that seems more uniquely Miltonic, echoing the Lady's wayward trip down "perplex't paths" in the *Mask* (37):

> thus I call'd, and stray'd I knew not whither,
> From where I first drew Aire, and first beheld
> This happie Light, when answer none return'd,
> On a green shadie Bank profuse of Flours
> Pensive I sate me down; there gentle sleep
> First found me, and with soft oppression seis'd
> My droused sense. (8.283–88)

This is exactly the point at which a Spenserian hero, "loosely displayd upon the grassie ground," would receive an unpleasant surprise.[40] While Adam believes he may be slipping back out of existence, however, he is untroubled by the sensation, and rightly so. If his wandering recalls the Lady's, his drowsy insouciance recalls Milton's stance in his "Letter to a Friend," where he protested that he had not "given up my selfe to dreame away my Yeares" like Endymion and included Sonnet 7 as evidence that his "tardie moving" was licensed by a higher power (*CPW* 1:319). In Adam's own sleep, he says a dream "gently mov'd / My fancy" (8.293–94), and the subsequent fit of poetical fury transported him to the garden, replete with fruits that "stirr'd in me sudden appetite" (8.308). At this point, Adam awoke, and "Here had new begun / My wandring," he says, "had not hee who was my Guide / Up hither, from among the Trees appeer'd / Presence Divine" (8.311–14).

As Kristin Pruitt observes, "Adam's admission that his wandering was forestalled by the appearance of the 'Guide' suggests the importance of divine instruction in his development."[41] But we should also emphasize that it affirms the value of the wandering and repose that first put him in contact with the divine. This marks the kind of departure from pedagogical orthodoxy that may by now be familiar: Ascham and the humanists, for example, had sought to eliminate such undirected exploration, because "We know by experience it selfe, that it is a mervelous paine, to finde oute but a short waie, by long wandering."[42] Reformers like Milton's associate Samuel Hartlib likewise anticipated the more pragmatic efforts of eighteenth- and nineteenth-century antipoverty campaigners to use mandatory literacy classes and moral training to "keepe the Children and others belonging to the Work-house, from wandring the Streets and Fields."[43] Adam's wandering education, however, utterly rejects the premises behind both the tradition and its reform.

In doing so, Milton turns his back on the new direction Locke would soon take pedagogical theory as he argued that we must not instruct the child's appetite "to wander" but must "subdue and master" it by balancing a "love of Credit, and an apprehension of Shame and Disgrace."[44] The distinction between this and Adam's education needs reiterating, because while it has been noted that God is an "ideal schoolmaster" in the poem, it does not quite follow, as Michael Allen argues, that this derives from his "balancing" of kindness and firmness.[45] God's pedagogy can be firm, but its greatest innovation is the way it indulges the capacity for childish play and error to facilitate genuinely free choice. "God," writes Milton in *Areopagitica*, "gives us minds that can wander beyond all limit and satiety" (*CPW* 2:528). In contrast to Locke's endorsement of shame and disgrace, Raphael will later tell Adam in the accents of many an American self-help guru that "Oft times nothing profits more / Then self esteem" (8.571).

"He rear'd me" (8.316), says Adam of the divine presence that wakes him from his dream, and the words surely imply not only physical assistance but also paternal nurture. Adam has already made progress: he's gone from observing physical phenomena, like the sun and the sky, to observing living creatures and inquiring about their maker. He has also begun exploring his body and self in a preliminary physical way, "Limb by Limb" (8.362), although he has not yet discovered the deeper principle of self that will allow him to speak with real authority and do more than intuitively repeat the names of the objects that he sees. This happens only after the divine presence whisks Adam out of "those Grammatic flats & shallows" (*CPW* 2:375), as Milton describes the preliminary rules in *Of Education*, informing him of the world's single "rigid interdiction," not to eat of the Tree of the Knowledge of Good and Evil (8.334). After learning the rule, he is plunged much deeper into a process of learning that will allow him to discover his own desire and channel it in ways that will reshape creation itself.

This begins with Adam's naming of the animals. Critics often cite the episode as an example of Adam's intuitive intelligence and have described his linguistic precision in terms of a burgeoning age of scientific rationalism.[46] As Leonard explains, God has endowed Adam and Eve in their prelapsarian state with "the reason to form an accurate language for themselves," and this ability allows Adam to discern that he does not just want to talk about Creation, but "wants someone to talk *to*."[47] Lest that make Adam, sans childish trips, seem too much the model of perfect adulthood, we must be alert to the way this realization emerges through gentle, pedagogical play. Adam's naming serves as a kind of exercise, a sensuous stimulation that engages his intellectual curiosity and leads him into a Socratic dialogue with his divine instructor:

> I nam'd them, as they pass'd, and understood
> Thir nature, with such knowledg God endu'd
> My sudden apprehension: but in these
> I found not what me thought I wanted still. (8.352–55)

There are only two things Adam still cannot name: the "Author of this Universe" and his own desire (8.360). The scene that follows is a remarkable innovation on existing biblical and theological accounts: God knows that Adam should not be alone, knows that the answer to his desire is "Eve," but makes Adam engage him in a mock debate to discover this for himself. Their dialogue is not at all unlike the kind of gentle discipline that allows the "young and pliant affections [to be] led" through the various stages of Milton's curriculum in *Of Education* (*CPW* 2:635) or the debate over "charming" divine philosophy conducted by the young brothers in the *Mask* (476). The "vision bright" firmly rebuts Adam's objection that he cannot find contentment "in solitude" (8.364), but he does so "with a smile more bright'nd" (8.368). From the start, this is clearly meant to be fun.

As it proceeds, the whole dialogue is clearly a form of play (appropriately, what God is doing would later be called "ribbing"). Its resemblance to the witty, joking dialogues between Erasmus's schoolboys and teachers in the *Colloquies* is surely more than coincidental; such ironic forms of play were central to the exercises Milton engaged in as a student and directed as a tutor. But as in the educational works explored in Chapter 5, the *proairesis* licensed by this play is astounding, and indeed for a moment it looks like the pejorative meaning of "heresy" is creeping back into Milton's pedagogical term. In an Erasmian colloquy like *De Lusu* ("Of Play"), which I discussed in the Introduction, the boys never go so far as to argue against their teacher's authority as they beg a playday – instead, they call on that authority, citing their tutor's own appreciation of leisure and the works of Plutarch he has given to them. The Father carefully explains to Adam, on the other hand, that solitude is not a problem, because the earth teems with animals that "come and play before" him (8.372), and this seems to be the final word: "So spake the Universal Lord, and seem'd / So ordering" (8.376–77).

Humbly but firmly, Adam challenges this seeming truth. The question he asks is a real progression, from the vaguest notion that something is missing to a desire for equal company, a society bound by harmony and pleasure: "Among unequals what societie / Can sort, what harmonie or true delight?"(8.383–84). Although this question is embedded in praise for his maker, it asserts the value of his own vision over and against any other seeming authority, including the Father's: one cannot help but recall the audacious question Milton posed to his musician father in *Ad Patrem*: "What good is finely tuned vocal music, if it lacks sense and measured speech? This befits a woodland choir, not Orpheus" (50–52).[48] Adam too proves that he is no parrot. As he asks for fellowship "fit to participate / All rational delight," he too gains the power to reshape the world with Orphic speech, giving voice to a wholly unprecedented human society (8.390–91).

The Father pushes back once more, but by now it is even more clear that he is "not displeas'd":

> A nice and suttle happiness I see
> Thou to thy self proposest, in the choice
> Of thy Associates, *Adam*, and wilt taste
> No pleasure, though in pleasure solitarie. (8.398–402)

His gentle discipline, which Adam characterizes simply as "freedom" (8.434), allows Adam to realize both God's incommensurability and his own "single imperfection" and need for "Collateral love, and deerest amitie," in ways that Satan, with all his rationalizing, never can (8.423, 426). Without the free exploration of this desire, God notes, all the "knowing" in the world cannot provide a true knowledge of self: "Thus farr to try thee, *Adam*, I was pleas'd, / And finde thee knowing not of Beasts alone, / Which thou hast rightly named, but of thy self" (8.437–39).[49] The point I wish to make is that this self is not the sole product of genius rationalism but of childish play. This is the state in which the world hangs pendent and man can assert his will even as he recognizes his interdependence.

The entire episode, of course, is enfolded in another scene of education between Adam and Raphael, who has come to instruct Adam and who now listens and learns as the first man describes his creation. Unlike Adam's first conversation with God, the pedagogical aspects of this conversation and of Michael's instruction of Adam in Books 11 and 12 have received due critical attention.[50] We will return to Michael's instruction at the end of this chapter, but it is worth reiterating here the sheer amount of angelic pedagogy in the book: Raphael descends in Book 5, to "advise" Adam (5.234), and their discussion continues through Book 8, while Michael helps Adam "attain the summe / Of wisdome" in the

final two books (12.575–76), which means that fully half of the epic is
overtly framed as educational discourse. Recalling those students that
Milton promises to leave "enflam'd with the study of learning, and the
admiration of virtue" and "infus[ed]" with "ardor" in *Of Education* (*CPW*
2:385), Adam regularly professes himself "fill'd / With admiration, and
deep Muse" or "Replete with joy and wonder" at the things the angels
reveal (7.51–52, 12.468). Adam's achievement of voice through his playful
debate with God, in other words, does not firmly ensconce him in rational adulthood but leaves him deeply sensitive to the strong passions that,
as we have seen throughout this book, are so clearly associated with youth.
It is also worth casting a glance back at the previous chapter and noting
that the same can be said of his angelic interlocutors, as seen in the "rosie
red" blush that suffuses Raphael's countenance when Adam asks him
whether Angels have sex (8.619). With this "striking glimpse of angelic
passion," Michael Schoenfeldt notes, "Milton here takes a primary signifier of postlapsarian erotic meaning … and asks it to represent an angelic
physiological response to a decidedly innocent question."[51] The vigor of
this response reflects Raphael's own youthfulness, and Adam's question
is indeed innocent, although not quite in the way that Schoenfeldt and
most other scholars have seen it. Because sex before the fall is not associated with sin, it is typical to describe Raphael's blush as an expression of
sinless ardor.[52] But Adam, like his descendant Jacob, is also wrestling with
the angel, asserting the value of a love for Eve that leaves him "still free"
to "follow what I approve" (8.610–11), and in this regard, Empson's quip
that the angel blushes because "he has been caught out talking nonsense"
about the worthlessness of human sexuality also holds true.[53] The question
is innocent, as are the heroic games that exercise the youth of heaven and
Adam's debate with God, but these are also the grounds on which truth
is discovered in a process surprisingly similar to its fallen equivalent in
Areopagitica and *Of Education*. If Raphael is caught out and blushes rosy
red, this is because he too enjoys his free time and learns from the experience.[54] He too allows himself to wander into unknown terrain.

Eve's Answering Looks

Recognizing the play in Adam's education highlights a flaw in those arguments that negatively compare Eve's shadowy entrancement at the pool
with his hearty rationalism. Mary Nyquist has perhaps written the rich-
est and most influential of these accounts, arguing that while Adam in
his conversations with Raphael "is revealed articulating the doctrine of

marriage, in Book IV's recollected self-mirroring Eve is portrayed enacting its discipline."⁵⁵ Eve's mimetic learning, in other words, demonstrates a new form of "subjectivity" associated with the female domestic sphere, a form of subjectivity that will be endlessly reiterated in future novels where heroines learn "the value of submitting desire to the paternal law."⁵⁶ Nyquist arrives at this conclusion by reading Eve's dalliance at the lake purely as a narcissistic fall, corrected when Eve learns the superiority of manly grace as embodied by a thoroughly adult Adam. Eve's "desire is clearly and unambiguously constituted by illusion, both in the sense of specular illusion and in the sense of error," Nyquist concludes – a version of "Neo-Platonic readings of the Narcissus myth [that] find in it a reflection of the 'fall' of spirit into matter."⁵⁷ But as we have seen, for Milton the immersion in a world of echoes and mirrors could in fact be a revolutionary resource, a necessary path to authoritative voice. In such a world "error" marks not insufficiency but nurture, just as the garden's rivers run "with mazie error under pendant shades" to feed "Flow'rs worthy of Paradise" (4.239–40). Again, this is not to deny the insight that Eve's first moments also affirm her lower hierarchical status: as shown in previous chapters, Milton's educational theories allow (even demand) a worldview that is at once flexible and stratified. Subjectivity is indeed gendered in *Paradise Lost*, and there is little doubt that it is structured according to masculinist assumptions that place the woman beneath the man even in a "mutual" relationship. But this is substantially different from relegating female subjectivity to a rigid "domestic sphere," as Nyquist depicts it – a subjectivity that is the end of a journey rather than its beginning.

Eve's education exemplifies "the sweetest and mildest manner" of paternal discipline that Milton described in *The Reason of Church Government* (*CPW* 1:837) and that we have seen in effect with Adam. Indeed, it takes that sweetness to a new level of sensuous literalism, as Eve awakens in a flowery bower, lulled by somnolent waters, and dallies with a watery image that God himself pronounces fair. Just as Adam's inceptive wandering has affinities with the Lady's self-discovery in Milton's *Mask*, Eve's scene of mirroring and airy voices could come straight from that earlier work. Like the Lady who reads herself in the myth of Echo and Narcissus, Eve anticipates the myth and becomes its source text:

> I first awak't, and found my self repos'd
> Under a shade of flours, much wondring where
> And what I was, whence thither brought, and how.
> Nor distant far from thence a murmuring sound
> Of waters issu'd from a Cave and spread

> Into a liquid Plain, then stood unmov'd
> Pure as th' expanse of Heav'n; I thither went
> With unexperienc't thought, and laid me downe
> On the green bank, to look into the cleer
> Smooth Lake, that to me seemd another Skie.
> As I bent down to look, just opposite,
> A Shape within the watry gleam appeard
> Bending to look on me, I started back,
> It started back, but pleas'd I soon returnd,
> Pleas'd it returnd as soon with answering looks
> Of sympathie and love; there I had fixt
> Mine eyes till now, and pin'd with vain desire,
> Had not a voice thus warnd me, What thou seest,
> What there thou seest fair Creature is thy self. (4.450–68)

As Diane McColley suggests, "several features of Milton's imagery make these united waters a metaphor for poetry."[58] The dense network of allusions in the passage recalls the waters of poetic inspiration invoked in *Lycidas*, the springs haunted by the muses in the invocation to Book 3, and "Siloa's Brook," which delights Milton's heavenly muse in the opening lines of the poem (1.11). This poetic mirror offers a form of pedagogical play, as Eve amuses herself with the shape in the water. As with the *Mask*'s Lady, the childishness of that play is important, marking this as a scene of licensed mirroring and echoing where voice can emerge, rather than as a scene of the "compulsive repetitions" that Regina Schwartz suggests characterize "Satan's narcissism."[59]

The child playing with a mirror was an extraordinarily common image to figure the child's mimetic being, as discussed in previous chapters. By 1485, it had in fact been combined with the Adamic child/apple trope, as shown in William Caxton's translation of Laurent's *Somme des Vices et Virtus:* "a chylde ... loveth better an apple or a myrrour than a royame [realm]."[60] Contemporary pamphlets like *Apples of Gold from the Tree of Life* made the same association in Milton's time: "The *naturall man* is just like a *Child*, that (*beholding his naturall face in a Glass*) thinks he sees *another* Childs *face*, and *not his own*."[61] There is an implication of ignorance in such descriptions, but nothing like the abject sinfulness or self-absorption that some critics have taken Eve's mirror-play to imply. Indeed, the most advanced pedagogical theories of the era pinned their hopes on this capacity for absorption, which indicated a rich potential rather than a disabling flaw.

Even before the voice of her father speaks, Eve begins to manifest this potential as the shape in the water looks back at her "with sympathie and love" (4.465). Just a moment earlier, Eve had truly been a blank slate, her "unexperienc't thought" as smooth and undisturbed as the surface of the lake, discreet only in her sense of separateness, bewildered about who or what she was. An instant later, quite on her own, she begins to experience the sympathy and love that will later join her to Adam and form the building blocks of human society; it is a sort of founding myth for the just society Cicero described as the outgrowth of familial affect, as discussed in Chapter 3. Satan's logical self-interest forecloses such experience, but in her wandering, turning, returning, and even mistaking, Eve demonstrates that in *Paradise Lost* being made sufficient to stand is a process rather than a state.

In this sense, Eve staring at her reflection in the lake, absorbed in its beauty, is Milton's prototypical childish reader. Her reverie is broken by a voice that gently explains "what there thou seest fair Creature is thy self" and directs her to follow "where no shadow staies / Thy coming" (4.468, 470–71). But this does not negate the value of the reverie, nor does it take on the "imperious" tone of Fish's hectoring narrator.[62] Rather than abandoning the play of image and reflection, the voice guides her to a more complex form of self-identification through mirroring: "Whose image thou art, him thou shall enjoy / Inseperablie thine, to him shalt beare / Multitudes like thy self" (4.471–73). This is not a simple correction of Eve's image play, but rather a re-formation of Echo and Narcissus, who in George Sandys's telling reflect one another in the kind of infinite regress witnessed when two mirrors are brought together: "the image of the voice so often rendered, is as that of the face reflected from one glasse to another; melting by degrees, and every reflection more weake and shady then the former."[63] For all the critical discussion of Eve's relation to Narcissus, this connection of Adam with Echo has not been emphasized. The description of Adam as "no shadow" in *Paradise Lost* (4.470) correlates closely with Sandys's description of Echo as "then a body, not a Voyce" and is a useful reminder of the habit of "dilation," or the "suspension or pendency of meaning" that Patricia Parker identifies as one of Milton's central poetic devices.[64] As she suggests, Milton regularly invokes classical figures in a way that allows the reader to hold in balance the continuity with and difference from classical models: here Adam, like Echo, is still a body, and he too will experience loss and pain, but unlike Echo this fall has not happened, in part because Eve is not yet the unworthy, Narcissistic object for whom he will sacrifice his voice. Where Sandys provides an image of infinite regress, Adam and Eve's reflection of one another offers infinite progress. Against Fish's contention that Milton creates such equations to allow the reader to make a false surmise, which he then reproves and corrects, Parker argues that these poetic structures poise the poem on the "threshold of choice."[65]

Eve's repeated recollection of this threshold state helps affirm its value. "That day," she says as she begins her account, "I oft remember" (4.449). Her memory of this moment, with its childish incompleteness, is everywhere different from Satan's deliberate forgetting of his own parental nurture, his false idea that freedom can be built on the proposition of autonomous individuals who spring from the ground fully formed.

As with the Lady's echoing in the *Mask*, this leads to her development of a powerful poetic voice. As McColley notes, although Eve "could have used her mirror as a pool of Narcissus, and trapped herself within herself, she uses it instead as a source of truth when, by a creative act of memory, she uses the experience to understand her calling and makes it into a poem."[66] In fact, it is through Eve's poetic memorialization that we hear Adam articulate a doctrine of individual freedom and social life based on mutuality rather than conquest or self-interest, as she relates the first words he speaks to her:

> to give thee being I lent
> Out of my side to thee, neerest my heart
> Substantial Life, to have thee by my side
> Henceforth an individual solace dear. (4.483–86)

The expression "individual solace" contains two meanings that seem diametrically opposed: in the sense of OED 1, "individual" means indivisible, of the same substance, or as Adam later describes it, "one Flesh, one Heart, one Soule" (8.499); in the sense of OED 3b, "individual" means special and distinct from all others, or as Adam later tells Raphael, "in her self compleat" (8.548). Milton's poem, however, does not ask us to choose one of these definitions in favor of the other, as Diana Benet does in promoting the idea that Adam here "is unable to credit any difference or space between Eve and himself."[67] Rather, Adam (or is it Eve?) gives voice to an affective social model that preserves the individual's perfect freedom by recognizing the need for mutual solace. It is hard to imagine an inceptive moment of society more different from either Hobbes's Leviathan state, where citizens "conferre all their power and strength upon one Man … submit their Wills, every one to his Will, and their Judgements to his Judgment" (*L* 2.17.227), or from Prynne's parliamentary Representation, where unambiguously adult men "resign up their Lives, Liberties, Estates, Laws, Religion into the hands" of their leaders.[68]

As Eve tells it, Adam's "gentle hand / Seisd" her own, but the whole weight of the poem hinges on the description of that gesture as "gentle" and the assurance that when she yields, it really is a choice and not just a conquest (4.488). As Melissa Sanchez notes, "Eve's acceptance of Adam as her image is also her acceptance of the humility on which republican government depends and which royal absolutism denies."[69] As I have been arguing, Milton actually recognizes that it is not merely royal absolutism that can deny such humility and mutuality: whether representation is monarchical or republican, political or poetic, Milton sees that it risks speaking for subjects by providing a false image of their adult self-sufficiency rather than making them fit to speak. Eve's poetic expression reverberates throughout the poem, echoing through the paradoxically "soft oppression" that Adam says "seis'd" him in his wandering and lulled him to sleep so he could experience the divine in his own flight of poetical fury (8.288). As he tells his own creation story, he continues the mirror play that allows God's creatures to discover themselves as free beings.

It is only when Eve forgets that such childish play has genuine integrity that she falls. She does not fall, in other words, because her education is insufficient, as Comenius describes it when he claims that with better training this childlike creature would have recognized that speaking serpents were an unnatural indication of "certain deceit" (*dolum certa*).[70] Such a view leads inevitably to the legal doctrine of *malitia supplet aetatem* as we have encountered it throughout this book, and it has been argued that Milton places Adam and Eve in exactly the double bind this doctrine implies, making full adult voice and agency contingent on lost innocence. Milton is dangerously close, thinks A. D. Nuttall, to endorsing the Gnostic heresy that Adam "actually was like a child until Satan and the tree of knowledge helped him to grow up."[71] But Milton avoids this heresy by spending so much time depicting the education of humans who are already created "Sufficient to have stood" (3.99). The process shows how childish obedience can be compatible with robust personal and intellectual growth, suggesting that an unimaginably free society might be constructed on the principle of fealty to God's image as written on the heart. Adam and Eve, in their discreet age yet still maturing, demonstrate the coexistence of affective filial ties with dynamic change.

Milton's Eve expresses this more clearly than anyone else in the poem when she first realizes the serpent has brought her to the forbidden tree:

> of this Tree we may not taste nor touch;
> God so commanded, and left that Command

> Sole Daughter of his voice; the rest, we live
> Law to our selves, our Reason is our Law. (9.652–55)

Eve's description of God's single command as the "Daughter of his voice" is an appropriately filial Hebraism, translating the rabbinic "*bat kol*," as John Hollander explains, "a phrase which means 'echo' in modern Hebrew, and which referred to a secondary, or derivative voice of the Holy Spirit."[72] Hollander cites the Neoplatonic poet Henry Reynolds (fl. 1628–31), who appended the following explanation to his own tale of Narcissus:

> *Ecco*, the Reflection of this divine breath, or Spirit upon us; or (as they interpret it) -*the daughter of the divine voice*; which through the beatifying splendor it shedds & diffuses through the Soule, is justly worthy to be reverenced and adored by us. This *Ecco* descending upon a *Narcissus*, or such a Soule as (impurely and vitiously affected) slights, and stops his eares to the Divine voice, or shuts his harte from divine Inspirations, through his being enamour'd of not himselfe, but his owne shadow meerely, and (buried in the ordures of the Sence) followes corporall shadowes, and flyes the light and purity of Intellectuall Beauty, he becoms thence … dispoyled … of his propper, native, and celestiall vertue, and ability.[73]

At least for a moment when she first sees the tree, Eve recognizes that the ability to speak with true inspiration derives from her own childish capacity for echoing and reflection – for valuing echoes as reflections rather than as laws. Ironically, her shadow play at the pool confirms this capacity for mimesis in a way that distances her from debilitating narcissism, while her use of masculine, mature reason will confirm her fall into the realm of Reynolds's "corporall shadowes."

This becomes clear from the moment that Milton's Eve, in contrast to the somewhat doltish figure in Comenius's version of the story, notices the "miracle" of the talking snake and makes a skeptical inquiry into the cause: "What may this mean? Language of Man pronounc't / By Tongue of Brute, and human sense exprest?" (9.553–54). Unlike the Edenic children in some other accounts who make an irrational or uninformed decision, Eve's rational ability to connect a set of seemingly factual conditions lays the cornerstone for Satan's success. He presents her with a set of data points: (1) fruit causes death; (2) snake eats fruit; (3) snake's life becomes more perfect, and she adeptly concludes that "death" is either a good thing or an idle threat.

Absent its affective anchor, this, however, is the kind of uninspired reason that Milton describes in the *Christian Doctrine*, where he notes that to credit reason over the divine light is to mistake "the shadow for the substance" (*CPW* 6:583). This is not a rejection of reason, but an insistence that it must be paired with other forms of knowing to be effica-cious; as in *Of Education*, the capacity for choice arises not from mature self-sufficiency but from childish wandering.[74] The problem with Eve's fall into narcissistic reasoning is not that she thinks *too much* of herself, but not enough, forgetting to see herself as an image of God and of Adam, forgetting that God's command itself is an echo of his voice, abandoning her part in the reflective play that is paradisal freedom. Satan presents a vision of Eve as idol, "a Goddess humane" (9.732) who is something to be viewed rather than an agent of speculation (a word that shares its root with the Latin *speculum*, or mirror). Instead of taking pleasure in her ability to reflect, rather than embody God, she begins to feel impaired, like Satan, as she contemplates the apparent ascent of another creature: "to us deni'd / This intellectual food, for beasts reserv'd?" (9.766–67). Gratitude turns into resentment as Eve begins to think of parental gifts in terms of econ-omies and exchange and of the Father's intellectual food as a commodity rather than a process of engagement. Even as Milton highlights her ratio-nal, adult capabilities, in other words, he demonstrates the collapse of the affective ties to God the Father that had allowed her to give voice to the poetic world she began discovering in her first created moments.

How else could she fail to distinguish Satan's "shew of Zeale and Love / To Man" (9.665–66) from the actual, felt experience of zeal and love? That mistaken identification of zeal strikingly recalls Thomas Bayly's oft-reprinted description of the "blind Zelots" who reenacted the fall of Adam and Eve by rebelling against King Charles.[75] For Bayly, only the king has the special privilege to listen to his heart above the law, because he is the mirror "wherein [God] beholds the representation of himself"; the people, on the other hand, are children commanded not to touch this "curious looking-glasse" of a king because "if they have the liberty to med-dle with it in the least degree, they may break it before they are aware."[76] Bayly conflates his metaphors in a familiar way; the rebels are both like children and like Adam and Eve, the king is both like a mirror and like the Tree of Knowledge. But he manages to convey very clearly the dangers of listening to the heart and of seeking the image and authority of God by examining our selves. The relationship between law and conscience, rela-tive to Milton's poem, is totally reversed.

Although his decision to eat the fruit has been praised as a "noble" act of love, Adam's inattention to his heart's true desire at the moment of his fall is just as profound as Eve's.[77] "I feel / The Link of Nature draw me," he intones, "Flesh of Flesh, / Bone of my Bone thou art" (9.913–14, 914–15). Despite couching his decision in terms of natural affection, he "remains under the spell of his own version of narcissistic idolatry," as William Kerrigan says, although this is not exactly, as Kerrigan adds, because Adam loves himself or the image of himself in Eve too much.[78] Adam makes no mention of "my Self," or "one Heart, one Soule," as he did in their first meeting (8.495, 8.499), and he has ceased to echo the meaning of "Individual solace" that maintains the integrity of personal judgment even as it recognizes mutuality. Instead, he offers a perfunctory anatomy lesson – flesh from flesh, bone from bone – and even this is wrong, because Eve has visibly changed from the untainted flesh he first embraced: "in her Cheek distemper flushing glowd" (9.887). Tellingly, he only misidentifies the bond of nature that draws him to sin *after* he reasons his way out of the affective moment of "horror chill / [that] Ran through his veins" when he first heard Eve's story (9.890–92). Adam is undeceived because his heart tells him what to do and he chooses not to listen, using his prodigious powers of reason to explain why God will not allow "Us his prime Creatures, dignifi'd so high" to fall (9.940). He begins to sound very adult here, but as he announces that he has "fixt [his] lot" (9.952) with Eve, he ironically also begins to echo the Satanic legions who gather to assent to Satan's plans, "Breathing united force with fixed thought" (1.560). With them, he fixes his thought and his lot, choosing the "perpetuall childhood of prescription" that Milton says God rejects for the children of liberty (*CPW* 2:514). His fall casts him and his progeny back into the grammatical flats and shallows.

Repairing the Ruins

It is finally Eve's recovery of her childish capacity for reflection that makes possible what John Shawcross has described as "the antithesis to narcissism that she exhibits as *Pardise Lost* ends (what may be epitomized as Milton's message to the world): that is, object love."[79] As is clear by now, I would revise the psychoanalytic model Shawcross so deftly employs to the Pauline one discussed in Chapter 5. Just as *Areopagitica* draws on 1 Corinthians 13.11–12 to assert that we must discover truth through a glass darkly and speak it with childish tongues, Eve's ability to recognize the Other and form a community as a free self depends not on her maturation out of childishness but on her recognition that childishness is an ongoing condition. Moreover, as we saw in the previous chapter, in *Paradise Lost* this is no longer something that separates Eve, in either her unfallen or fallen condition, from the Angels and the Son, but something that unites her to them.

Milton makes this abundantly clear in Book 10, when Eve facilitates the survival of the human race, becoming the first human embodiment of the epic's new brand of heroism. Humbling herself before her guilty, disdainful spouse, she offers to "importune Heaven, that all / The sentence from thy head remov'd may light / On me" (10.933–35), a gesture that recapitulates the Son's self-sacrifice from Book 3, where he asks the Father to let the full weight of man's sin fall "on mee" (3.237). Here we see the moral component of Aeneas's valor sublimed from its martial relics. Like the Son's request that the Father "Account mee man" (3.238), it is specifically made possible by Eve's powers of representation and reflection, the ability to take on the traits and responsibilities of another without, in the manner of Hobbesean representation, subsuming that person's ability to choose. As Kevis Goodman suggests, "Now *Eve* is the pool, as it were, holding up to Adam a reflection of his own despair."[80] Except she surely reflects more than despair. Her childish mimesis reflects the divine presence still remaining in Adam and in the world around them both. And once again she gives voice to a principle that he will later echo: God works his justice, Adam affirms to Michael, "by small / Accomplishing great things, by things deemd weak / Subverting worldly strong, and worldly wise" (12.566–68). This is the "argument / Not less but more Heroic" than the previous epics Milton claims to surpass (9.13–14), because where those epics commemorate societies that rise from a state of war, his proposes a society that rises from the bonds of natural affection.

Adam defensively responds to Eve that "if Prayers / Could alter high Decrees, I to that place / Would speed before thee" (10.952–54), and Dennis Danielson has noted that in this moment he seems "like a child – or a childish adult – who hears a good idea and then rebukes himself for not having thought of it first."[81] Danielson is talking about Adam's petulance, but his comparison may be more apt than even he realizes. Adam is not only childish in his fit of pique but also in the subsequent response in which his "heart relent[s]" to Eve's gesture before his mind rationally determines its efficacy or its worth (10.940). Danielson shows that Eve's offer to bear Adam's sin, like Christ's, allows us to see through the "telescope of typology" how Adam could have made a different choice when he joined Eve in sin: he could have anticipated and imitated her sacrifice, which anticipates and imitates Christ's.[82] This would have required not less self-love, or less love for her, but a truer kind of love that recognized the value of the self in its ability to reflect the divine. By the same token, here he begins to mirror Eve's own example, and ultimately his decision to seek forgiveness at their place of judgment echoes her own humble offer of penitent return.

Soon the formal education of Adam and Eve has begun again. Ann Baynes Coiro explains that in the final two books of the poem, the archangel Michael instructs the fallen Adam in a way that "exactly parallels, down to the smallest detail, the 'methodological course' that Milton delineated" in *Of Education*.[83] That is, he grounds this education on sensible things, first showing Adam the revelations of history in the vision of Book 11, then progressing to a more advanced level of moral education in the narrated lecture of Book 12. Adam is not always the ideal student: he frequently lapses into the kind of thinking associated with hormone-driven schoolboys, as when he responds with delight to the "Beavie of fair Women, richly gay / In Gems and wanton dress" (11.582–83), and Michael must sharply reprimand his misogynistic suggestion that "the tenor of Mans woe / Holds on the same, from Woman to begin" (11.632–33).[84] But by the end, Adam proclaims that this "perplext" path has cleared his eyes and his heart (12.275). Most importantly – and this is something Coiro does not note – this educational process draws on mimetic notions of childhood to engage Adam in the events of history and fit him for his own role in it. Adam responds to the vision of his progeny drowned in the general flood with the complete mimetic absorption that had made children exemplars of poetic response since Aristotle:

> How didst thou grieve then, *Adam*, to behold
> The end of all thy Ofspring, end so sad,
> Depopulation; thee another Floud,
> Of tears and sorrow a Floud thee also drown'd,
> And sunk thee as thy Sons. (11.754–77)

The wrenching emotional experience recalls the one Milton described to his childhood friend Charles Diodati in Elegy 1, where he explained that on a break from the "barren fields" (*nuda arva*) of Cambridge he had been "ravished completely" (*totum rapiunt*) by his own independent course of poetic education, including drama that "pleases to have watched with suffering, / as there is sweet bitterness in tears" (13, 39–40).

Likewise, as Adam begins to model a godly patriarchy through his participation in such dramatic and narrative experiences, it is tempting to think that Milton recalled his own role of playing the "Father" as a young student in the Cambridge salting that he retrieved for publication years later, in 1673–74. This work, labeled "juvenilia" and divided into the sixth *Prolusion* and "At a Vacation Exercise," was discussed in the Introduction as an example of the way boys in grammar school and beyond were encouraged to play at their adult roles. But with Adam's education we have come full circle. "How comes it that I have so suddenly been made a Father!?," Milton exclaims in the *Prolusion* (*C* 12:240; *CPW* 1:283), and he continues this inquiry into the power of mimesis to transform the self in the "Vacation Exercise," where "imperfect words with childish tripps / Half unpronounc't, slide through my infant-lipps / Driving dum silence from the portal dore" (3–5). This playful performance of adulthood has real educative power – Milton assumes the persona of the Aristotelian Ens, or Being, and identifies his sons as the Aristotelian categories of Substance, Quantity, Relation, and Quality. But as he notes, "I do not wish to be excessively tiresome, my children [*gnati*], in giving advice to you, lest I should seem to have bestowed more labor [*operoso*] in educating you than in begetting you" (*C* 12:244; *CPW* 1.286). Creativity and authority finally depend on the efficacy of mimetic play rather than the solemnity of rigorous advice. The same can be said of this part of Michael's education, which leaves Adam "fatherly displeased" and prompts a visceral response to earth's first tyrant, Nero: "O execrable Son so to aspire / Above his Brethren, to himself assuming / Authoritie usurpt" (12.64–66). Adam has learned a lesson that will be long in coming to his children.

As Michael explains, the filial principle that so effortlessly enabled Adam and Eve's prelapsarian freedom will need to be won again in a world that will only slowly pass from Old Testament law to New Testament grace:

> With purpose to resign them in full time
> Up to a better Cov'nant, disciplin'd
> From shadowie Types to Truth, from Flesh to Spirit,
> From imposition of strict Laws, to free
> Acceptance of large Grace, from servil fear
> To filial, works of law to works of Faith. (12.300–06)

This is a coming-of-age process, as Milton characterized it in the *Doctrine and Discipline of Divorce*, where he explains that the Old Testament law, "as a strict Schoolmaster ... punisht every trespasse without indulgence," but now the Gospel corrects "by admonition and reproof only, in free and mature age, which was punisht with stripes in the childhood and bondage of the Law" (*CPW* 2:353). As Michael's narration reaches this climactic moment, Fish claims that "Adam's education, tied to his discovery of what is comprehended in the prophecy of the seed, and tracing out the pattern of history, ends here."[85] But as in Milton's *Mask* and his political writings, coming of age in *Paradise Lost* is never complete. Although they are not in childhood and bondage as they leave Paradise, Adam and Eve remain childish in a way that accords with the free and mature age imagined for God's people in *The Doctrine and Discipline of Divorce*.

Despite all his education, Adam accepts the childish state Paul discusses in 1 Corinthians 13 as his own, because he must dwell in "this transient World, the Race of time / Till time stand fixt" (12.554–55). But rather than casting Adam into a position of passive, infantile obedience, this acceptance propels him into the free enterprise of childish exploration as he departs Paradise with Eve, "hand in hand with wandring steps and slow" (12.648). That penultimate line captures beautifully the affective register of Milton's ideal education, the priority it gives to wandering and pendency, and the idea that this process remains necessarily incomplete until Christ's second coming finally brings an end to childish things. In the wake of all this angelic instruction, Milton's citation of Daniel 12.3 in *The Christian Doctrine* seems apt: "teachers shall shine like the brightness of the heavens, and those who justify many, like the stars, for ever and ever" (*CPW* 6:569). It reminds us that these scenes of education are enfolded in a larger pedagogical effort of justifying many by justifying the "wayes of God to men," as Milton proposes to do at the beginning of his epic (1.26). This, if we return to Parker's concept of "dilation," is perhaps the poem's most lasting achievement – not to lecture its reader, or even to make him fall, but to provide a space to wander awhile through Eden and discover the gentle discipline that points the way back.

The final depiction of "Our lingring Parents," with all the weight of the poem behind it, is a rich alternative to Hobbes's mushroom men and an equally rich rejoinder to those ill-fated patriarchal theories that depicted Adam as earth's only king. Like Hobbes's depiction of the state of nature, it is resolutely about individuals' motivation to join in league together, a choice and not an inheritance. But unlike Hobbes's account, Milton's never proclaims an absolute equality: Eve is frustratingly absented from Adam's prehistory lessons, provided instead with a still more gentle and abstract education while she sleeps and dreams. Nor does Milton's poem attempt to reduce or explain away the contingencies of childhood. Rather, it goes to some lengths to depict a form of discipline that engages these contingencies and finds in them the building blocks of adult responsibility. The societal vision this licenses for Milton, as we have seen in previous chapters, admits hierarchy in a way that the modern liberal ideal seeks to deny. But Milton's fiction also seems more honest than the contemporary notion that we all suddenly become equal at the predetermined age of sixteen, eighteen, or twenty-one. Grappling with the complex forces that enable claims to a personal, political self, Milton's poem suggests that even in Eden the creation of the human is not a singular event but a perplexed path.

In the final scene of Milton's poem, Adam and Eve face their own vast prospect of undiscovered truth, with the world "all before them, where to choose" (12.646). But the poem resists a proto-Romantic glorification of the child's perception as thoroughly as it resists the notion that we can ever completely put away childish things. Rather than looking forward to Locke, then, it offers a rich final statement on the way writers throughout the seventeenth-century drew on concepts of childhood to figure the relationship between poetic and political power. For Milton, the limitations of our first parents' perception are as important as its efficacy, and this is the central fact not only of mortal knowledge but also of this fragile, miniature society. In a poem that has been full of the voices of men and angels, Milton does not depict his young humans speaking, but touching, "hand in hand" (12.648). Their wordless gesture recalls, with a difference, Jonson's silent boy actor and Prynne's voiceless people. In the infancy of the world, all is appropriately hushed, and although their way is "solitarie" (12.649), they are not alone.

Epilogue
"Children Gathering Pebbles on the Shore"

In 1609, when the first childish trips slid through Milton's infant lips and the Children of the Blackfriar's performed *Epicoene*, King James claimed to govern as a "natural father" to his people, whose political obligation derived from birth rather than consent.[1] By 1675, the year after Milton's death, the Crown's own attorney had affirmed the right of the King's subjects not to have taxes imposed "but by the common consent," a transformation that would shortly be confirmed by the Glorious Revolution of 1688.[2] Throughout this book, I've argued that childhood was used to figure this development and the obstacles to it. Literally voiceless, or *infans*, the child speaks his transformation from infant to subject into being, and during the era of English revolution this moment became the focus of intense poetic and political scrutiny.

In Jonson's *Epicoene* we see childhood as a period that can seemingly be extended without end, as the play offers to channel the child's natural mimetic tendencies in the service of the absolutist state, fashioning subjects who can parrot their author's voice but not speak with their own. At the same time, *Epicoene*'s rocky performance history aptly demonstrates the capacity of childish play to elude such discipline. For this reason, both Prynne and Hobbes attempt to eliminate the vast, gray area of childish becoming from the political discourse: both envision forms of consent in which subjects would resign their voices to those who represented them, and both seek to make the binding power of this consent absolute. For Prynne this means severing the links between poetic and political representation, making it clear that adult subjects give their voices in a rational act untainted by the vagaries of poetic imitation. For Hobbes it means redefining consent to encompass the acceptance of nurture by diminutive children, promoting a didactic "Culture of their mindes" that will eliminate poetical fury from the child's training (*L* 2.31.399). Milton fiercely resisted such efforts throughout his career. In his works, the liminal zone between childhood and adulthood is a space of tremendous poetic and

186

political power. It is here that play is liberated and heresy flourishes in its positive sense of free choice.

Milton's sense that coming of age is an ongoing, even recursive project warns against mapping the processes of maturation too neatly onto a larger historical narrative in the mode of Whig history. Nevertheless, the decline in filial deference observed by Aubrey and others during the Civil War coincided with the introduction of many voices to the national discourse, and they often claimed a newfound authority for the experiences and perceptions of youth. The Digger visionary Gerrard Winstanley, for example, repeatedly described the dawning, empowered, collective self he hoped to cultivate as a "Man-Child," invoking the childish stage that created so much havoc in the common law.[3] Like Hobbes, he claimed parents governed their children only by consent, although he invoked this idea to oppose authoritarian rule in a way that explicitly rejects Hobbesian force:

> By this choyce, they make him not only a Father, but a Master and a Ruler. And out of this root springs up All Magistrates and Officers.... For here take notice, That though the children might not speak, yet their weakness and simplicity did speak, and chose their Father to be their Overseer.[4]

For Winstanley as for Milton, 2 Corinthians 12.9–10 provides an appropriate motto: "my strength is made perfect in weakness."

As discussed in Chapter 5, the Quakers emerged during this time as well, and the statesman and controversialist Roger Williams (1606–83) had good reason to dismiss their dissenting voices as the "pratling of *Children* and *Parrets*."[5] The group arguably had its genesis when George Fox (1624–91) broke off his apprenticeship at age nineteen, after a sustained drinking session with his peers, and began the wandering travels that would consume the next several years of his life. The renowned Quaker preacher Richard Farnworth (c. 1630–66) experienced his spiritual awakening at age sixteen and was soon dismissed by his employer Thomas Lord for refusing to worship with the family, while James Parnell (1636–56) left his family at age fifteen and began drawing thousands to sermons where he became known as the "quaking boy."[6] In the 1670s, children's revivals swept the country, and during this time Milton's own young amanuensis, Thomas Ellwood (1639–1713), began solidifying his identification as a Quaker through a series of violent encounters with his father. For the young Ellwood, the greatest challenge to his growing faith was the realization that he must not "make a Difference between my Father and all other Men."[7]

Probing their earliest memories for signs of God's inner light, Quakers like Ellwood emphasized the child's unalloyed perception and integrity.

But despite their shared sense that the childish sensibility might be a locus for choice and dissent, this is both where they begin to diverge from Milton and where they begin to anticipate the Romantic child cult that William Empson identifies as one of his versions of pastoral.[8] The Romantic pastoral child is "in the right relation to Nature, not dividing what should be unified," and "its intuitive judgment contains what poetry and philosophy must spend their time labouring to recover."[9] Empson suggests that this Romantic figure combines "the virtues of the poet and the scientist" in a kind of childish empiricism, because it is the "small observer, like the child, who does least to alter what he sees and therefore sees most truly."[10] Indeed, long before the Victorians took up the mantle of childish perception, Isaac Newton (1642–1727) reportedly described his career in just these terms: "to myself I seem to have been only like a boy playing on the seashore, and diverting myself now and then finding a smoother pebble or a prettier shell than ordinary, whilst the great ocean of truth lay all undiscovered before me."[11] This is both a statement of modesty and of method: the child's simplicity is an empirical asset, a capacity for absorption in the small, knowable details that form the outer bounds of vast truths. If this shared sensibility helps explain the burgeoning Quaker membership of the Royal Society, however, it also begins to leave behind the complications of malice and original sin that define the questions of this book and Milton's answers to them.[12]

This is of a piece with Locke's masterful move to sever the child's epistemological and political significance, which I suggested in the Introduction as a turning point away from political theory that seriously engaged concepts of childhood and poetics to address questions of political voice. For Locke, children's limited experience excludes them from the political sphere:

> *Children*, I confess are not born in this full state of *Equality*, though they are born to it. Their Parents have a sort of Rule and Jurisdiction over them when they come into the World, and for some time after, but 'tis but a temporary one. The Bonds of this Subjection are like the Swadling Cloths they are wrapt up in, and supported by, in the weakness of their Infancy. Age and Reason as they grow up, loosen them till at length they drop quite off, and leave a man at his own free disposal.[13]

Born without the equal capacity for consent that defines Locke's polity, the child's consent is "tacit and scarce avoidable" but his obligation is no less secure (or lengthy: Locke's notes for a utopian society propose that this extended innocence would last "till 40 years old").[14] Locke's children are quite distinct from his version of Adam, who was "created a perfect Man, his Body and Mind in full possession of their Strength and Reason."[15] Even as this disqualifies Locke's children from making political choices, it makes them ideal models of education, inquiry, and observation, and he attacks scholastic principles of innate knowledge by asserting that the child's understanding of any truth, like the establishment of any fact, "depends upon collection and observation," a simple, individualistic work of "framing and collecting."[16] Accordingly, the child's encounter with the apple no longer restages an encounter with original sin but rather functions as an empirical lesson: "the child, when part of his Apple is taken away, knows it better in that particular instance, than by this General Proposition, the whole is equal to all of its parts; and that if one of these have need to be confirmed to him by the other the general has more need to be let into his mind by the particular, than the particular by the general."[17] Education aims for simple productivity rather than for staging an agonistic battle of virtue and vice. This leaves no place for childish wandering, and Locke proposes in his *Essay on the Poor Law* that children caught idly wasting their time should be sent to workhouses that would combine the virtues of school and factory. In a master stroke of efficiency that would have delighted Comenius, he even suggests that the "same fire that warms the room" for the children's labor will serve to heat their "warm water-gruel."[18]

In the eighteenth century such ideas about the proper occupation of children generated a new literature that attempted to complete Comenius's project of purging educational texts of disruptive and unseemly material. In this "sanitization" of children's literature, as Andrew O'Malley describes it, romance narratives and chapbook adventures from folklore were stripped of their disruptive elements and children's literature took a distinctively prescriptive turn.[19] I would even suggest that the attempt to depoliticize the child – to elide the scene of becoming examined in this book from the liberal narrative – generates the category of children's literature as we know it. Isaac Watts's *Divine Songs, Attempted in Easy Language for the Use of Children*, "undeniably the most popular book of children's verse ever published," is a fine example of the genre's development.[20] First published in 1715, *Divine Songs* sets children's literature and the child's reading experience apart from faction, party, controversy, or politics: "you will find here nothing that savours of a party: the children of high and low degree; of the Church of England, or dissenters; baptized in infancy or not, may all join together in these songs."[21] Rather than raising the child up, Watts has "endeavoured to sink the language to the level of a child's understanding."[22] Rather than flirting with malice, the children in his text are "cleanly and harmless as doves or as lambs," and they speak only to announce that "my tongue obeys, / And angels shall rejoice, / To hear their mighty Maker's praise / Sound from a feeble voice."[23]

In this literature, the child's mind remains a blank slate, or undyed wool, but without the taint of original sin, a move that sets it a world apart from the ethical and moral battlefield encountered by Milton's children, where we "bring not innocence into the world, we bring impurity much rather" (*CPW* 2:515). In the grandest of ironies, Milton's own work was caught up in the vortex and translated into *The Story of Paradise Lost for Children* in 1828. "I fear it will be very difficult to form *Paradise Lost* into a suitable tale for children," announces a character named "Mamma," who nevertheless forges ahead with a robust editorial program to protect her children's innocence by firmly distinguishing biblical fact from Milton's "poetical embellishment."[24] For the ideal reader of such literature, the coming-of-age moment becomes less fraught with moral peril, but it also dissipates as a locus for dissent or meaningful consent. As Patricia Meyer Spacks suggests, the troublesome childish period between infancy and adulthood disappears as this literature suggests that "the young should be thought of, should think of themselves, as children until the very moment at which they assume full adult responsibility."[25] The young are required "not to grow but to yield," and maturity is marked not by struggle but by acceptance of adult authority.[26]

Only when we understand the difference between this and Milton's use of childhood can we appreciate why Stanley Fish is not quite right to suggest that the Son in *Paradise Regained* is the perfect Miltonic hero because he stubbornly insists on doing "nothing at all."[27] The challenge in Milton, as Fish sees it, is to make oneself a passive vessel for the Father's will, and the Son does this perfectly, refusing to do anything but stand. At almost exactly the same time that Newton was describing himself as a diminutive child gathering pebbles, however, the Son in *Paradise Regained* was announcing that any man who reads without "a spirit and judgment equal or superior" is no better than a "spunge; / As children gathering pebbles on the shore" (4.324, 329–30). This is not a rejection of childishness as such, but of diminutive childhood as a figure of passive innocence. The Son discovers his superior judgment only by wondering "where will this end?" as he is "Wandring this woody maze" (2.245–46), another version of the perplexed paths navigated by the childish actors in Milton's *Mask* and the world of choice that lies before Adam and Eve at the end of *Paradise Lost*. Like them, the Son in *Paradise Regained* has grown "to youth's full flowr" (1.67), although Satan tempts him repeatedly with the idea that he might achieve a kind of instant adulthood or that he is already a belated man. "Thy years are ripe, and over-ripe," Satan taunts (3.31), but the Son maintains his childish freedom, neither a little lamb nor a fully formed adult. To do so is, literally, a balancing act, as the Son teeters on his "uneasie station" on the temple spire until he is relieved by a host of angels (4.584). And then, as soon as he has rested and refreshed himself with food, he begins tracing his path back "Home to his Mother's house," wandering childishly once more through a world of temptations and trials that he meets with perfect freedom (4.639). In doing so, he reflects the image of the Father and the example of Eve, discovering a voice that will "begin to save mankind" (4.635).

Notes

INTRODUCTION

1 Ferdinando Nicolls, *The Life and Death of Mr. Ignatius Jurdain* (London: 1654/55), 16. See also Frances B. Troup, "An Exeter Worthy and His Biographer," *Report and Transactions of the Devonshire Association* 29 (1897): 350–77; and Mark Stoyle, *From Deliverance to Destruction: Rebellion and Civil War in an English City* (Exeter: University of Exeter Press, 1996), 19–37.

2 Ignatius Jordan to Thomas Lake, June 1618, PRO S.P. 14/97/140, fol. 171. I have modernized some of the letter's more archaic spelling; a full transcription, without the patent included by Jordan or other contextual documents quoted later in the chapter, is reproduced in John M. Wasson (ed.), *Records of Early English Drama: Devon* (Toronto: University of Toronto Press, 1986), 188–89.

3 The edict, from April 1658, is reproduced in W. Cotton and Henry Woollcombe, *Gleanings from the Municipal and Cathedral Records Relative to the History of the City of Exeter* (Exeter, 1877), 167.

4 Jordan, PRO S.P. 14/97/140, fol. 170.

5 Virginia Gildersleeve suggests child actors were "tacitly allowed special privileges" because they were "not technically regarded as professional actors," in *Government Regulation of the Elizabethan Drama* (New York: Columbia University Press, 1908), 196. The company's patent maintains this amateur pose and is reproduced in Glynne Wickham, Herbert Berry, and William Ingram (eds.), *English Professional Theatre, 1530–1660* (Cambridge: Cambridge University Press, 2000), 271–73.

6 Jordan, PRO S.P. 14/97/140, fol. 170.

7 Undated letter "to all mayors, sheriffs, bayliffs," PRO S.P. 14/97/140, fol. 172. The letter seems to be a draft, but appears in the manuscript with the other two documents relating to the incident.

8 Jacques Rancière, *Dis-agreement: Politics and Philosophy*, trans. Julie Rose (Minneapolis: University of Minnesota Press, 1999), 50. See also Aristotle's distinction between noise and "the power of speech," in *Politica*, trans. Benjamin Jowett, in *The Works of Aristotle*, ed. W. D. Ross, 12 vols. (Oxford: Clarendon Press, 1921), vol. 10, 1253a.

9 George Wither, *Opobalsamum Anglicanum* (London, 1646), 12. See Derek Hirst, *The Representative of the People?: Voters and Voting in England Under the Early Stuarts* (Cambridge: Cambridge University Press, 1975), 18–20. For Wither's poetry and politics, see David Norbrook, *Writing the English Republic: Poetry, Rhetoric, and Politics 1627–1660* (Cambridge: Cambridge University Press, 1999), 140–58.

10 Rancière, *Dis-agreement*, 50.

11 Thomas Elyot, *The Boke Named the Governor* (London, 1531), sig. G1r-v.

12 Lawrence Stone, *The Family, Sex, and Marriage in England, 1500–1800* (New York: Harper and Row, 1977), 175.

13 Philippe Ariès, *Centuries of Childhood: A Social History of Family Life*, trans. Robert Baldick (New York: Vintage, 1965), 38. First published as *L'Enfant et la vie familiale sous l'ancien régime* (Paris: Librairie Plon, 1960).

14 Lloyd deMause, "The Evolution of Childhood," *The History of Childhood*, ed. Lloyd deMause (London: Jason Aronson, 1974), 1.

15 John Donne, "Death's Duel," *The Sermons of John Donne*, ed. Evelyn M. Simpson and George R. Potter, 10 vols. (Berkeley: University of California Press, 1962), vol. 10, p. 232; Richard Baxter, *A Treatise of Conversion* (London, 1657), 71.

16 See Baxter, *A Treatise of Conversion*, 71. More common than Baxter's staunch anti-Pelagianism was the diplomatic balancing act handed down from Augustine, who carefully noted that infants are "as innocent as can be," a formulation that credited their relative purity even while acknowledging their inheritance of original sin, in *The City of God*, trans. John Healey (London: 1610), bk. 22, ch. 22, p. 904.

17 Linda A. Pollock, *Forgotten Children: Parent-child Relations from 1500– 1900* (Cambridge: Cambridge University Press, 1983). See also Ralph A. Houlbrooke, *The English Family: 1450–1700* (London: Longman, 1984) and the significant revision of Stone's family history by Alan Macfarlane, *Marriage and Love in England: 1300–1840* (Oxford: Blackwell, 1986).

18 Nicholas Orme, *Medieval Children* (New Haven: Yale University Press, 2001), 130.

19 Margaret L. King, "Concepts of Childhood: What We Know and Where We Might Go," *Renaissance Quarterly* 60 (2007): 393. See also C. John Sommerville, *The Discovery of Childhood in Puritan England* (Athens: University of Georgia Press, 1992).

20 Leah S. Marcus, *Childhood and Cultural Despair: A Theme and Variations in Seventeenth-Century Literature* (Pittsburgh: University of Pittsburgh Press, 1978), 41.

21 John Earle, *Micro-cosmographie* (London, 1628), sig. B1r. The book was reprinted thirteen times in quick succession and also was popular in manuscript, copied, for example, in Folger MS V.a. 345.

22 Aristotle, *Poetics*, trans. Stephen Halliwell, Loeb Classical Library (Cambridge, MA: Harvard University Press, 1995), sec. 48b, p. 37. For Aristotle on the child's mind as a tabula rasa, see *De Anima*, trans. Hugh Lawson-Tancred (New York: Penguin, 1987), bk. 3, ch. 4, p. 204. Aristotle's imagery of clean

wax tablets and blank pages became common currency via Aquinas, and the scholastic principle that *nihil est in intellectu nisi quod prius fuerit in sensu* remained commonplace throughout the reformation. See Thomas Aquinas, *Summa Theologiae: Latin Text and English Translation*, trans. Timothy Suttor, 61 vols. (London: Blackfriars, 1970), vol. 11, part 1a., q. 79, art. 3, pp. 153–54; Duns Scotus, in *Super Universalia Porphyrii Questiones, Opera Omnia*, ed. Luke Wadding, 26 vols. (Farnborough: Gregg International Publishers, 1969), vol. 1, q. 3, p. 71; and Martin Luther, *Lectures on Romans*, trans. Wilhelm Pauck (Westminster: John Knox Press, 1961), 69.

23 Michael Witmore, *Pretty Creatures: Children and Fiction in the English Renaissance* (Ithaca: Cornell University Press, 2007), 5, 193.

24 *Ibid.*, 7.

25 Brian Vickers, "The Age of Eloquence," *History of European Ideas* 5 (1984): 427–37. See also Wayne A. Rebhorn's introduction to *Renaissance Debates on Rhetoric*, ed. Wayne A. Rebhorn (Ithaca: Cornell University Press, 2000), 1–13; and Neil Rhodes, *The Power of Eloquence and English Renaissance Literature* (New York: St. Martin's Press, 1992).

26 Pierre Bourdieu and Jean-Claude Passeron, *Reproduction in Education, Society and Culture*, trans. Richard Nice (London: Sage, 1977), xi. See also Richard Halpern, *The Poetics of Primitive Accumulation: English Renaissance Culture and the Genealogy of Capital* (Ithaca: Cornell University Press, 1991); Lisa Jardine and Anthony Grafton, *From Humanism to the Humanities* (Cambridge, MA: Harvard University Press, 1986); and Mary Thomas Crane, *Framing Authority: Sayings, Self, and Society in Sixteenth-Century England* (Princeton: Princeton University Press, 1993).

27 Richard Mulcaster, *The First Part of the Elementarie* (London, 1582), 18; Roger Ascham, *The Scholemaster, or Plaine and Perfite Way of Teachyng Children* (1570), in *English Works*, ed. William Aldis Wright (Cambridge: Cambridge University Press, 1904), 236; Charles Hoole, *A New Discovery of the Old Art of Teaching School* (London, 1661), sig. A4v.

28 John Donne, *A Sermon Preached at St. Paul's in the Evening, November 23, 1628,* in *Fifty Sermons* (London, 1649), 391. For a similar progression, see Thomas Gataker, *David's Instructer: A sermon preached at the visitation of the Free-Schole at Tunbridge in Kent* (London, 1620), 19, and John Brinsley, *A Consolation for Our Grammar Schooles* (London, 1622), 17.

29 Halpern, *Poetics of Primitive Accumulation*, 28.

30 Gordon J. Schochet, *The Authoritarian Family and Political Attitudes in 17th Century England: Patriarchalism in Political Thought*, 2nd ed. (London: Transaction, 1988). See also Johann P. Sommerville, *Politics and Ideology in England 1603–1640* (London: Longman, 1986); and Kevin Sharpe, *Remapping Early Modern England: The Culture of Seventeenth-Century Politics* (Cambridge: Cambridge University Press, 2000), 104–07.

31 Ascham, *Scholemaster*, 205.

32 Some prototypical New Historicist analyses of sovereign power include Stephen Greenblatt, *Shakespearean Negotiations: The Circulation of Social*

Energy in Renaissance England (Berkeley: University of California Press, 1988); Louis Montrose, *The Purpose of Playing: Shakespeare and the Cultural Politics of the Elizabethan Theatre* (Chicago: University of Chicago Press, 1996); and Stephen Orgel, *The Illusion of Power: Political Theatre in the English Renaissance* (Berkeley: University of California Press, 1975).

33 Mark A. Kishlansky, *Parliamentary Selection: Social and Political Choice in Early Modern England* (Cambridge: Cambridge University Press, 1986), 8. See also John K. Gruenfelder, *Influence in Early Stuart Elections, 1604–1640* (Columbus: Ohio State University Press, 1981).

34 Hirst, *Representative of the People?*, 4.

35 Su Fang Ng, *Literature and the Politics of Family in Seventeenth-Century England* (Cambridge: Cambridge University Press, 2007); Erin Murphy, *Familial Forms: Politics and Genealogy in Seventeenth-Century English Literature* (Newark: University of Delaware Press, 2011); Melissa E. Sanchez, *Erotic Subjects: The Sexuality of Politics in Early Modern English Literature* (Oxford: Oxford University Press, 2011). See also Rachel Weil, *Political Passions: Gender, the Family, and Political Argument in England, 1680–1714* (Manchester: Manchester University Press, 1999); Margaret J. M. Ezell, *The Patriarch's Wife: Literary Evidence and the History of the Family* (Chapel Hill: University of North Carolina Press, 1987); and Susan D. Amussen, *An Ordered Society: Gender and Class in Early Modern England* (Oxford: Basil Blackwell, 1988).

36 See also Wendy Wall, *Staging Domesticity: Household Work and English Identity in Early Modern Drama* (Cambridge: Cambridge University Press, 2002); and Katharine Gillespie, *Domesticity and Dissent in the Seventeenth Century: English Women's Writing and the Public Sphere* (Cambridge: Cambridge University Press, 2004).

37 Francis Bacon, *Certain Considerations Touching the Better Pacification and Edification of the Church of England*, in *Resuscitatio* (London, 1657), 241. See also the comparison of children, idiots, and animals in Thomas Hobbes, *Leviathan*, 2.26.317. For "muted groups" who may speak only through the prism of a dominant group's sociolinguistic order, see Edwin Ardener, "Belief and the Problem of Women," in *Perceiving Women*, ed. Shirley Ardener (New York: John Wiley and Sons, 1975), 1–27, and Elaine Showalter, "Feminist Criticism in the Wilderness," *Critical Inquiry* 8 (1981): 179–205.

38 For the widespread Renaissance belief in the "mysterious power inherent in language," see Rhodes, *The Power of Eloquence*, 29.

39 Rebecca W. Bushnell, *A Culture of Teaching: Early Modern Humanism in Theory and Practice* (Ithaca: Cornell University Press, 1996), 19.

40 Gerrard Winstanley, "The New Law of Righteousness," in *The Complete Works of Gerrard Winstanley*, ed. Thomas N. Corns, Ann Hughes, and David Loewenstein, 2 vols. (Oxford: Oxford University Press, 2009), vol. 1, p. 534.

41 Gerrard Winstanley, "Declaration to the Powers of England (The True Levellers Standard Advanced)," in *The Complete Works*, 2:8.

42 Witmore, *Pretty Creatures*, 5.

43 Marcus, *Childhood and Cultural Despair*, 120; Witmore, *Pretty Creatures*, 7, 9, 10, 14, 23. For other discussions of preadolescent children, see Robert Pattison, *The Child Figure in English Literature* (Athens: University of Georgia Press, 1978); Michael Shapiro, *Children of the Revels: The Boy Companies of Shakespeare's Time and Their Plays* (New York: Columbia University Press, 1977); and Joy Leslie Gibson, *Squeaking Cleopatras: The Elizabethan Boy Player* (Phoenix Mill: Sutton, 2000).

44 Paul Griffiths, *Youth and Authority: Formative Experiences in England, 1560–1640* (Oxford: Clarendon Press, 1996), 9.

45 Ilana Krausman Ben-Amos, *Adolescence and Youth in Early Modern England* (New Haven: Yale University Press, 1994), 8.

46 William Shakespeare, *As You Like It*, in *The Norton Shakespeare*, ed. Stephen Greenblatt et al., 2nd ed. (New York: Norton, 2008), 2.7.142–43, 2.7.147.

47 Orme suggests this remains true, although childhood in the past was "less distinct from adulthood than it is today," *Medieval Children*, 3.

48 Anna Davin, "What is a Child?," in *Childhood in Question: Children, Parents, and the State*, eds. Anthony Fletcher and Stephen Hussey (Manchester: Manchester University Press, 1999), 19.

49 Henry Cuffe, *The Differences of the Ages of Mans Life Together with the Originall Causes* (London, 1607), 117–18. Italics in original.

50 *Ibid.*, 118.

51 John Shirley, *A Short Compendium of Chirurgery* (Cambridge, 1678), 8.

52 Notably, such views placed Christ's crucifixion, at the traditional age of thirty-three, just at the threshold of adulthood, or the period "now commonly thought … the flower & perfection of mans age," according to George Hakewill, *An Apologie of the Power and Providence of God in the Government of the World* (Oxford, 1627), 162. Pythagoras's division of the eighty years of life into four equal segments also remained influential, as in the popular English translation of Wawrzyniec Goslicki, *The Counsellor* (London, 1598): "Childhood should last till twentie, youth other twentie, mans estate other twentie, and olde age doth determine all, after the fourth twentie" (139). Goslicki later says children do not achieve full adult discretion until age forty-nine (140).

53 Matthew Hale, *Historia Placitorum Coronae*, 2 vols. (London: 1800), vol. 1, ch. 3, p. 22; Edward Coke, *The First Part of the Institutes of the Laws of England, or a Commentary Upon Littleton*, 10th ed. (London, 1703), bk. 2, ch. 4, sec. 103.

54 Keith Thomas, "Age and Authority in Early Modern England," *Proceedings of the British Academy* 62 (1997): 214. See also Ben-Amos, *Adolescence and Youth*, 5.

55 *Reformatio Legum Ecclesiasticarum*, ed. Edward Cardwell (Oxford: Oxford University Press, 1850), 44. Canon 100 of the Canons of 1603 revised this requirement slightly to mandate parental consent only before age twenty-one, although canon 103 continued to emphasize the need for parental consent for most marriages. See Martin Ingram, *Church Courts, Sex and Marriage in England, 1570–1640* (Cambridge: Cambridge University Press, 1987), 135.

56 For typical standards of filial deference, see William Perkins, *Christian Oeconomie or A Short Survey of the Right Manner of Erecting and Ordering a Familie According to the Scriptures* (London, 1609), 5, 147–49; and Thomas Cobbet, *A Fruitfull and Usefull Discourse Touching the Honour due from Children to Parents* (London, 1656), sig. A2v. See also Peter Laslett, *Family Life and Illicit Love in Earlier Generations* (Cambridge: Cambridge University Press, 1977), 177.

57 John Aubrey, *Aubrey's Brief Lives*, ed. Oliver Lawson Dick (Ann Arbor: University of Michigan Press, 1949), xxxii–xxxiii. See also Isaac Watts, *Treatise on the Education of Children and Youth*, 2nd ed. (London, 1769), 158.

58 For the traditional sacramental view that even the youngest child is joined to the church in baptism because he "believes not of himself but through others," see Thomas Aquinas, *Summa Theologiae: Latin Text and English Translation*, 61 vols., trans. James Cunningham (London: Blackfriars, 1975), vol. 57, 3a.68, p. 9. Calvin rejected baptism as a sacrament but insisted on its importance as "God's sign, communicated to a child as by an impressed seal," in *Institutes of the Christian Religion*, ed. John T. McNeill, trans. Ford Lewis Battles, 2. vols. (Philadelphia: The Westminster Press, 1960), vol. 2, bk. 4, sec. 9, p. 1332.

59 This is the wording in the 1549 Book of Common Prayer. The 1652 revision included the phrase "*sondry kindes of* sin"; see F. E. Brightman (ed.), *The English Rite: Being a Synopsis of the Sources and Revisions of the Book of Common Prayer*, 2 vols. (London: Rivingtons, 1921), vol. 2, pp. 778–79.

60 *Year Books of the Reign of King Edward III: Years 11 and 12*, ed. and trans. Alfred Horwood (London: Longman, 1883), 627.

61 See Anthony Platt and Bernard L. Diamond, "The Origins of the 'Right and Wrong' Test of Criminal Responsibility and Its Subsequent Development in the United States: An Historical Survey," *California Law Review* 54 (1966): 1227–60.

62 *Year Books of the Reign of King Edward III*, 627.

63 Thomas Granger, *A Familiar Exposition or Commentarie on Ecclesiastes* (London, 1621), 166. See also John Cotta, *A Short Discoverie of the Unobserved Dangers of Severall Sorts of Ignorant and Inconsiderate Practisers of Physicke* (London, 1612), 30.

64 "innocent, adj. and n.," OED 3b.

65 Bartholomaeus Anglicus, *Batman Uppon Bartholome His Booke De Proprietatibus Rerum*, trans. Stephen Batman (London, 1582), sig. O1r.

66 John Spencer, *Kaina Kai Palaia, Things New and Old, or, A Store-house of Similies, Sentences, Allegories, Apophthegms, Adagies, Apologues* (London, 1658), 479. For other descriptions of the test, see John Bramhall, *A Sermon Preached at Dublin upon the 23 of Aprill, 1661 Being the Day Appointed for His Majesties Coronation* (London, 1661), 25, and John Boys, *An Exposition of the Dominical Epistles and Gospels…the Winter Part from the First Adventuall Sunday to Lent* (London, 1610), 479.

67 John Tombes, *An Apology* (London, 1646), 154.

68 Holly Brewer, *By Birth or Consent: Children, Law, and the Anglo-American Revolution in Authority* (Chapel Hill: University of North Carolina Press, 2005), 197.

69 Seventeenth-century women even sometimes voted in parliamentary elections, as shown by Sara Mendelson and Patricia Crawford, *Women in Early Modern England, 1550–1720* (Oxford: Oxford University Press, 1998), 56.

70 Brewer, *Birth or Consent*, 2.

71 See Griffiths, *Youth and Authority*, 5; and E. A. Wrigley and R. S. Schofield, *Population History of England 1541–1871* (Cambridge: Cambridge University Press, 1989), 216.

72 Plato, *Republic*, trans. Paul Shorey, in *The Collected Dialogues*, ed. Edith Hamilton and Huntington Cairns (Princeton: Princeton University Press, 1962), 395d, p. 640.

73 Richard Baxter, *A Treatise of Episcopacy* (London, 1680), 128. See also Fynes Moryson, who notes that "Children like Parrats, soone learne forraigne languages, and sooner forget the same," in *An Itenerary* (London, 1617), 2–3.

74 John Locke, *An Essay Concerning Human Understanding*, ed. Roger Woolhouse (London: Penguin, 1997), bk. 3 ch. 2 sec. 7, p. 366.

75 Locke formulates this patriarchal theory under the heading "Lex Naturae" in his journal entry for July 15, 1678, Bodleian Library MS Locke f. 3, 201–02.

76 Locke, *Two Treatises on Government*, 2nd ed., ed. Peter Laslett (Cambridge: Cambridge University Press, 1992), bk. 2 sec. 75, p. 318.

77 Locke, *Two Treatises*, 2.119.348.

78 The most important later development of Locke's tacit consent came from John Rawls, who explained that "An unfortunate mistake of the idea of social contract was to suppose that political obligation does require some such act, or at least, to use language which suggests it. It is sufficient that one has knowingly participated in and accepted the benefits of a practice acknowledged to be fair," in "Justice as Reciprocity," *Collected Papers*, ed. Samuel Freeman (Cambridge, MA: Harvard University Press, 1999), 210. Such ideas undergird Rawls's formation of the hypothetical "original position" in *A Theory of Justice* (Cambridge, MA: Harvard University Press, 1971).

79 See Andrew O'Malley, *The Making of the Modern Child: Children's Literature and Childhood in the Late Eighteenth-Century* (New York: Routledge, 2003) and Alan Richardson, "Wordsworth, Fairy Tales, and the Politics of Children's Reading," *Romanticism and Children's Literature in Nineteenth-Century England*, ed. James Holt McGavran Jr. (Athens: University of Georgia Press, 2009), 48–49.

80 Warren W. Wooden, *Children's Literature of the English Renaissance* (Lexington: University Press of Kentucky, 1986), 88.

81 *Goody Two Shoes* (London, 1765); Eliza Weaver Bradburn, *The Story of Paradise Lost, for Children* (London, 1828). For the impact and content of these works, see Seth Lerer, *Children's Literature: A Reader's History from Aesop to Harry Potter* (Chicago: University of Chicago Press, 2008), 105–06, and Jonathan

Sircy, "Educating Milton: *Paradise Lost*, Accommodation, and the *Story of Paradise Lost, for Children*," *Milton Quarterly* 45 (2011): 172–86.

82 Edmund Spenser, "A Letter of the Authors Expounding his *Whole Intention in the Course of thie Worke*," in *The Faerie Queene*, ed. A. C. Hamilton, Hiroshi Yamashita, and Toshiyuki Suzuki, 2nd ed. (London: Longman, 2001), 714.

83 O'Malley, *Making of the Modern Child*, 22. For Romantic children "as a race apart," see Judith Plotz, *Romanticism and the Vocation of Childhood* (New York: Palgrave, 2001), xv.

84 William Wordsworth, "Ode (There Was a Time)," *Selected Poetry*, ed. Stephen Gill (Oxford: Oxford University Press, 2008), 85, 107.

85 Richard Mulcaster, *Positions Wherin those Primitive Circumstances Be Examined Which are Necessarie for the Training up of Children* (1581), ed. Robert Herbert Quick (New York: Longmans, 1888), 57.

86 For the expansion of schooling, see Kenneth Charlton and Margaret Spufford, "Literacy, Society, and Education," in *The Cambridge History of Early Modern English Literature*, eds. David Loewenstein and Janel Mueller (Cambridge: Cambridge University Press, 2002), 25; Darryll Grantley, *Wit's Pilgrimage: Drama and the Social Impact of Education in Early Modern England* (Aldershot: Ashgate, 2000), 3–25; and Joan Simon, *Education and Society in Tudor England* (Cambridge: Cambridge University Press, 1966).

87 Ascham, *The Scholemaster*, 184, 187.

88 Witmore, *Pretty Creatures*, 23.

89 Erasmus, *Declamatio De Pueris Statim ac Liberaliter Instituendis*, in *Opera Omnia*, 10 vols. (Hildesheim: Georg Olms, 1961), vol. 1, p. 509: "ut diximus, invitat infantulos nativa quaedam imitandi voluptas, cujus vestigium aliquod videmus & in sturnis ac psittacis. Quid Poetarum fabulis amoenis?" For a contemporary translation, see Richard Sherry, *A Treasise of Schemes and Tropes* (London, 1550), sig. N6r.

90 Thomas Bastard, "De puero balbutiente," *Chrestoleros* (London, 1598), 177.

91 Henry Peacham, *The Compleat Gentleman* (London, 1634), 24.

92 Brinsley, *A Consolation*, 26, 12. See also Hoole, *The New Discovery*, 142.

93 This was the schoolmaster's excuse in Bloxworth, Dorset, when he ran afoul of church authorities for staging children's performances in the Parish church, as found in Rosalind Conklin Hays and C. E. McGee (eds.), *Records of Early English Drama (REED): Dorset* (Toronto: University of Toronto Press, 1999), 137. For performances by less known but dramatically important schools, see T. H. Vail Motter, *The School Drama in England* (New York: Longmans, 1929).

94 The *Records of Early English Drama* richly documents these play days. See, for example, Mark C. Pilkinton (ed.), *REED: Bristol* (Toronto: University of Toronto Press, 1997), 77, 147; Sally L. Joyce and Evelyn S. Newlyn (eds.), *REED: Cornwall* (Toronto: University of Toronto Press, 1999), 137, 199; James M. Gibson (ed.), *REED: Kent, Diocese of Canterbury*, 2 vols. (Toronto: University of Toronto Press, 2002), vol. 1, pp. 191, 283, 287; David Galloway (ed.), *REED: Norwich* (Toronto: University of Toronto Press, 1984), 21, 52, 54. See also Foster Watson, *The English Grammar Schools to 1600: Their Curriculum and Practice* (Cambridge: Cambridge University Press, 1908), 315–320.

95 Thomas Hobbes, *Elements of Law*, 2. 9.8.184; John Lyly, *Euphues, the Anatomy of Wit* (London, 1578), sig. B1v. On Lyly's use of humanist educational tropes, see Richard A. McCabe, "Wit, Eloquence, and Wisdom in *Euphues: the Anatomy of Wit*," *Studies in Philology* 81 (1984), 299–324.

96 For the marketing of these works as juvenilia, see Sarah Knight, "Milton's Forced Themes," *Milton Quarterly* 45 (2011): 145–60.

97 See John K. Hale, "Milton Plays the Fool: The Christ's College Salting, 1628," *Classical and Modern Literature* 20 (2000): 51–70.

98 Desiderius Erasmus, *Colloquia Familiaria*, in *Opera Omnia*, 10 vols. (Hildesheim: Georg Olms, 1961), vol. 1, p. 645. Optimistic educationists detailed rules to ensure that barring out was done in "a peaceable and loving manner," as in Charles Hoole, *New Discovery*, 294. See Keith Thomas, *Rule and Misrule in the Schools of Early Modern England* (Reading: University of Reading Press, 1976), 33.

99 Erasmus, *Colloquia*, 646: "P: Quis erit fideiussor aut sponsor, isthuc futurum? C: Ego captis mei periculo non dubitem esse sponsor. P: Imo culi periculo potius. Scio quam non sit tutum tibi credere, tamen hic periculum faciam, quam sis bonae fidei. Si dederis verba, posthac nequicquam mecum egeris. Ludant, sed gregatim in campis."

100 See Thomas Blount, *Nomo-lexicon, a Law Dictionary* (London, 1670).

101 Erasmus, *Colloquia*, 646: "ne divertant ad compotationes, aut alia nequiora."

102 See Keith Thomas, "Children in Early Modern England," *Children and Their Books: A Celebration of the Work of Iona and Peter Opie*, eds. Gillian Avery and Julia Briggs (Oxford: Clarendon, 1989), 45–77, and Thomas, *Rule and Misrule*, 24.

103 Erasmus, *Colloquia*, 645.

104 Robert Weimann, *Authority and Representation in Early Modern Discourse* (Baltimore: Johns Hopkins University Press, 1996), 4, 109.

105 See William Burton (trans.), *Seaven Dialogues Very Pleasant and Delightfull for all Persons* (London, 1624). The French schoolmaster Mathurin Cordier's *Colloquiorum Scholasticorum* were nearly as popular as those by Erasmus, and editors gathered the works of Vives, Erasmus, and other humanists in collections like *Familiara Colloquia* (London, 1673). For the literary reputation of the colloquies and their centrality as an educational resource "for two centuries or more," see Wallace K. Ferguson, "Works of Erasmus," in *Collected Works of Erasmus: Literary and Educational Writings*, ed. Craig R. Thompson, 7 vols. (Toronto: University of Toronto Press, 1978), vol. 1, pp. xi–xiv.

106 Charles Hoole, *Children's Talk* (London, 1697), 23. Hoole's book was first published in 1659; the copy from which I quote is held by the Folger library, call number 167–097q. Practice alphabets and scribbles seem to indicate a youthful annotator.

107 Lerer, *Children's Literature*, 80. See also Gillian Adams, "In the Hands of Children," *The Lion and the Unicorn* 29 (2004): 38–51. For the important observation that children's marginal doodles suggest that they used books

as scrap paper more often than they "annotated" them, see H. J. Jackson, *Marginalia: Readers Writing in Books* (New Haven: Yale University Press, 2001), 19–21.

108 The phrase is from Joanna Picciotto, *Labors of Innocence in Early Modern England* (Cambridge, MA: Harvard University Press, 2010), 630n.205. See also her argument that "by the seventeenth century, 'popular' festivity had become a largely 'top-down' affair" (87–88).

109 Nigel Smith, *Is Milton Better than Shakespeare?* (Cambridge, MA: Harvard University Press, 2008), xvi.

110 Stanley Fish, *How Milton Works* (Cambridge, MA: Harvard University Press, 2001), 14.

111 Augustine, *City of God*, 22.29.915.

112 Peter C. Herman, "Paradigms Lost, Paradigms Found: The New Milton Criticism," *Literature Compass* 2 (2005): 1–26.

113 Carole Pateman, *The Problem of Political Obligation: A Critique of Liberal Theory* (Berkeley: University of California Press, 1985), 82.

CHAPTER I. COMING OF AGE ON STAGE

1 John Gauden, *Hiera Dakrya, Ecclesiae Anglicanae Suspiria* (London, 1659), 284.

2 James I, *The True Law of Free Monarchies*, in *The Political Works of James I*, ed. Charles Howard McIlwain (Cambridge, MA: Harvard University Press, 1918), 85. Until 1752, England used the Old Style Calendar with the new year beginning on March 25 instead of January 1, as was the case in most European countries. This sometimes created confusion, as with Jonson's play, which he dated 1609 although it probably debuted in January or February of 1610 in the New Style Calendar. To eliminate ambiguity, in such cases dates provided are Old Style/New Style.

3 For Charles II's republication of works like Richard Mocket's *God and the King*, see Gordon J. Schochet, *The Authoritarian Family and Political Attitudes in 17th Century England: Patriarchalism and Political Thought*, 2nd ed. (London: Transaction, 1988), 88–89.

4 Lisa Jardine, *Still Harping on Daughters: Women and Drama in the Age of Shakespeare* (London: Harvester, 1983), 18.

5 Stephen Orgel, *Impersonations: The Performance of Gender in Shakespeare's England* (Cambridge: Cambridge University Press, 1996), 70. Dympna Callaghan broaches the subject, but rather than querying the historical meaning of the boys' childishness, she primarily offers a Lacanian reading of the way the boys shaped masculine gender by enacting a female "lack," in *Shakespeare Without Women: Representing Gender and Race on the Renaissance Stage* (London: Routledge, 2000), 67–74. Other important accounts that examine the boys' appeal without interrogating their status as children are Mary Bly's *Queer Virgins and Virgin Queans on the Early Modern Stage* (Oxford: Oxford University Press, 2000); Phyllis Rackin, "Androgyny,

Mimesis, and the Marriage of the Boy Heroine on the English Renaissance Stage," *PMLA* 102 (1987): 29–41; and Anthony Dawson, "Performance and Participation," *The Culture of Playgoing in Shakespeare's England: A Collaborative Debate*, ed. Anthony Dawson and Paul Yachnin (Cambridge: Cambridge University Press, 2001), 11–37.

6 Orgel, *Impersonations*, 29, 103.

7 Michael Shapiro, *Children of the Revels: The Boy Companies of Shakespeare's Time and Their Plays* (New York: Columbia University Press, 1977), 108.

8 Shapiro, *Children of the Revels*, 104.

9 Michael Witmore, *Pretty Creatures: Children and Fiction in the English Renaissance* (Ithaca: Cornell University Press, 2007), 96; Claire M. Busse, "'Pretty Fictions' and 'Little Stories': Child Actors on the Early Modern Stage," in *Childhood and Children's Books in Early Modern Europe, 1550–1800*, eds. Andrea Immel and Michael Witmore (New York: Routledge, 2006), 86.

10 Peter Stallybrass, "Transvestism and the 'Body Beneath': Speculating on the Boy Actor," in *Erotic Politics: Desire on the Renaissance Stage*, ed. Susan Zimmerman (London: Routledge, 1992), 68; italics in the original.

11 For the view that these were essentially the same company, see Edel Lamb, *Performing Childhood in the Early Modern Theatre: The Children's Playing Companies, 1599–1613* (Basingstoke: Palgrave Macmillan, 2009), 10–12. For the alternative, see Richard Dutton, "The Revels Office and the Boy Companies, 1600–1613: New Perspectives," *English Literary Renaissance* 32 (2002): 324–51, and Bly, *Queer Virgins*, 28–34. For our purposes the most important fact is that the companies all shared key personnel, such as the manager Robert Keysar and child actors like Nathan Field, who were impressed or apprenticed early in the company's history.

12 Lorraine Helms argues that Field played Epicoene based on several pieces of "circumstantial evidence," including his "epicoene good looks" and Chapman's reference to Field's "Acted woman"; see "Roaring Girls and Silent Women: The Politics of Androgyny on the Jacobean Stage," in *Women in Theatre*, Themes in Drama 11, ed. James Redmond (Cambridge: Cambridge University Press, 1989), 73n26.

13 Richard Dutton, introduction to *Epicene, or the Silent Woman*, by Ben Jonson (Manchester: Manchester University Press, 2003), 7.

14 Ben Jonson, *The Entertainment at Britain's Burse*, ed. James Knowles, in *Re-Presenting Ben Jonson: Text, History, Performance*, ed. Martin Butler (Houndmills, Basingstoke: Macmillan, 1999), 134 (fol. 144v).

15 Two copies of the bond exist, Dulwich College Mun. 47 and Ms. XVIII. 9, both transcribed in *Henslowe Papers, Being Documents Supplementary to Henslowe's Diary*, ed. Walter W. Greg (London: A. H. Bullen, 1907), 18, 111.

16 Mark Eccles, "Brief Lives: Tudor and Stuart Authors," *Studies in Philology* 79 (1982): 10.

17 The annotation, in what appears to be a seventeenth-century hand, also identifies Hugh Attawell as Sir Amorous la Foole, as discussed in James A. Riddell, "Some Actors in Ben Jonson's Plays," *Shakespeare Studies* 5 (1969): 285–98.

18 Two months after the play's first performance, on March 10, 1609/10, Christopher Davell and Robert Browne, who may have been the Queen's Revels shareholder of the same name, signed a bond for Barksted to appear at sessions as a consequence of the arrest; see Eccles, "Brief Lives," 10.

19 *Ibid.*, 10.

20 See Mark Eccles, "Elizabethan Actors I: A-D," *Notes & Queries* 236 (1991): 39.

21 For example, if the printed cast list for Beaumont and Fletcher's *The Coxcomb* represents the company in 1608, the early performances of that play included twenty-two-year-old Joseph Taylor, christened 1586, and Robert Benfield, who was old enough to christen his own child on February 21, 1609/10; see Lucy Munro, *The Children of the Queen's Revels: A Jacobean Theatre Repertory* (Cambridge: Cambridge University Press, 2005), 41. For the view that actors in the Children of Paul's were nineteen to twenty years old when they dissolved in 1606, see Reavley Gair, *The Children of Pauls: The Story of a Theatre Company, 1553–1608* (Cambridge: Cambridge University Press, 1982), 159. Boy actors in adult companies played women well into their late teens and twenties, and at least one, Hugh Clarke, continued after he was married, as shown by David Kathman, "How Old Were Shakespeare's Boy Actors?," *Shakespeare Survey* 58 (2005): 220–46.

22 Kathryn Schwarz, *Tough Love: Amazon Encounters in the English Renaissance* (Durham: Duke University Press, 2000), 27.

23 Andrew Gurr, *The Shakespearean Stage, 1574–1642*, 4th ed. (Cambridge: Cambridge University Press, 2009), 67.

24 Lamb, *Performing Childhood*, 40.

25 *Ibid.*, 8. See Judith Butler, *Gender Trouble: Feminism and the Subversion of Identity* (London, Routledge, 1999), 9–10.

26 Plutarch, *Plutarch's Moralia*, ed. and trans. Frank Cole Babbitt, 15 vols. (Cambridge, MA: Harvard University Press, 1960), vol. 1, 57, 171. For Plutarch's influence, see D. A. Russell, *Plutarch* (London: Duckworth, 1973), 143–48. For a comprehensive list of the Latin, English, French, Spanish, and Italian versions of Plutarch see Robert Aulotte, *Amyot et Plutarque: La Tradition des Moralia au XVIe Siècle* (Geneva: Librairie Droz, 1965), 325–62.

27 See Lynn D. Wardle, "Rethinking Marital Age Restrictions," *Journal of Family Law* 22 (1983): 1–20; and Frederick Pollock and Frederic Maitland, *History of English Law Before the Time of Edward I*, 2nd ed., 2 vols. (Cambridge: Cambridge University Press, 1899), vol. 2, 390–93.

28 Edward Coke, *The First Part of the Institutes of the Laws of England, or a Commentary Upon Littleton*, 10th ed. (London, 1703), bk. 1, ch. 5, sec. 36.

29 Bertolt Brecht, *Schriften Zum Theater*, ed. Werner Hecht, 7 vols. (Frankfurt: Suhrkamp Verlag, 1963), vol. 5, 177.

30 Jonathan Goldberg, *James I and the Politics of Literature: Jonson, Shakespeare, Donne, and their Contemporaries* (Baltimore: Johns Hopkins University Press, 1983), 85.

31 James I, "The Kings Verses," Folger MS V.b.303, fol. 264. For a list of MS variants of this poem, see James Craigie (ed.), *The Poems of James VI of Scotland*, 2 vols. (Edinburgh: Scottish Text Society, 1958), vol. 2, p. 262n15.

32 James I, "King's Verses," fol. 265.

33 Lamb, *Performing Childhood*, 3, 40.

34 Henry Cuffe, *The Differences of the Ages of Mans Life Together with the Originall Causes* (London, 1607), 117.

35 *Ibid.*, 117–18.

36 Munro, *Children of the Queen's Revels*, 52.

37 *Ibid.*, 13.

38 James I, *Proceedings in Parliament, 1610*, ed. Elizabeth Read Foster, 2 vols. (New Haven: Yale University Press, 1966), vol. 2, 103–04, 107.

39 See Mark A. Kishlansky, *Parliamentary Selection: Social and Political Choice in Early Modern England* (Cambridge: Cambridge University Press, 1986), 10.

40 Joseph Hall, *The Contemplations upon the History of the New Testament* (London, 1661), 495. For other examples, see Richard Younge, *Apples of Gold from the Tree of Life* (London, 1654), 3, and Laurent, *Somme des Vices et Vertus*, trans. William Caxton (Westminster, 1485), sig. H2r.

41 See Holly Brewer, *By Birth or Consent: Children, Law, and the Anglo-American Revolution in Authority* (Chapel Hill: University of North Carolina Press, 2005), 26–31.

42 John Tey, June 13, 1610, *Parliamentary Debates in 1610*, ed. Samuel Gardiner (London, 1862), 55.

43 *Proceedings in Parliament, 1610*, 2:147.

44 George More, June 13, 1610, *Parliamentary Debates*, 55.

45 Juan Luis Vives, *De Tradendis Disciplinis*, in *Joannis Ludovici Vivis Valentini Opera Omnia*, ed. G. Mayans y Siscár, 8 vols. (Benedicti Monfort, 1745; rept. London: Gregg Press, 1964), vol. 6, bk. 2, ch. 2, 285.

46 Coke, *First Part of the Institutes*, 3.4.323.

47 *Ibid.*, 2.4.104. For Coke's personal interest in limiting children's consent after his own daughter rejected the marriage he had arranged, see Deborah G. Burks, "'I'll Want My Will Else': *The Changeling* and Women's Complicity with Their Rapists," *ELH* 62 (1995): 759–90.

48 For the documents that licensed the "taking" of children, see E. K. Chambers (ed.), "Commissions for the Chapel," *Malone Society Collections* 1.4/5 (1911): 357–63.

49 The deposition is reproduced in Frederick Gard Fleay, *A Chronicle History of the London Stage: 1559–1642* (New York: Burt Franklin, 1890), 129.

50 *Ibid.*, 131.

51 *Ibid.*, 131.

52 Both the school's charter and the legal case of the "inveigled" boys are in the Canterbury Cathedral Archives and are transcribed in James M. Gibson (ed.), *REED: Kent, Diocese of Canterbury* (Toronto: University of Toronto Press, 2002), 191, 227–28.

53 For evidence that binding apprentices in child and adult companies was more about protecting valuable property than about training, see Robert Barrie, "Elizabethan Play-Boys in the Adult London Companies," *SEL* 48 (2008): 237–57; and David Kathman, "Grocers, Goldsmiths, and Drapers: Freemen and Apprentices in the Elizabethan Theater," *Shakespeare Quarterly* 55 (2004): 1–49.

54 The deposition is now lost or miscataloged at the PRO, but was transcribed by Charles W. Wallace in the early twentieth century, and this transcription can be found at the Huntington Library, mssWallace papers, Box 9, Folder 13B.

55 *Ibid.*

56 The original bill and return for this lawsuit are at PRO REQ-2-681 and are described in G. E. Bentley, "The Salisbury Court Theatre and its Boy Players," *Huntington Library Quarterly* 40 (1977): 129–49. For the subsequent discovery of other documents important to the case, including the papers binding Hammerton as a Draper's apprentice, see Kathman, "Grocers, Goldsmiths, and Drapers," 1–49.

57 Bly, *Queer Virgins*, 123.

58 Lamb, *Performing Childhood*, 37.

59 William Shakespeare, Sonnet 20, *The Norton Shakespeare*, ed. Stephen Greenblatt et al., 2nd ed. (New York: W. W. Norton, 2008), 12.

60 Bruce R. Smith, *Homosexual Desire in Shakespeare's England: A Cultural Poetics* (Chicago: University of Chicago Press, 1994). For the insight that "what determined the shared and recurring features of homosexual relationships was the prevailing distribution of power, economic power and social power, not the fact of homosexuality itself," see Alan Bray, *Homosexuality in Renaissance England* (London: Gay Men's Press, 1982), 56. For the heteroerotic version of the same dynamic, see Arthur F. Marotti, "'Love Is Not Love': Elizabethan Sonnet Sequences and the Social Order," *ELH* 49 (1982): 396–428.

61 James I, May 17, 1620, Letter to George Villiers, *King James and Letters of Homoerotic Desire*, ed. David M. Bergeron (Iowa City: University of Iowa Press, 1999), 149.

62 Smith, *Homosexual Desire*, 51.

63 Edward Coke, *The Third Part of the Institutes of the Laws of England* (London, 1797), ch. 10, 58. See Smith, *Homosexual Desire*, 51, 194.

64 Richard Brathwaite, "The Age for Apes," in *The Honest Ghost* (London, 1658), 139–40.

65 Johan Huizinga, *Homo Ludens: A Study of the Play Element in Culture*, trans. Johan Huizinga and R. F. C. Hull (London: Routledge, 1998), 13.

66 Plutarch, *Moralia*, 1.16.57.

67 Leah S. Marcus, *Childhood and Cultural Despair: A Theme and Variations in Seventeenth-Century Literature* (Pittsburgh: University of Pittsburgh Press, 1978), 75.

68 William Prynne, *Histrio-Mastix* (London, 1633), 916.

69 *Ibid.*, 171–72.

70 John Rainolds, *Th' Overthrow of Stage-Plays* (London, 1599), 17.

71 Orgel, *Impersonations*, 39.

72 Karl Young, "William Gager's Defence of the Academic Stage," *Transactions of the Wisconsin Academy of Sciences, Arts and Letters* 18 (1916): 614. Young's article includes the full text of Gager's work.

73 See Chambers (ed.), "Commissions for the Chapel," 360.

74 For the records of the payments see the *Calendar of the Manuscripts of the Most Honourable the Marquess of Salisbury*, 24 vols. (London: HMSO, 1976), vol. 24, 168. This was a "rare example of children being paid for their efforts," as noted by Lamb, *Performing Childhood*, 14. Scott McMillin has argued that Field's efforts were scribal grunt work done for Jonson, in "Jonson's Early Entertainments: New Information from Hatfield House," *Renaissance Drama*, NS 1 (1968): 153–66. But it seems unlikely that merely copying the script, which only runs to about three thousand words, would have required such intensive, all-night effort.

75 Nathan Field, "To my lov'd friend M. John Fletcher, on his Pastorall," *The Faithfull Shepheardesse* (London, 1610?), sig. A3r.

76 Nathan Field, *A Woman is a Weathercock* (London, 1612), sig. A4r.

77 Matthew Hale, *Historia Placitorum Coronae*, 2 vols. (London: 1800), vol. 1, 24, 26, 629.

78 Horace, *The Satires of Horace*, ed. Arthur Palmer (London: Macmillan, 1968), 1.4.101.

79 See Horace, *Satires*, 1.4.73–74.

80 See Hugh Gazzard, "'Those Graue Presentments of Antiquitie': Samuel Daniel's *Philotas* and the Earl of Essex," *Review of English Studies* 51 (2000): 423–50.

81 Sir Edward Hoby to Sir Thomas Edmondes, March 7, 1605, *The Court and Times of James I*, ed. Thomas Birch, 2 vols. (London, 1848), vol. 1, 60–61.

82 Letter from the French Ambassador, Antoine Lefèvre de la Boderie, to Pierre Brulart de Puisieux, Marquis de Sillery, April 8, 1608, Appendix 2a in *The Conspiracy and Tragedy of Byron*, ed. and trans. John Margeson (Manchester: Manchester University Press, 1988), 276–77. For the original French, see E. K. Chambers (ed.), *The Elizabethan Stage*, 4 vols. (Oxford: Oxford University Press, 1923), vol. 3, p. 257–58.

83 Thomas Lake to Robert Lord Salisbury, March 11, 1608, *Malone Society Collections* 2.2, ed. W. W. Greg (Oxford: Oxford University Press, 1923), 149.

84 Thomas Heywood, *An Apology for Actors* (London, 1612), sig. G3v.

85 *Ibid.*, sig. G3v. Rival playwrights understood the dynamic, and some scholars suggest that *Hamlet*'s lines about the "little eyases" who jeopardize the livelihood of adult actors may be a later addition responding to the boys' increasingly risky behavior. See Roslyn L. Knutson "Falconer to the Little Eyases: A New Date and Commercial Agenda for the 'Little Eyases' Passage in *Hamlet*," *Shakespeare Quarterly* 46 (1995): 1–31.

86 Charles Hoole, *An Easie Entrance to the Latine Tongue* (London, 1649), 130.

87 The epicene could also gesture toward other kinds of childish indeterminacy, so that the "Epicoene" believer who wavers in his religious loyalty, for example, is compared to "a strange, stigmaticke, mishapen, halfe-borne, halfe-unborne child," in Thomas Adams, *Mystical Bedlam* (London, 1615), 72.

88 See Foster (ed.), *Proceedings in Parliament*, 2:54n4.

89 Thomas Dekker, *The Guls Horne-Booke* (London, 1609), 29. See Bly, *Queer Virgins*, 65–70.

90 The speaker of Donne's "Elegy 11: To His Mistress," for example, darkly warns his mistress that if she follows him dressed as a male page "th'indifferent Italian" will "haunt thee with such lust, and hideous rage, / As Lot's fair guests were vex'd," in *John Donne's Poetry*, ed. Donald Dickson (New York: Norton, 2007), 38, 40–41.

91 Michele De Filippis, "The Literary Riddle in Italy to the End of the Sixteenth Century," *University of California Publications in Modern Philology* 34 (1948): 13.

92 For early iterations of this riddle see Thomas A. Green (ed.), "Catch Question," *Folklore: An Encyclopedia of Beliefs, Customs, Tales, Music, and Art* (Santa Barbara: ABC-Clio, 1998), 117. Giovanni Straparola's sixteenth-century *Le piacevoli notti* – perhaps the most famous collection of Italian riddles in Jonson's time – includes dozens of variations on this theme.

93 Thomas Middleton, *Father Hubburds Tales*, in *Collected Works of Thomas Middleton*, ed. Gary Taylor and John Lavagnino (Oxford: Oxford University Press, 2007), 159.

94 Phillip Stubbes, *The Anatomie of Abuses* (London, 1583), sig. L8v.

95 Cyprian makes his comment in his epistle to Euchratius, *Sancti Cypriani Episcopi Opera*, eds. G. F. Diercks et al., 6 vols. (Turnhout: Brepols Publishers, 1994), vol. 3B, 6. The passage was often cited, as in John Northbrooke, *Spiritus est Vicarius Christi in Terra* (London, 1577), 75.

96 See, for example, the argument that *Epicoene* points to fundamental gender instabilities in a way that "would have been a matter of manifest anxiety if the play had not been performed by children, who represented indeterminacy in its least threatening form," in Richmond Barbour, "'When I Acted Young Antinous': Boy Actors and the Erotics of Jonsonian Theatre," *PMLA* 110 (1995): 1015.

97 See W. W. Greg, "Was there a 1612 Quarto of *Epicene*?," *The Library* 15 (1934): 310–13; Dutton, introduction, 72–75; and David Riggs, *Ben Jonson: A Life* (Cambridge, MA: Harvard University Press, 1989), 156.

98 Jonathan Sawday, "Re-writing a Revolution: History, Symbol and Text in the Restoration," *The Seventeenth Century* 7 (1992): 187.

99 *A Satyr upon the Mistresses*, in J. W. Ebsworth (ed.), *The Roxburghe Ballads*, 9 vols. (Hertford: The Ballad Society, 1885), vol. 5, 130.

100 Edmond Dillon, *To the Kings Most Excellent Majesty* (London, 1664), 10.

101 See Dale B. J. Randall, *Winter Fruit: English Drama 1642–1660* (Lexington: University Press of Kentucky, 1995), 374.

102 The prologue is reproduced in Robert Gale Noyes, *Ben Jonson of the English Stage, 1660–1776* (Cambridge, MA: Harvard University Press, 1935), 175–76. James's comparison of himself to a mirror is in *Proceedings in Parliament 1610*, 2:103.

103 Noyes, *Ben Jonson*, 176.

104 Colly Cibber, *An Apology For the Life of Colly Cibber*, ed. B. R. S. Fone (Ann Arbor: University of Michigan Press, 1968), 71.

105 Samuel Pepys, 18 August 1660, *The Diary of Samuel Pepys*, ed. Robert Latham and William Matthews, 10 vols. (Berkeley: University of California Press, 1970), vol. 1, 224.

CHAPTER 2. CHILDREN, LITERATURE, AND THE
PROBLEM OF CONSENT

1 Oliver Arnold, *The Third Citizen: Shakespeare's Theater and the Early Modern House of Commons* (Baltimore: The Johns Hopkins University Press, 2007), 26.
2 *Ibid.*, 29. For the idea of the public theatre as a "cultural arena ... whose unprecedented development, both in physical space and social organization, encouraged a social critique," see Annabel Patterson, *Shakespeare and the Popular Voice* (Cambridge, MA: Blackwell, 1989), 10. See also Andrew Hadfield, *Shakespeare and Republicanism* (Cambridge: Cambridge University Press, 2005), 73. For the qualification that theatre was less a mouthpiece for republicanism or absolutism than "a space in which playgoers could practice thinking about how power works in the political domain," see Jeffrey S. Doty, "Shakespeare's *Richard II*, 'Popularity,' and the Early Modern Public Sphere," *Shakespeare Quarterly* 61 (2010): 185.
3 Arnold, *Third Citizen*, 2.
4 William Shakespeare, *Coriolanus*, in *The Norton Shakespeare*, ed. Stephen Greenblatt et al., 2nd ed. (New York: W. W. Norton, 2008), 2.3.4–5.
5 Arnold, *Third Citizen*, 9.
6 Shakespeare, *Coriolanus*, 2.3.175, 3.1.30.
7 *Ibid.*, 20; Patterson, *Shakespeare and the Popular Voice*, 127; emphasis in the original.
8 James I, "The Kings Verses," Folger MS V.b.303, fol. 264–65.
9 Arnold, *Third Citizen*, 10.
10 January 4, 1649, *Journal of the House of Commons* 6 (1802): 110.
11 See William Prynne, *The Soveraigne Power of Parliaments and Kingdoms* (London, 1643).
12 William Prynne, *Minors No Senators, or a Briefe Discourse Proving That Infants Under the Age of 21 Yeares Are Uncapable in Point of Law of Being Members of Parliament*, 1st ed. (London, 1646), 8.
13 Andrew Thrush, "Introductory Survey," *The House of Commons, 1604–29*, 6 vols. (Cambridge: Cambridge University Press for the History of Parliament Trust, 2010), vol. 1, 65.
14 Holly Brewer, *By Birth or Consent: Children, Law, and the Anglo-American Revolution in Authority* (Chapel Hill: University of North Carolina Press, 2005), 26.
15 See Clive Holmes, "Colonel King and Lincolnshire Politics, 1642–46," *The Historical Journal* 16 (1973): 471–74.
16 Prynne, *Minors No Senators*, 4.
17 Hanna Fenichel Pitkin, *The Concept of Representation* (Berkeley: University of California Press, 1972), 35, 93.
18 *Ibid.*, 110.
19 *Ibid.*, 110.
20 *Ibid.*, 101.
21 Quentin Skinner, "Hobbes on Representation," *European Journal of Philosophy* 13 (2005): 155–84.

22 Henry Parker, *Jus Populi* (London, 1644), 18.

23 See also Parker's (anonymous) descriptions of the "Art and peaceable Order" of representation in *Observations Upon Some of his Majesties Late Answers and Expresses* (London, 1642), 15.

24 Parker, *Jus Populi*, 18.

25 Prynne, *Minors No Senators*, 15 and *Histrio-Mastix* (London, 1633), 48. The figure of the cipher as a metaphor for political representation was a fairly common one that could serve either a laudatory or pejorative function: Polixines, in Shakespeare's *Winter's Tale*, claims that his "thanks" are magnified thousands of times because "like a cipher, / Yet standing in rich place, I multiply" (1.2.6–7); William Davenant disparages court counselors for "adding Cyphers" to already sufficient monarchical power, in *Gondibert* (1651), ed. David F. Gladish (Oxford: Clarendon, 1971), 2.2.14; and Milton uses the term to disparage monarchs as mere figureheads in *The Readie and Easie Way* (*CPW* 7:426).

26 Prynne, *Minors No Senators*, 13.

27 Howard Thomas, Earl of Suffolk, to the Treasurer and Chamberlains of Walden, 23 February 1603/4, British Library Egerton MS 2644, fol. 138.

28 James Welwood, *Memoirs of the Most Material Transactions in England for the Last Hundred Years Preceding the Revolution in 1688*, 6th ed. (London, 1718), 226.

29 Francis Bacon, "A Letter to the King Advising Him to Call a Parliament," 1615, *The Letters and The Life of Francis Bacon*, ed. James Spedding, 7 vols. (London: Longmans, 1869), vol. 5, 181.

30 November 28, 1621, *Proceedings and Debates of the House of Commons, in 1620 and 1621. Collected by a Member of That House,* 2 vols. (Oxford: Clarendon Press, 1766), vol. 2, 227.

31 See February 13, 1626, *Proceedings in Parliament, 1626*, eds. William B. Bidwell and Maija Jansson, 2 vols. (New Haven: Yale University Press, 1992), vol. 2, 25.

32 Prynne, *Minors No Senators*, 11, 14.

33 *Ibid.*, 9.

34 William M. Lamont, *Marginal Prynne, 1600–1669* (London: Routledge, 1963), 41.

35 Prynne, *Minors No Senators*, 9.

36 William Prynne, *Minors No Senators ... As Now Reprinted With Some Inlargements*, 2nd ed. (London, 1661), 16.

37 Prynne, *Minors No Senators*, 3.

38 Prynne, *Histrio-Mastix*, 867, 916.

39 Prynne, *Minors No Senators*, 3.

40 *Ibid.*, 6.

41 Prynne, *Histrio-Mastix*, 788.

42 Prynne, *Minors No Senators*, 3.

43 Michael Witmore, *Pretty Creatures: Children and Fiction in the English Renaissance* (Ithaca: Cornell University Press, 2007), 35.

44 Prynne, *Histrio-Mastix*, 908.

45 Prynne, *Minors No Senators*, 10.

46 *Ibid.*, 14–15.

47 Brewer, *By Birth or Consent*, 30. For the bill, see the entry for December 16, 1653, *Acts and Ordinances of the Interregnum, 1642–1660*, eds. C. H. Firth and R. S. Rait, 3 vols. (London: HMSO, 1911), vol. 2, 817.

48 See for example George Savile, *Some Cautions Offered to the Consideration of Those Who Are to Chuse Members to Serve in the Ensuing Parliament* (London, 1695), 16.

49 Prynne, *Minors No Senators*, 1, 7.

50 For humanist anxiety over "soft and effeminate" poetry, see Richard Helgerson, *The Elizabethan Prodigals* (Berkeley: University of California Press, 1976), 35; Frances E. Dolan, "Taking the Pencil out of God's Hand: Art, Nature, and the Face-Painting Debate in Early Modern England," *PMLA* 108 (1993): 224–39; and Mary Ellen Lamb, "Apologizing for Pleasure in Sidney's Apology for Poetry: The Nurse of Abuse Meets the Tudor Grammar School," *Criticism* 36 (1994): 499–519.

51 See Walter J. Ong, "Latin Language Study as a Renaissance Puberty Rite," *Studies in Philology* 56 (1959): 103–24.

52 Philip Sidney, "The Defence of Poesie," *Prose Works of Sir Philip Sidney*, ed. Albert Feuillerat, 4 vols. (Cambridge: Cambridge University Press, 1962), vol. 3, 29.

53 *Ibid.*, 20.

54 *Ibid.*, 20.

55 Prynne, *Histrio-Mastix*, 79. Prynne is translating freely from Isidore of Seville, *Sententiae*, ed. Pierre Cazier (Turnhout: Brepols, 1998), bk. 3, ch. 13, sec. 2.

56 Prynne, *Histrio-Mastix*, 79.

57 Philip Sidney, *The Poems of Sir Philip Sidney*, ed. William A. Ringler (Oxford: Clarendon, 1962), 11.6–8.

58 Richard Helgerson, *Self-Crowned Laureates: Spenser, Jonson, Milton, and the Literary System* (Berkeley: University of California Press, 1983), 61.

59 John Smith, *The Mysterie of Rhetorique Unvail'd* (London, 1656), 251–52.

60 Bartholomaeus Anglicus, *Batman Uppon Bartholome His Booke De Proprietatibus Rerum*, trans. Stephen Batman (London, 1582), sig. O1r. The close associations of childhood, language, and destabilizing desire make it tempting to invoke Lacan's notion that language constructs desire as an effect of the child's frustrated attempt to make "his need pass through the defiles of the signifier," as described in *Écrits*, trans. Bruce Fink (New York: Norton, 2006), 525. In early modern writing, however, desire is both an inborn condition of childhood and a characteristic of a very specific, poetic discourse; as men age and embrace more serious pursuits, their capacity for authoritative speech is meant to close the "gap opened up by the effect of signifiers" and eliminate wayward desire (*Ibid.*, 525).

61 Stephen Gosson, *The Schoole of Abuse* (London, 1579), title page.

62 See Katherine Duncan-Jones, *Sir Philip Sidney: Courtier Poet* (London: Hamish Hamilton, 1991), 232–35; and Arthur F. Kinney, *Markets of*

Bawdrie: The Dramatic Criticism of Stephen Gosson (Salzburg: Institute for English Language and Literature, 1974).

63 Gosson, *Schoole of Abuse*, sig. A6r.

64 For Gosson as a prodigal writer, see Helgerson, *Elizabethan Prodigals*, 66–69.

65 Richard Mulcaster, *Positions Wherein those Primitive Circumstances Be Examined Which are Necessarie for the Training up of Children* (1581), ed. Robert Herbert Quick (New York: Longmans, 1888), 141.

66 Roger Ascham, *The Scholemaster, or Plaine and Perfite Way of Teachyng Children* (1570), in *English Works*, ed. William Aldis Wright (Cambridge: Cambridge University Press, 1904), 189; Henry Peacham, *The Compleat Gentleman* (London, 1634), 22.

67 See Rebecca W. Bushnell, *A Culture of Teaching: Early Modern Humanism in Theory and Practice* (Ithaca: Cornell University Press, 1996), 73–116; and Mary Thomas Crane, *Framing Authority: Sayings, Self, and Society in Sixteenth-Century England* (Princeton: Princeton University Press, 1993), 68–70.

68 Mulcaster, *Positions*, 270. For the performances of Mulcaster's boys see Joy Leslie Gibson, *Squeaking Cleopatras: The Elizabethan Boy Player* (Phoenix Mill: Sutton, 2000), 173.

69 James G. Turner, *Schooling Sex: Libertine Literature and Erotic Education in Italy, France, and England, 1534–1685* (Oxford: Oxford University Press, 2003), 42.

70 Gosson, *Schoole of Abuse*, sig. A6r.

71 *Ibid.*, sig. A6r.

72 Anonymous, *A Second and Third Blast of Retrait from Plaies and Theaters* (London, 1580), 110–11. For the theory that the tract was actually authored by the playwright Anthony Munday, see Nora Johnson, *The Actor as Playwright in Early Modern Drama* (Cambridge: Cambridge University Press, 2003), 84–121.

73 John Stockwood, *A Sermon Preached at Paules Crosse on Barthelmew Day* (London, 1578), 23.

74 John Stockwood, *A Very Fruiteful Sermon Preched at Paules Crosse the Tenth of May Last* (London, 1579), sig. K5v.

75 See Jacqueline Miller's discussion of theories of mimesis whereby the audiences is "infected" by the literary work or the rhetor, "The Passions Signified: Imitation and the Construction of Emotions in Sidney and Wroth," *Criticism* 43 (2001): 407–21.

76 Anonymous, *A Second and Third Blast*, 104.

77 Gosson, *Schoole of Abuse*, sig. A6v.

78 Prynne, *Histrio-Mastix*, 174.

79 *Ibid.*, 314–15, 515.

80 *Ibid.*, 145.

81 Prynne, *Minors No Senators*, 9.

82 *Ibid.*, 8.

83 Arnold, *Third Citizen*, 34.

84 Prynne, *Minors No Senators ... As Now Reprinted*, sig. A2r.

85 Arnold, *Third Citizen*, 190. See also Ilana Krausman Ben-Amos, *The Culture of Giving: Informal Support and Gift-Exchange in Early Modern England* (Cambridge: Cambridge University Press, 2008), 171–75.

86 Mark Knights, *Representation and Misrepresentation in Later Stuart Britain: Partisanship and Political Culture* (Oxford: Oxford University Press, 2006), 177. For specific examples, see John K. Gruenfelder, *Influence in Early Stuart Elections, 1604–1640* (Columbus: Ohio State University Press, 1981), 19–21, and Kishlansky, *Parliamentary Selection*, 196.

87 Prynne, *Minors No Senators ... As Now Reprinted*, sig. A2r.

88 "The Englysh Anarchye," Folger MS V.B. 303, f. 325. A version of this poem is printed with substantial variations in W. Walker Wilkins (ed.), *Political Ballads of the Seventeenth and Eighteenth Centuries*, 2 vols. (London: Longman, 1860).

89 See Duncan-Jones, *Sir Philip Sidney*, 44–62.

90 See Robert Filmer, *The Free-holder's Grand Inquest*, in *Patriarcha and Other Writings*, ed. Johann P. Sommerville (Cambridge: Cambridge University Press, 1991), 69–130.

91 William Prynne, *The Third Tome of an Exact Chronological Vindication and Historical Demonstration of our British, Roman, Saxon, Norman, English Kings Supreme Ecclesiastical Jurisdiction* (London, 1665), sig. A2v. For Prynne's view of this text as his crowning contribution to the discourse of sovereignty, see William Lamont, *Puritanism and Historical Controversy* (Montreal: McGill-Queen's University Press, 1996), 67–68.

92 Prynne, *Minors No Senators*, 10.

93 Charles Herle, *A Fuller Answer to a Treatise Written by Doctor Ferne* (London, 1642), 25.

94 See Deborah Baumgold, *Hobbes's Political Theory* (Cambridge: Cambridge University Press, 1988), 45–48.

95 Prynne, *Minors No Senators*, 10.

96 *Ibid.*, 11–12.

97 Anthony Ashley Cooper, Earl of Shaftesbury, *Some Observations Concerning the Regulating of Elections for Parliament* (London, 1689), 13.

CHAPTER 3. CONTRACT'S CHILDREN

1 Jacques Rancière, *Dis-agreement: Politics and Philosophy*, trans. Julie Rose (Minneapolis: University of Minnesota Press, 1999), 50.

2 Philip Abbott, "The Three Families of Thomas Hobbes," *The Review of Politics* 43 (1981), 243; Su Fang Ng, *Literature and the Politics of Family in Seventeenth-Century England* (Cambridge: Cambridge University Press, 2007), 94. See also Gilbert Meilaender, "'A Little Monarchy': Hobbes on the Family," *Thought* 53 (1978): 401–15; Gordon J. Schochet, *The Authoritarian Family and Political Attitudes in 17th Century England: Patriarchalism in Political Thought*, 2nd ed. (London: Transaction, 1988), 225–43; Carole Pateman,

The Sexual Contract (Stanford: Stanford University Press, 1988), 19–37; and Nancy J. Hirschmann, *Gender, Class, and Freedom in Modern Political Theory* (Princeton: Princeton University Press, 2008), 29–77.

3 Thomas Hobbes, "To the Reader," *The Illiads and Oddysses of Homer*, in *The English Works of Thomas Hobbes*, ed. William Molesworth, 11 vols. (London: Longman, 1839–45), vol. 10, v.

4 See Leo Strauss, *The Political Philosophy of Hobbes: Its Basis and Genesis*, trans. Elsa M. Sinclair (Chicago: University of Chicago Press, 1952); John W. N. Watkins, *Hobbes's System of Ideas: A Study in the Political Significance of Philosophical Theories*, 2nd ed. (London: Hutchinson, 1973); David P. Gauthier, *The Logic of Leviathan: The Moral and Political Theory of Thomas Hobbes* (Oxford: Clarendon, 1969); and Jean Hampton, *Hobbes and the Social Contract Tradition* (Cambridge: Cambridge University Press, 1986).

5 See Howard Warrender, *The Political Philosophy of Hobbes: His Theory of Obligation* (Oxford: Clarendon, 1957).

6 For an especially deft update and revision of the Warrender thesis, see Deborah Baumgold, *Hobbes's Political Theory* (Cambridge: Cambridge University Press, 1988). For the historical-contextual approach as a response to Warrender, see Quentin Skinner's important essay, "The Ideological Context of Hobbes's Political Thought," *The Historical Journal* 9 (1966): 268–317. This approach is developed by Johann P. Sommerville, *Thomas Hobbes: Political Ideas in Historical Context* (Basingstoke: Macmillan, 1992), and Deborah Baumgold, *Contract Theory in Historical Context: Essays on Grotius, Hobbes, and Locke* (Leiden: Brill, 2010).

7 David Johnston, *The Rhetoric of Leviathan: Thomas Hobbes and the Politics of Cultural Transformation* (Princeton: Princeton University Press, 1989), 98; Quentin Skinner, *Reason and Rhetoric in the Philosophy of Hobbes* (Cambridge: Cambridge University Press, 1997), 5.

8 Cicero, *De Finibus Bonorum et Malorum*, ed. L. D. Reynolds (Oxford: Clarendon, 1998), bk. 5, ch. 23, sec. 64, 182: "In omni autem honesto de quo loquimur nihil est tam inlustre nec quod latius pateat quam coniunctio inter homines hominum et quasi quaedam societas et communicatio utilitatum et ipsa caritas generis humani. Quae nata a primo satu, quod a procreatoribus nati diliguntur et tota domus coniugio et stirpe coniungitur, serpit sensim foras, cognationibus primum, tum adfinitatibus, deinde amicitiis, post vicinitatibus, tum civibus et iis qui publice socii atque amici sunt, deinde totius complexu gentis humanae. Quae animi adfectio … iustitia dicitur." Pufendorf cites the passage but does not quote it, in *The Law of Nature and Nations* (London, 1749), bk. 2, ch. 2, sec. 2, 100.

9 See Cicero, *De Oratore*, ed. H. Rackham, Loeb Classical Library, 2 vols. (Cambridge, MA: Harvard University Press, 1941), vol. 2, bk. 3, ch. 53, sec. 204.

10 Thomas Wilson, *The Arte of Rhetorique* (London, 1553), sig. Bb3v.

11 John Bramhall, *The Serpent Salve or A Remedie for the Biting of an Aspe Wherein the Observators Grounds are Discussed* (London, 1643), 105.

12 Schochet, *Patriarchalism in Political Thought*, 90–91.

13 Thomas Bayly, *The Royal Charter Granted Unto Kings by God Himself and Collected Out of His Holy Word in Both Testaments* (London, 1649), 92.

14 The Authorized Version of 1611, commissioned by King James, emphasizes the "nursing father" in ways the popular Geneva bible did not; in the Geneva version of Numbers 11.12, for example, Moses carries his people "as a nurse beareth ye sucking child." For a medieval romance version of the monstrous, toothy child see *Sir Gowther*, in *The Middle English Breton Lays*, ed. Anne Laskaya and Eve Salisbury (Kalamazoo: Medieval Institute, 1995), 120–36.

15 See Alan Stewart, *The Cradle King: The Life of James VI and I* (New York: St. Martin's, 2003), 206.

16 See also *DC* 11.5.183 and *L* 2.43.610.

17 Ng, *Literature and the Politics of Family*, 45.

18 For the description of Charles's death as a parricide, see Claudius Salmasius, *Defensio Regia pro Carolo I* (Paris, 1649), 26–27.

19 See Victoria Kahn, *Wayward Contracts: The Crisis of Political Obligation in England, 1640–1674* (Princeton: Princeton University Press, 2004), 67–69 and 83–111. For the sixteenth-century origins of this "discourse of indiscernible – and thus potentially uncontainable – dissent," see Lowell Gallagher, *Medusa's Gaze: Casuistry and Conscience in the Renaissance* (Stanford: Stanford University Press, 1991), 2.

20 Pateman, *Sexual Contract*, 45–50. See also Carole Pateman, "'God Hath Ordained to Man a Helper': Hobbes, Patriarchy, and Conjugal Right," *Feminist Interpretations and Political Theory*, eds. Mary Lyndon Shanley and Carole Pateman (Cambridge: Polity Press, 1991), 50–74.

21 Thomas Hobbes, *The Art of Rhetoric* (London: 1681), 70–71.

22 Strauss, *Political Philosophy*, 30–43.

23 See *EL* 2.1.6.111, as well as Hobbes's description of fear as "the Passion to be reckoned upon" in *L* 1.14.200. For the most thorough treatment of Hobbes's passion of fear, see Strauss, *Political Philosophy*, 12.

24 Hampton, *Hobbes and the Social Contract*, 35. See also Gregory S. Kavka, *Hobbesian Moral and Political Theory* (Princeton: Princeton University Press, 1986), 179; and George Schedler, "Hobbes on the Basis of Political Obligation," *Journal of the History of Philosophy* 15 (1977): 167.

25 Hampton, *Hobbes and the Social Contract*, 39.

26 Hobbes, *Art of Rhetoric*, 74.

27 Pateman, *Sexual Contract*, 49.

28 Hugo Grotius, *De Jure Belli ac Pacis* (1625), ed. William Whewell, 3 vols. (Cambridge: Cambridge University Press, 1853), vol. 2, bk. 2, ch. 11, sec. 4: "Quod autem fit animo non deliberato, id nos quoque ad vim obligandi non credimus pertinere." For the much-debated question of whether and how much Grotius influenced Hobbes, see Martin Harvey, "Grotius and Hobbes," *British Journal for the History of Philosophy* 14 (2006): 27–50.

29 Grotius, *De Jure Belli*, vol. 2, 2.11.5: "Ideo et furiosi, et amentis, et infantis nulla est promissio. Aliud censendum de minoribus, hi enim etsi non satis

firmum judicium habere credantur, ut et foeminae, id tamen nec perpetuum est, nec per se sufficit ad actus vim elidendam. Quando autem puer ratione uti incipiat, non potest certo definiri: sed ex quotidianis actibus, aut etiam ex eo quod communiter in quaque regione accidit, desumendum est."

30 See Hamilton Vreeland, *Hugo Grotius: The Father of the Modern Science of International Law* (New York: Oxford University Press, 1917), 24; and Charles S. Edwards, *Hugo Grotius, The Miracle of Holland: A Study in Political and Legal Thought* (Chicago: Nelson Hall, 1981), 1–3.

31 Grotius, *De Jure Belli*, 1:2.5.1.

32 *Ibid.*, 1:2.5.1.

33 *Ibid.*, 1:2.5.5.

34 *Ibid.*, 1:2.5.8.

35 Victoria Silver, "Hobbes on Rhetoric," *The Cambridge Companion to Hobbes*, ed. Tom Sorell (Cambridge: Cambridge University Press, 1996), 340.

36 Robert Filmer, *Observations Concerning the Originall of Government, upon Mr. Hobs 'Leviathan', Mr. Milton against Salmasius, H. Grotius 'De Jure Belli'*, in *Patriarcha and Other Writings*, ed. Johann P. Sommerville (Cambridge: Cambridge University Press, 1991), 228.

37 *Ibid.*, 228.

38 Filmer, *The Anarchy of a Limited or Mixed Monarchy*, in *Patriarcha and Other Writings*, 142.

39 *Ibid.*, 142.

40 *Ibid.*, 142.

41 Filmer, *Observations Concerning the Original of Government*, 192.

42 William Prynne, *Minors No Senators*, 1st ed. (London, 1646), 10.

43 My translation of *DC* 8.1.160: "Ut redeamus iterum in statum naturalem, consideremusque homines tanquam si essent iamiam subito e terra (fungorum more) exorti & adulti, sine omni unius ad alterum obligatione."

44 Skinner, *Reason and Rhetoric*, 303–15. For the axiomatic method of later contract theory, see the "original condition" of John Rawls, a "purely hypothetical situation" where "no one knows his place in society, his class position or social status, nor does any one know his fortune in the distribution of natural assets and abilities," in *A Theory of Justice* (Harvard: Harvard University Press, 1971), 12. For Cadmus and the dragon's teeth see Ovid, *Metamorphoses*, ed. Frank Justus Miller, Loeb Classical Library, 2 vols. (Harvard: Harvard University Press, 1916), vol. 1, 3.103–30.

45 Mary Nyquist, "Hobbes, Slavery, and Despotical Rule," *Representations* 106 (2009): 4.

46 Pateman, *Sexual Contract*, 47.

47 Nyquist, "Hobbes," 4.

48 Strauss, *Political Philosophy*, 124–25.

49 Nyquist, "Hobbes," 9. For the English edition's translation, see Thomas Hobbes, *De Cive: The English Version*, ed. Howard Warrender (Oxford: Clarendon, 1983), 9.7.124.

50 Nyquist, "Hobbes," 17.

51 Filmer, *Observations Upon Aristotle's Politiques*, in *Patriarcha and Other Writings*, 236–37.

52 Jon Parkin, *Taming the Leviathan: The Reception of the Political and Religious Ideas of Thomas Hobbes in England 1640–1700* (Cambridge: Cambridge University Press, 2007), 12.

53 See Vere Chappell's introduction to *Hobbes and Bramhall on Liberty and Necessity*, ed. Vere Chappell (Cambridge: Cambridge University Press, 1999), ix–xxiv; and Samuel I. Mintz, *The Hunting of Leviathan: Seventeenth-century Reactions to the Materialism and Moral Philosophy of Thomas Hobbes* (Cambridge: Cambridge University Press, 1962).

54 John Bramhall, *Castigations of Mr. Hobbes His Last Animadversions in the Case Concerning Liberty and Universal Necessity* (London, 1657), 531.

55 Bramhall, *Castigations*, 534.

56 William Lucy, *Observations, Censures, and Confutations of Notorious Errours in Mr. Hobbes His Leviathan and Other His Bookes* (London, 1663), 137; Thomas Tenison, *The Creed of Mr. Hobbes Examined in a Feigned Conference Between Him and a Student in Divinity* (London, 1670), 131–32.

57 John Eachard, *Mr. Hobbs's State of Nature Considered in a Dialogue Between Philautus and Timothy* (London, 1672), 79.

58 John Bramhall, *A Defence of True Liberty from Antecedent and Extrinsecall Necessity Being an Answer to a Late Book of Mr. Thomas Hobbs of Malmsbury* (London, 1655), 190.

59 *Ibid.*, 225.

60 See also Tenison, *The Creed of Mr. Hobbes*, 132; and Lucy, *Observations*, 139.

61 Bramhall, *Castigations*, 531.

62 *Ibid.*, 471.

63 Thomas Hobbes, *Of Libertie and Necessitie* (London, 1654), 8.

64 Parkin, *Taming the Leviathan*, 56.

65 Hobbes, *Of Libertie and Necessitie*, 11–12.

66 See *DC*, praefatio, 81; and Hobbes, *De Cive: The English Version*, "The Author's Preface," 33.

67 See Richard Tuck, "Warrender's *De Cive*," in *Thomas Hobbes: Critical Assessments*, ed. Peter King (London: Routledge, 1992), 423–26. See also Richard Tuck and Michael Silverthorne's introduction to *On the Citizen*, by Thomas Hobbes (Cambridge: Cambridge University Press, 1998), xxxvii.

68 See Howard Warrender's introduction to *De Cive: The Latin Version*, 1–5.

69 Baumgold, *Hobbes's Political Theory*, 1.

70 Roger Ascham, *The Scholemaster, or Plaine and Perfite Way of Teachyng Children* (1570), in *English Works*, ed. William Aldis Wright (Cambridge: Cambridge University Press, 1904), 205.

71 John Brinsley, *Ludus Literarius, or the Grammar School* (London, 1612), 278, 276.

72 Pateman, *Sexual Contract*, 2, 3.

73 See, for example, Richard Baxter, *The Catechizing of Families* (London, 1683).

74 Abbott, "The Three Families of Thomas Hobbes," 246.

75 Samuel Rutherford, *Lex, Rex* (London, 1644), 225.

76 Peter O. King, "Thomas Hobbes's Children," *The Philosopher's Child: Critical Perspectives in the Western Tradition*, ed. Susan M. Turner and Gareth B. Matthews (Rochester: University of Rochester Press, 1998), 72.

77 Thomas Hobbes, *Leviathan, sive de Materia, Forma, & Potestate Civitatis Ecclesiasticae et Civilis* (London, 1676), 2.20.100. The use of "debet," to owe as a debt, is not an inevitable word choice. There are other ways to say that "one owes life" to another, such as Cicero's formulation, "through whom he lives [*propter quos vivit*]," in "Pro Milone Oratio," *Orationes*, ed. Albert Clark, 2nd ed., 6 vols. (Oxford: Clarendon, 1916), vol. 2, 22.

78 Schochet, *Patriarchalism in Political Thought*, 241–42. See also Abbot, "The Three Families of Thomas Hobbes," 246.

79 Hobbes, *Leviathan, sive de Materia, Forma, & Potestate*, 2.30.160.

80 For a nearly identical description of the child's mind, see Hobbes's fellow member of the Great Tew Circle, John Earle, *Micro-cosmographie* (London, 1628), sig. B1v.

81 Skinner, *Reason and Rhetoric*, 363.

82 Thomas Hobbes, "The Answer of Mr. Hobbes to Sir Will. D'Avenant's Preface Before Gondibert," in *Gondibert*, ed. David F. Gladish (Oxford: Clarendon, 1971), 45.

83 See *EL* 1.10.52. For the argument that *Leviathan* attempts to limit the destabilizing passion of vainglory, or "the pathology of mimetic desire," by harnessing the romance imagination within contractual bounds, see Kahn, *Wayward Contracts*, 170.

84 William Davenant, *Gondibert*, ed. David F. Gladish (Oxford: Clarendon, 1971), "The Author's Preface to his Much Honor'd Friend, M. Hobbes," 7.

85 *Ibid.*, 38.

86 *Ibid.*, 13.

87 *Ibid.*, 2.8.22.

88 For the argument that the close relationship between Hobbes and Davenant helps account for *Leviathan*'s return to rhetoric, see Ted H. Miller, "The Uniqueness of *Leviathan*: Authorizing Poets, Philosophers, and Sovereigns," *Leviathan After 350 Years*, ed. Tom Sorell and Luc Foisneau (Oxford: Oxford University Press, 2004), 75–103.

89 Hobbes, "To the Reader," *The Illiads and Oddysses of Homer*, 10:v.

CHAPTER 4. "PERPLEX'T PATHS"

1 J. Martin Evans, *The Miltonic Moment* (Lexington: University Press of Kentucky, 1998), 5.

2 Patricia A. Parker, *Inescapable Romance: Studies in the Poetics of a Mode* (Princeton: Princeton University Press, 1979), 118. For poetic pendency as a manifestation of Milton's "anally retentive personality," see John T. Shawcross, *John Milton: The Self and the World* (Lexington: University Press of Kentucky, 1993), 66; for a feminist reading, see Mary Loeffelholz, "Two Masques of

Ceres and Proserpine: *Comus* and *The Tempest*," in *Re-membering Milton*, ed. Mary Nyquist and Margaret W. Ferguson (London: Methuen, 1988), 37.

3 See David Norbrook, "The Reformation of the Masque," in *The Court Masque*, ed. David Lindley (Manchester: Manchester University Press, 1984), 94–110; Georgia B. Christopher, "The Virginity of Faith: *Comus* as a Reformation Conceit," *ELH* 43 (1976): 479–99; Maryann Cale McGuire, *Milton's Puritan Masque* (Athens: University of Georgia Press, 1983), 6; and Cedric C. Brown, *John Milton's Aristocratic Entertainments* (Cambridge: Cambridge University Press, 1985).

4 Jonson, *Pleasure Reconciled to Virtue* (7:485); Thomas Carew, *Coelum Brittanicum* (London, 1640), 212.

5 Victoria Kahn, *Machiavellian Rhetoric: From the Counter-Reformation to Milton* (Princeton: Princeton University Press, 1994), 196–97.

6 For the relation of the *Mask* to Michaelmas, see Brown, *Milton's Aristocratic Entertainments*, 38–40, and William B. Hunter, "The Liturgical Context of Comus," *ELN* 10 (1972): 11–15.

7 Brown, *Milton's Aristocratic Entertainments*, 40–41.

8 John Boys, *The Third Part from S. John Baptists Nativitie to the Last Holie Day in the Whole Yeere [Exposition of the Festivall Epistles and Gospels Used in Our English Liturgie]* (London, 1615), 110.

9 *Ibid.*, 110.

10 *Ibid.*, 110.

11 *Ibid.*, 110–11.

12 *Ibid.*, 114.

13 Leah S. Marcus, *Childhood and Cultural Despair: A Theme and Variations in Seventeenth-Century Literature* (Pittsburgh: University of Pittsburgh Press, 1978), 41, 75.

14 Boys, *Third Part*, 113.

15 Barbara K. Lewalski, "Milton's *Comus* and the Politics of Masquing," in *The Politics of the Stuart Court Masque*, ed. David Bevington and Peter Holbrook (Cambridge: Cambridge University Press, 1998), 314.

16 A. S. P. Woodhouse, "The Argument of Milton's *Comus*," *University of Toronto Quarterly* 11 (1942): 46–71. For an argument that subsumes much of this debate, suggesting that manifestations of grace and providence permeate the *Mask* in various forms, see Brown, *Milton's Aristocratic Entertainments*, 122–23.

17 See also the claims for the *Mask*'s theological orthodoxy in Catherine Gimelli Martin, "The Non-Puritan Ethics, Metaphysics, and Aesthetics of Milton's Spenserian Masque," *Milton Quarterly* 37 (2003): 215–44.

18 Gordon Campbell and Thomas N. Corns, *John Milton: Life, Work, and Thought* (Oxford: Oxford University Press, 2008), 84.

19 See Herbert Berry, "The Miltons and the Blackfriar's Playhouse," *Modern Philology* 89 (1992): 510–14.

20 Keith Thomas, "Age and Authority in Early Modern England," *Proceedings of the British Academy* 62 (1997): 205–48.

21 Stephen M. Fallon, *Milton's Peculiar Grace: Self-Representation and Authority* (Ithaca: Cornell University Press, 2007), 60. See also Barbara K. Lewalski, *The Life of John Milton: A Critical Biography* (Oxford: Blackwell, 2000), 74.

22 See Campbell and Corns, *John Milton*, 67.

23 For a suggestive account of Randolph's fame and influence on Milton, see Ann Baynes Coiro, "Anonymous Milton, or A *Maske* Masked," *ELH* 71 (2004): 609–29.

24 Michael Drayton, *Endimion and Phoebe Ideas Latmus* (London, 1595), sig. G1v. For the classical heritage and literary afterlife of Endymion, see David Bevington's introduction to *Endymion*, by John Lyly (Manchester: Manchester University Press, 1996), 9–11.

25 Milton, *Facsimile of the Manuscript of Milton's Minor Poems: Preserved in the Library of Trinity College, Cambridge*, ed. William Aldis Wright (Cambridge: Cambridge University Press, 1899), fol. 7.

26 For romance as a genre defined by error, see Patricia A. Parker, *Inescapable Romance: Studies in the Poetics of a Mode* (Princeton: Princeton University Press, 1979), 16–53.

27 Roy Flannagan, introduction to *A Maske*, by John Milton, *The Riverside Milton* (Boston: Houghton-Mifflin, 1998), 111.

28 *The Statutes at Large*, 14 vols. (London, 1786), vol. 2, 4–5 Philip and Mary, C8, 499–500.

29 *Statutes at Large*, 4–5 P &M, C8, 500.

30 Matthew Hale, *Historia Placitorum Coronae*, 2 vols. (London: 1800), vol. 1, 660.

31 *Ibid.*, 1:25.

32 Stephen Orgel, "The Case for Comus," *Representations* 81 (2003): 32.

33 For Egerton's position as a shaping force on the *Mask*, see G. F. Sensabaugh, "The Milieu of *Comus*," *John Milton: 20th-Century Perspectives*, ed. J. Martin Evans, 5 vols. (New York: Routledge: 2003), vol. 2, 268–82.

34 J. C. Maxwell, "*Comus*, Line 37," *Notes and Queries* 9 (1959): 364.

35 Virgil, *The Aeneid of Virgil*, 2 vols., ed. R. D. Williams (London: Macmillan, 1972), vol. 2, 9.181.

36 *Ibid.*, 9.391–92.

37 Joseph Glanvill, *Essays on Several Important Subjects in Philosophy and Religion* (London, 1676), 15–16.

38 Boys, *Third Part*, 110.

39 Desiderius Erasmus, *Declamatio de Pueris Statim ac Liberaliter Instituendis*, in *Opera Omnia*, 10 vols. (Hildesheim: Georg Olms, 1961), vol. 1, 493.

40 *Ibid.*, 494: "Si qua Thessala mulier esset, qua malis artibus posset & conaretur filium tuum in suem aut lupum vertere, none putares nullum supplicium fatis dignum illius scelere?"

41 John Brinsley, *A Consolation for our Grammar Schooles* (London, 1622), 26, 12.

42 Roger Ascham, *The Scholemaster* (1570), in *The English Works*, ed. William Aldis Wright (Cambridge: Cambridge University Press, 1904), 222.

43 *Ibid.*, 227.

44 *Ibid.*, 228.

45 Erica Fudge, *Perceiving Animals: Humans and Beasts in Early Modern English Culture* (Urbana: University of Illinois Press, 2002), 70–71. See also S. J. Wiseman, "Hairy on the Inside: Metamorphosis and Civility in English Werewolf Texts," *Renaissance Beasts: Of Animals, Humans, and Other Wonderful Creatures*, ed. Erica Fudge (Urbana: University of Illinois University Press, 2004), 50–57.

46 See Leo Miller, "Milton's Clash with Chappell: A Suggested Reconstruction," *Milton Quarterly* 14 (1980): 77–87; and J. Milton French (ed.), *The Life Records of John Milton*, 5 vols. (New Brunswick: Rutgers University Press, 1949–58), vol. 1, 106. On the (almost certainly apocryphal) story that Milton was "whipt" by Chappell, see Arthur Sherbo, "More on Milton's Rustication," *Milton Quarterly* 18 (1984): 22–24.

47 Milton's much-discussed invocations of Orpheus include *Lycidas* (58–63), *Paradise Lost* (7.32–38), and *Il Penseroso* (3). Such repetition signals a "recurrent anxiety" according to Harold Bloom, *A Map of Misreading* (Oxford: Oxford University Press, 2003), xv. See also Clifford Davidson, "The Young Milton, Orpheus, and Poetry," *English Studies* 59 (1978): 27–34; Stanley Fish, *How Milton Works* (Cambridge, MA: Belknap-Harvard, 2001), 295–300; and Michael Lieb, *Milton and the Culture of Violence* (Ithaca: Cornell University Press, 1994), 59–80.

48 See Virgil, *Georgics*, in *Virgil*, ed. and trans. H. Rushton Fairclough and rev. G. P. Goold, Loeb Classical Library, 2 vols. (Cambridge, MA: Harvard University Press, 1999), vol. 1, 4.522.

49 Milton, *Ad Patrem*, 50–52: "Denique quid vocis modulamen inane juvabit, / Verborum sensusque vacans, numerique loquacis? / Silvestres decet iste choros, non Orphea cantus."

50 J. Andrew Hubbell, "Comus: Milton's Re-Formation of the Masque," *Spokesperson Milton: Voices in Contemporary Criticism*, eds. Charles W. Durham and Kristin Pruitt McColgan (Selinsgrove: Susquehanna University Press, 1994), 204.

51 See Patricia Vicari, "The Triumph of Art, the Triumph of Death: Orpheus in Spenser and Milton," *Orpheus: The Metamorphosis of a Myth*, ed. John Warden (Toronto: University of Toronto Press, 1982), 207–30.

52 Boys, *Third Part*, 114.

53 *Ibid.*, 112.

54 See Hilda L. Smith, "Humanist Education and the Renaissance Concept of Woman," *Women and Literature in Britain, 1500–1700*, ed. Helen Wilcox (Cambridge: Cambridge University Press, 1999), 16–27.

55 For example, Robert Codrington says educated ladies "afford great pleasure in their Conversation to others," in *The Second Part of Youths Behaviour: Or Decency in Conversation Amongst Women* (London, 1672), 2.

56 William Shullenberger, "Tragedy in Translation: The Lady's Echo Song," *English Literary Renaissance* 33 (2003): 405. See also C. L. Barber, "A Mask

Presented at Ludlow Castle: The Masque as a Masque," *A Mask at Ludlow: Essays on Milton's Comus*, ed. John S. Diekhoff (Cleveland: Case Western Reserve University Press, 1968), 188–206; Louise Simons, "'And Heaven Gates Ore My Head': Death as Threshold in Milton's Masque," *Milton Studies* 23 (1987): 53–96; and Angus Fletcher, *The Transcendental Masque: An Essay on Milton's Comus* (Ithaca: Cornell University Press, 1972), 198–202.

57 George Sandys, *Ovid's Metamorphosis Englished, Mythologized and Represented in Figures* (Oxford, 1632), 106.

58 Orgel, "The Case for Comus," 40.

59 George Herbert, "Heaven," in *The Complete English Poems*, ed. John Tobin (London: Penguin, 1991), 12–13.

60 Lawes's setting of the song is reproduced by Hubert J. Foss, "The Airs of the Songs by Henry Lawes with His Version of the Words," in *A Maske at Ludlow: Essays on Milton's Comus*, ed. John S. Diekhoff (Cleveland: Case Western University Press, 1968), 241–50.

61 Orgel, "The Case for Comus," 40–41.

62 *Ibid.*, 40–41.

63 For explorations of the idea of mirroring and echo as part of the masque's deeper structure, see Simons, "And Heaven's Gates," 59; John Hollander, *The Figure of Echo: A Mode of Allusion in Milton and After* (Berkeley: University of California Press, 1981); and Jonathan Goldberg, *Voice Terminal Echo: Postmodernism and English Renaissance Texts* (New York: Methuen, 1986), 133–38.

64 Orgel, "The Case for Comus," 37. See also Jacqueline Disalvo, "Fear of Flying: Milton on the Boundaries Between Witchcraft and Inspiration," *ELR* 18 (1988): 114–37.

65 John Milton, *A Maske: The Earlier Versions*, ed. S. E. Sprott (Toronto: University of Toronto Press, 1973), TMS 167. Sprott provides parallel transcriptions of the Trinity Manuscript (TMS), Bridgewater Manuscript (BMS), and 1637 printing in this edition.

66 Leah S. Marcus, *The Politics of Mirth: Jonson, Herrick, Milton, Marvell, and the Defense of Old Holiday Pastimes* (Chicago: Chicago University Press, 1986), 189.

67 Fish, *How Milton Works*, 157.

68 *Ibid.*, 32.

69 Milton, *A Maske: The Earlier Versions*, TMS 167.

70 The Bridgewater MS is a presentation copy with an elaborate title page, but it seems to represent the closest thing we have to the performance text. For the authoritative account relating the various manuscripts to the order of the *Mask*'s composition, see S. E. Sprott's introduction to Milton, *A Maske: The Earlier Versions*, 3–33.

71 Milton, *A Maske: The Earlier Versions*, BMS 242.

72 For the development of counterpoint, see Edward E. Lowinsky, "Music in the Culture of the Renaissance," *Journal of the History of Ideas* 15 (1954): 509–53. For counterpoint as a literary trope, see Christle Collins Judd, *Reading*

Renaissance Music Theory: Hearing with the Eyes (Cambridge: Cambridge University Press, 2000), 41–50.

73 In addition to Fish's idea that Comus and the Lady represent diametrically opposed worldviews, see John D. Cox, "Poetry and History in Milton's Country Masque," *ELH* 44 (1977): 627, and Jesse G. Swan, "Imbodies and Imbrutes: Constructing Whiteness in Milton's *A Maske Presented at Ludlow Castle,*" *Clio* 33 (2004): 367–406.

74 William Shullenberger, *The Lady in the Labyrinth: Milton's* Comus *as Initiation* (Madison: Farleigh Dickinson University Press, 2008), 141.

75 See editorial glosses of "home-felt" in Stephen Orgel and Jonathan Goldberg (eds.), *John Milton: The Major Works* (Oxford: Oxford University Press, 1990), 764n51; John Carey (ed.), *Milton: Complete Shorter Poems,* 2nd ed. (London: Longman, 1997), 194n261; Roy Flannagan (ed.), *The Riverside Milton* (Boston: Houghton Mifflin, 1998), 135n171.

76 For Ferdinand's greeting of Miranda ("O you wonder!"), see William Shakespeare, *The Tempest,* in *The Norton Shakespeare,* ed. Stephen Greenblatt et al., 2nd ed. (New York: W. W. Norton, 2008), 1.2.427. See also John M. Major, "*Comus* and the *Tempest,*" *Shakespeare Quarterly* 10 (1959): 177–83.

77 For Evans, see Leah Marcus, "The Earl of Bridgewater's Legal Life: Notes toward a Political Reading of *Comus,*" *Milton Quarterly* 21 (1987): 13–23; and Leah S. Marcus, "Justice for Margery Evans: A 'Local' Reading of *Comus,*" *Milton and the Idea of Woman,* ed. Julia M. Walker (Urbana: University of Illinois Press, 1988), 66–85. For the Castlehaven Scandal, see Barbara Breasted, "*Comus* and the Castlehaven Scandal," *Milton Studies* 3 (1971): 201–24; and Rosemary Karmelich Mundhenk, "Dark Scandal and the Sun-Clad Power of Chastity: The Historical Milieu of Milton's *Comus,*" *SEL* 15 (1975): 141–52.

78 See Cynthia B. Herrup, *A House in Gross Disorder: Sex, Law, and the 2nd Earl of Castlehaven* (Oxford: Oxford University Press, 2001), 73–86.

79 Hale, *Historia Placitorum Coronae,* 1:660.

80 See, for example, Catherine Thomas, "Chaste Bodies and Poisonous Desires in Milton's *Mask,*" *SEL* 46 (2006): 450; and Ross Leasure, "Milton's Queer Choice: Comus at Castlehaven," *Milton Quarterly* 36 (May 2002): 63–86.

81 "unharboured, adj.," OED 2; "unblenched, adj.," OED 1; "arbitrate, v.," OED 2.b.

82 Carey (ed.), *Complete Shorter Poems,* 201n422, 201n423.

83 *Ibid.,* 201n420, 202n425, 202n428.

84 *Ibid.,* 202n431–6, 202n467; "embody, v.," OED 2; "imbrute, v.," OED 2.

85 Shakespeare, Sonnet 130, in *The Norton Shakespeare,* 6.

86 Fish, *How Milton Works,* 157.

87 Brown, *Milton's Aristocratic Entertainments,* 92.

88 "Words," the hermetic magus Cornelius Agrippa argued, "are the fittest medium betwixt the speaker and the hearer, carrying with them not only the conception of the mind, but also the vertue of the speaker with a certain efficacy unto the hearers, and this often-times with so great a power, that often-times they change not only the hearers, but also other bodies,

and things that have no life," in *Three Books of Occult Philosophy*, trans. J. F. (London, 1651), 152.

89 Milton, *A Maske: The Earlier Versions*, BMS 750.

90 *Ibid.*, TMS 803, 696. The passage containing the line "O my simplicity" is marked out heavily and replaced with a pasted leaf, as can be seen in Milton, *Facsimile of the Manuscript*, fol. 22, fol. 20.

91 See Coiro, "Anonymous Milton," 609–29. For the title page, see John Milton, *John Milton's Complete Poetical Works Reproduced in Photographic Facsimile*, ed. Harris Francis Fletcher, 4 vols. (Urbana: University of Illinois Press, 1943), vol. 1, 263.

92 *Ibid.*, 189–92.

93 *Ibid.*, 56. I have described this process in greater detail in the forthcoming "Revising Childhood in Milton's Ludlowe *Maske*," in *Young Milton: The Emerging Author, 1620–1642*, ed. Edward Jones (Oxford: Oxford University Press).

94 Blair Hoxby, "The Wisdom of Their Feet: Meaningful Dance in Milton and the Stuart Masque," *English Literary Renaissance* 37 (2007): 95.

95 Stella P. Revard, *Milton and the Tangles of Neara's Hair: The Making of the 1645 Poems* (Columbia: University of Missouri Press, 1997), 64.

96 Louis L. Martz, "The Rising Poet, 1645," *The Lyric and Dramatic Milton: Selected Papers from the English Institute*, ed. Joseph Summers (New York: Columbia University Press, 1965), 20.

CHAPTER 5. "CHILDREN OF REVIVING LIBERTIE"

1 Stanley Fish, *How Milton Works* (Cambridge, MA: Harvard University Press, 2001), 14, 189.

2 Barbara K. Lewalski, "Barbara K. Lewalski on Why Milton Matters," *Milton Studies* 44 (2005): 17. See also David Norbrook, "*Areopagitica*, Censorship, and the Early Modern Public Sphere," in *British Literature: 1640–1789, A Critical Reader*, ed. Robert DeMaria, Jr. (Oxford: Blackwell, 1999), 13–39. For a survey of the long roots of this continuing debate, see John T. Shawcross, "Spokesperson Milton," in *Spokesperson Milton: Voices in Contemporary Criticism*, eds. Charles W. Durham and Kristin Pruitt McColgan (Selinsgrove: Susquehanna University Press, 1994), 5–17.

3 Richard Halpern, *The Poetics of Primitive Accumulation: English Renaissance Culture and the Genealogy of Capital* (Ithaca: Cornell University Press, 1991), 38. Lisa Jardine and Anthony Grafton agree that humanism cultivated a "properly docile attitude toward authority," in *From Humanism to the Humanities* (Cambridge, MA: Harvard University Press, 1986), xiv. See also Catherine Belsey, *The Subject of Tragedy: Identity and Difference in Renaissance Drama* (London: Methuen, 1985), 125; and Catherine Belsey, *John Milton: Language, Gender, Power* (Oxford: Blackwell, 1988).

4 Rebecca W. Bushnell, *A Culture of Teaching: Early Modern Humanism in Theory and Practice* (Ithaca: Cornell University Press, 1996), 19.

5 See Timothy Raylor, "New Light on Milton and Hartlib," *Milton Quarterly* 27 (1993): 19–30.

6 See Mark Greengrass, Michael Leslie, and Timothy Raylor (eds.), *Samuel Hartlib and Universal Reformation: Studies in Intellectual Communication* (Cambridge: Cambridge University Press, 1994).

7 James G. Turner, *Schooling Sex: Libertine Literature and Erotic Education in Italy, France, and England, 1534–1685* (Oxford: Oxford University Press, 2003), 47.

8 See Robert E. Stillman, *The New Philosophy and Universal Languages in Seventeenth-Century England: Bacon, Hobbes, and Wilkins* (Lewisburg: Bucknell University Press, 1996), 14; and James G. Turner, "The Visual Realism of Comenius," *History of Education* 1 (1972): 113–38.

9 Jan Amos Comenius, *Orbis Pictus: A Facsimile of the First English Edition of 1659*, trans. Charles Hoole, ed. John E. Sadler (London: Oxford University Press, 1968), 88.

10 Jan Amos Comenius, *Didactica Magna*, in *Opera Didactica Omnia*, 3 vols., (Amsterdam, 1657; repr. Prague: Czechoslovak Academy of Sciences, 1957), vol. 1, ch. 6, sec. 5, 35: "Homini jam ante lapsum Scholam fuisse in Paradiso apertam, in qua sensim proficeret ... nam nec incessus nec loquela, nec ratiocinatio defuit: cognitionem tamen rerum, quae & quanta ab experientia venit, defuisse."

11 Joanna Picciotto, *Labors of Innocence in Early Modern England* (Cambridge, MA: Harvard University Press, 2010), 36.

12 Barbara K. Lewalski, *The Life of John Milton: A Critical Biography*, rev. ed. (Oxford: Blackwell, 2002),173.

13 Comenius, *Orbis Pictus*, 92.

14 This is an instance of "humanism converting through scientific revolution into modernity," as described by Angelica Duran, *The Age of Milton and the Scientific Revolution* (Pittsburgh: Duquesne University Press, 2007), 114.

15 Comenius, *Didactica Magna*, 16.35.76: "per interiorum partium poros alimentum subministrat." For familiar descriptions of children's minds as impressionable "wax" (*ceram*) or "moist and pliant" (*humidum & molle*), see *Ibid.*, 7.5.37.

16 Stillman, *The New Philosophy*, 36.

17 Comenius, *Didactica Magna*, 25.14.153; *Ibid.*, 25.10.151: "jocularem Plautum, lascivum Catullum, impurum Ovidium, impium ... Lucianum, obscaenum Martialem."

18 *Ibid.*, 25.19.156: "mixta quam optimis eduliis aut potionibus."

19 *Ibid.*, 25.14.153: "inebriat & in soporem collocat incautas mentes, illisque monstrosarum opinionum, periculosarum tentationum, teterrimarumque cupiditatum, somnia inducit."

20 Comenius, *Didactica Magna*, 32.2–5.185–86: "Inter consuetam & usurpatam hactenus, navamque hanc, instituendi formam, id appreat discriminis, quod inter ustitatam olim Libros multiplicandi artem Calamo & repertam post, usitatamque nunc jam, Typis, esse videmus. Nempe, ut quemadmodum

Typographiae ars, quanquam difficilior, sumptuosior, operosior, longe tamen ad celerius, certius, elegantius, libros exscribendum accomodatior: ita Methodus haec nova, quamvis initio difficultatibus terret, recepta tamen serviat erudiendis longe pluribus, certiorique cum profectu, & majore voluptate.... Fere modis scientias inscribi mentibus quibus externe illinuntur chartis. Quae causea est, cur non inepte fingi possit, & Didacticae huic novae adaptari nomen, ad nomen *Typographiae* alludens *didacografia*." My translation here is indebted to M. W. Keatinge (ed. and trans.), *The Great Didactic*, by Jan Amos Comenius (London: Adam and Charles Black, 1896), 439–41.

21 Comenius, *Didactica Magna*, 32.17.188. The passage also recommends that "our eyes must follow them wherever they turn" (*oculis comitandi sunt quoquo se vertunt*), a phrasing that would have suited Foucault's analysis of the Panopticon perfectly. See Michel Foucault, *Discipline and Punish: The Birth of the Prison*, trans. Alan Sheridan (New York: Vintage, 1979), 200–28.

22 Comenius, *Didactica Magna*, 23.7.134.

23 Belsey, *The Subject of Tragedy*, 125.

24 See Thomas Festa, *The End of Learning: Milton and Education* (New York: Routledge, 2006), 60–61; and Stanley E. Fish, *Surprised by Sin: The Reader in Paradise Lost* (Berkeley: University of California Press, 1967), 1–56.

25 Roger Ascham, *The Scholemaster* (1570), in *The English Works*, ed. William Aldis Wright (Cambridge: Cambridge University Press, 1904), 229.

26 Edward Phillips, "The Life of Mr. John Milton," in *The Early Lives of Milton*, ed. Helen Darbishire (New York: Barns and Noble, 1932), 60. Milton recommends these authors in *CPW* 2:395–96.

27 See Glenn Sucich, "'Not Without Dust and Heat': Alchemy and *Areopagitica,*" *Uncircumscribed Mind: Reading Milton Deeply*, eds. Charles W. Durham and Kristin A. Pruitt (Selinsgrove: Susquehanna University Press, 2008), 46–48.

28 Nigel Smith, "*Paradise Lost* and Heresy," *The Oxford Handbook of Milton*, eds. Nicholas McDowell and Nigel Smith (Oxford: Oxford University Press, 2009), 510. See also Nigel Smith, "Areopagitica: Voicing Contexts, 1643–5," in *Politics, Poetics and Hermeneutics in Milton's Prose*, eds. David Loewenstein and James Grantham Turner (Cambridge: Cambridge University Press, 1990), 107.

29 Ann Baynes Coiro, "'To repair the ruins of our first parents': *Of Education* and Fallen Adam," *SEL* 28 (1988): 133.

30 J. Milton French (ed.), *Life Records of John Milton*, 5 vols. (New Brunswick: Rutgers University Press, 1949–58; repr. New York: Gordian Press, 1966), vol. 2, 104.

31 See Smith, "Voicing Contexts," 108–13.

32 Phillip J. Donnelly, *Milton's Scriptural Reasoning: Narrative and Protestant Toleration* (Cambridge: Cambridge University Press, 2009), 37.

33 A. D. Nuttall argues that Milton does not, in fact, avoid the blasphemous theological implications in such moments and that this is the drama of his work, in *The Alternative Trinity: Gnostic Heresy in Marlowe, Milton, and Blake* (Oxford: Oxford University Press, 2007), 129–45. Although this remains a

minority view, it is an important reminder of the boldness of Milton's pedagogical assumptions.

34 Edmund Spenser, "A Letter of the Authors Expounding His *Whole Intention in the Course of thie Worke*," in *The Faerie Queene*, ed. A. C. Hamilton, Hiroshi Yamashita, and Toshiyuki Suzuki, 2nd ed. (London: Longman, 2001), 714.

35 For antinomian use of Paul's scripture, see Tom Hayes, "Diggers, Ranters, and Women Prophets: The Discourse of Madness and the Cartesian Cogito in Seventeenth-Century England," *Clio* 26 (1996): 29–50, and Paul M. Dowling, *Polite Wisdom: Heathen Rhetoric in Milton's Areopagitica* (Lanham: Rowman and Littlefield, 1995), 56. For Fish's contention that neither good nor bad books are "causally related to a virtuous result," see *How Milton Works*, 197.

36 Smith, "Areopagitica: Voicing Contexts," 103.

37 John Saltmarsh, *The Smoke in the Temple* (London, 1646), 14. For a similarly radicalizing use of the scripture by the radical antinomian John Everard, see his "Of Milk for Babes; and of Meat for Strong Men," in *The Gospel Treasury Opened* (London, 1657), 217. See also the characterization of the *saeculum* as the "time that the man-child began to speak like a child growing up toward manhood," by Gerrard Winstanley, *A Declaration to the Powers of England* (*The True Levellers Standard Advanced*), in *The Complete Works of Gerrard Winstanley*, ed. Thomas N. Corns, Ann Hughes, and David Loewenstein, 2 vols. (Oxford: Oxford University Press, 2009), vol. 2, 7.

38 C. John Sommerville, *The Discovery of Childhood in Puritan England* (Athens: University of Georgia Press, 1991), 16. See also Susan Brigden, "Youth and the English Reformation," *Past and Present* 95 (1982): 37–40.

39 For protests by apprentices, see Joad Raymond, *The Invention of the Newspaper: English Newsbooks, 1641–49* (Oxford: Oxford University Press, 1996), 115. For an account of young Quaker leaders including George Fox, Richard Farnworth (age sixteen), and the "quaking boy" James Parnell, who left his family at age fifteen, see Rosemary Moore, *The Light in their Consciences: The Early Quakers in Britain, 1646–66* (University Park: Pennsylvania State University Press, 2000).

40 For the intolerant Milton, see John Illo, "The Misreading of Milton," *Radical Perspectives in the Arts*, ed. Lee Baxandall (Harmandsworth: Penguin, 1972), 178–92.

41 See my "'Exactest proportion': The Iconoclastic and Constitutive Power of Metaphor in Milton's Prose Tracts," *ELH* 76 (2009): 399–417.

42 Robert Filmer, *Observations Concerning the Originall of Government, upon Mr. Hobs Leviathan, Mr. Milton against Salmasius, Mr. Grotius De Jure Belli*, in *Patriarcha and Other Writings*, ed. Johann P. Sommerville (Cambridge: Cambridge University Press, 1991), 197.

43 January 4, 1649, *Journal of the House of Commons* 6 (1802): 110.

44 See Blair Worden, *The Rump Parliament, 1648–53* (Cambridge: Cambridge University Press, 1974), 23.

45 See Laura Lunger Knoppers, "Late Political Prose," *A Companion to Milton*, ed. Thomas N. Corns (Oxford: Blackwell, 2001), 309–25.

46 Sharon Achinstein, *Milton and the Revolutionary Reader* (Princeton: Princeton University Press, 1994), 8.

47 *Ibid.*, 19.

48 Richard Mulcaster, *Positions Wherin those Primitive Circumstances Be Examined Which are Necessarie for the Training up of Children* (1581), ed. Robert Herbert Quick (New York: Longmans, 1888), 141.

49 For the common charge that royalist religion and propaganda had bewitched and charmed the people, see David Loewenstein, *Representing Revolution in Milton and His Contemporaries: Religion, Politics and Polemics in Radical Puritanism* (Cambridge: Cambridge University Press, 2001), 78–79.

50 Robert Filmer's *Patriarcha* is the consummate example, but see also John Bramhall, *The Serpent Salve or A Remedie for the Biting of an Aspe Wherein the Observators Grounds are Discussed* (London, 1643), 105, and Thomas Bayly, *The Royal Charter Granted Unto Kings by God Himself and Collected Out of His Holy Word in Both Testaments* (London, 1649), 92.

51 Quentin Skinner, "John Milton and the Politics of Slavery," *Milton and the Terms of Liberty*, eds. Graham Parry and Joad Raymond (Cambridge: D. S. Brewer, 2002), 3. The very capacity of someone else to impinge on your will, in other words, makes you a slave, whether they do so or not. As Henry Parker asked, if law is contingent on "the Kings meere discretion, wherein doth [the English citizen] excell the Captives condition?," in *The Case of Shipmony* (London, 1640), 109.

52 Henry Parker, *A Letter of Due Censure, and Redargution to Lieut. Col. John Lilburne* (London, 1650), 39.

53 Barbara K. Lewalski, "How Radical Was the Young Milton?," *Milton and Heresy*, eds. Stephen B. Dobranski and John P. Rumrich (Cambridge: Cambridge University Press, 2008), 49. Even Christopher Hill, the most influential champion of Milton's radicalism, admitted that Milton was at times "highly elitist, [with] little but contempt for the uneducated," in *Milton and the English Revolution* (London: Faber and Faber, 1977), 248.

54 Hugh Jenkins, "Quid Nomine Populi Intelligi Velimus: Defining the 'People' in *The Second Defense*," *Milton Studies* 46 (2007): 194.

55 For the idea that the praise of Cromwell is relatively straightforward, see Robert Thomas Fallon, "*A Second Defence*: Milton's Critique of Cromwell?," *Milton Studies* 39 (2000): 167–83; for the alternative view, see David Armitage, "John Milton: Poet Against Empire," *Milton and Republicanism*, eds. David Armitage, Armand Himy, and Quentin Skinner (Cambridge: Cambridge University Press, 1995), 206–25; Blair Worden, "Milton and Marchamont Nedham," *Milton and Republicanism*, 156–80; and David Loewenstein, "Milton and the Poetics of Defense," *Politics, Poetics, and Hermeneutics in Milton's Prose*, eds. David Loewenstein and James Grantham Turner (Cambridge: Cambridge University Press, 1990), 171–92.

56 Su Fang Ng, *Literature and the Politics of Family in Seventeenth-Century England* (Cambridge: Cambridge University Press, 2007), 73.

57 Ranulf de Glanvill, *The Treatise on the Laws and Customs of the Realm of England, Commonly Called Glanvill*, ed. and trans. G. D. G. Hall (Oxford: Oxford University Press, 1994), bk. 7, ch. 9, 166.

58 William Empson, *Milton's God*, rev. ed. (Cambridge: Cambridge University Press, 1981), 130.

59 "Critical pedagogy" attempts to cultivate "habits of thought, reading, writing, and speaking which go beneath surface meaning, first impressions, dominant myths, official pronouncements, traditional clichés, [and] received wisdom," according to Ira Shor, *Empowering Education: Critical Teaching for Social Change* (Chicago: University of Chicago Press, 1992), 129. *Pedagogy of the Oppressed* is the translated title of the book that established the field of critical pedagogy, Paulo Freire's *Pedagogia do Oprimido* (São Paulo: Paz & Terra, 1970).

60 Stephen M. Fallon, *Milton's Peculiar Grace: Self-Representation and Authority* (Ithaca: Cornell University Press, 2007), 38–39.

61 Aristotle, *On Rhetoric: A Theory of Civic Discourse*, trans. George A. Kennedy (New York: Oxford University Press, 1991), bk. 1, ch.2, sec. 4, 38. See also John S. Diekhoff, "The Function of the Prologues of *Paradise Lost*," *PMLA* 57 (1942): 697–704.

62 James G. Turner, "Milton among the Libertines," *Milton, Rights and Liberties*, eds. Christophe Tournu and Neil Forsyth (Berne: Peter Lang, 2007), 454.

63 Fish, *How Milton Works*, 197.

64 Fallon, *Peculiar Grace*, 174.

65 Alexander More, "The Public Faith of Alexander More," *CPW* 4:1106.

66 See the discussion of the *Pro Se Defensio*'s debt to Aretino and the French pornographer Nicholas Chorier in Turner, "Milton Among the Libertines," 452.

67 For the classical precedent "encouraging a form of wit – *sales* or 'salty things' – that combined mental brilliance with sauciness and salacity," see Turner, *Schooling Sex*, 170–71.

68 Milton is quoting Cicero, *De Oratore*, ed. H. Rackham, Loeb Classical Library, 2 vols. (Cambridge, MA: Harvard University Press, 1941), vol. 1, bk. 2, ch. 56, sec. 227.

CHAPTER 6. "YOUTHFUL BEAUTY"

1 John Dryden, "To the Right Honourable Roger Earl of Orrery," in *The Works of John Dryden*, eds. John Smith, H. T. Swedenberg, Jr., et al., 20 vols. (Berkeley: University of California Press, 1965), vol. 8, 101. For Dryden and Hobbes, see Maximillian Novak, "John Dryden's Politics: The Rabble and Sovereignty," *John Dryden (1631–1700): His Politics, His Plays, and His Poets*, ed. Claude Rawson and Aaron Santesso (Newark: University of Delaware Press, 2004), 86–106.

2 Joad Raymond, *Milton's Angels: The Early-Modern Imagination* (Oxford: Oxford University Press, 2010), 269.

3 Alastair Fowler (ed.), *Milton: Paradise Lost*, 2nd ed. (London: Longman, 1998), 208n636.

4 Roy Flannagan (ed.), *Paradise Lost*, in *The Riverside Milton* (Boston: Houghton Mifflin, 1998), 435n167. See also Roland Mushat Frye, "Milton's *Paradise Lost* and the Visual Arts," *Proceedings of the American Philosophical Society* 120 (1976): 240.

5 Henry Vaughan, "The Retreat," *Complete Poems*, ed. Alan Rudrum (London: Penguin, 1995), 2.

6 See Raymond, *Milton's Angels*, 89–124; Feisal G. Mohamed, *In the Anteroom of Divinity: The Reformation of Angels from Colet to Milton* (Toronto: University of Toronto Press, 2008); and the still useful Robert H. West, *Milton and the Angels* (Athens: University of Georgia Press, 1955).

7 Regina M. Schwartz, *Remembering and Repeating: Biblical Creation in Paradise Lost* (Cambridge: Cambridge University Press, 1988), 5.

8 See Hobbes, *DC* 8.1.160.

9 See Stephen M. Fallon, *Milton Among the Philosophers: Poetry and Materialism in Seventeenth-Century England* (Ithaca: Cornell University Press, 1991), 206–22.

10 C. S. Lewis, *A Preface to Paradise Lost* (Oxford: Oxford University Press, 1961), 98.

11 *Ibid.*, 95.

12 John Rogers, *The Matter of Revolution: Science, Poetry, & Politics in the Age of Milton* (Ithaca: Cornell University Press, 1996), 123.

13 *Ibid.*, 123, 110–11.

14 See Henry Cuffe, *The Differences of the Ages of Mans Life Together with the Originall Causes* (London, 1607), 117–18.

15 William Empson, *Milton's God*, rev. ed. (Cambridge: Cambridge University Press, 1981), 59.

16 *Ibid.*, 60.

17 For Milton's heaven as a militarized zone, see Amy Boesky, "Milton's Heaven and the Model of the English Utopia," *SEL* 36 (1996): 91–110.

18 Empson, *Milton's God*, 110.

19 Stanley Fish, *How Milton Works* (Cambridge, MA: Harvard University Press, 2001), 191.

20 "innure, v.¹," OED 1.

21 See also Margaret Olofson Thickstun, *Milton's Paradise Lost: Moral Education* (Houndmills: Palgrave Macmillan, 2007), 70–80.

22 William B. Hunter, Jr. "Milton on the Exaltation of the Son: The War in Heaven in *Paradise Lost*," *ELH* 36 (1969): 215–31; Christopher Kendrick, *Milton: A Study in Ideology and Form* (London: Methuen, 1986), 137. Milton's ambiguity navigates a thorny exegetical tradition, according to Richard S. Ide, "On the Begetting of the Son in *Paradise Lost*," *SEL* 24 (1984): 141–55. In *The Christian Doctrine*, Milton explains that the Son is both begotten in a literal sense, out of the Father's own substance, and in the later, metaphorical sense seen in *Paradise Lost* when he is exalted and confirmed as "Son" (*CPW* 6:204–12).

23 For the relationship between prelapsarian and postlapsarian time, see Valerie Carnes, "Time and Language in Milton's *Paradise Lost*," *ELH* 37 (1970): 517–39, and Amy Boesky, "*Paradise Lost* and the Multiplicity of Time," *A Companion to Milton*, ed. Thomas N. Corns (Oxford: Blackwell, 2001), 380–93.

24 Sherry Lutz Zivley, "The Thirty-Three Days of *Paradise Lost*," *Milton Quarterly* 34 (2000): 116–26.

25 Raymond, *Milton's Angels*, 303–04.

26 Sir John Fortescue, *The Governance of England*, ed. Charles Plummer (Oxford: Clarendon, 1885), 121. See also Ernst H. Kantorowicz, *The King's Two Bodies: A Study in Medieval Political Theology* (1957; repr. Princeton: Princeton University Press, 1997), 7–10.

27 Paul Raffield, *Images and Cultures of Law in Early Modern England: Justice and Political Power, 1558–1660* (Cambridge: Cambridge University Press, 2004), 178.

28 *Ibid.*, 178.

29 Raymond, *Milton's Angels*, 272.

30 *Ibid.*, 269; Richard H. Fulmer, "From Law to Love: Young Adulthood in Milton's *Paradise Lost*," *American Imago* 63 (2006): 26, 30.

31 For Satan's gradual intellectual descent see S. Musgrove, "Is the Devil an Ass?," *Review of English Studies* 21 (1945): 302–15. For early arguments that Milton more aggressively "degraded" Satan, see C. H. Herford, *Dante and Milton* (Manchester: Manchester University Press, 1924), 34–35, and A. J. A. Waldock, *Paradise Lost and Its Critics* (Cambridge: Cambridge University Press, 1947), 91–92.

32 "inferior, adj.," OED2.

33 For an argument that Satan's cringing behavior marks his fall rather than demonstrating God's appreciation of toadying, see John Leonard, "'Once Fawn'd and Cring'd': A Song and Dance About Satan's Servility," *Milton Quarterly* 19 (1985): 101–05.

34 See J. B. Broadbent, *Some Graver Subject: An Essay on* Paradise Lost (New York: Barnes and Noble, 1960), 115; and Michael Wilding, *Dragon's Teeth: Literature in the English Revolution* (Oxford: Clarendon, 1987), 205–31.

35 Sharon Achinstein, *Milton and the Revolutionary Reader* (Princeton: Princeton University Press, 1994), 54.

36 Mark A. Kishlansky, *Parliamentary Selection: Social and Political Choice in Early Modern England* (Cambridge: Cambridge University Press, 1986), 225.

37 Lord Monboddo, *Of the Origin and Progress of Language*, 6 vols. (Edinburgh: 1773–92), vol. 2, p. 356–57. John Leonard alerted me to this source, discussed in his forthcoming survey of critical response to *Paradise Lost* for the Duquesne/Columbia Variorum edition of Milton's poems.

38 William Shakespeare, *Coriolanus*, in *The Norton Shakespeare*, ed. Stephen Greenblatt et al., 2nd ed. (New York: W. W. Norton, 2008), 2.3.4–5.

39 Jacques Rancière, *Dis-agreement: Politics and Philosophy*, trans. Julie Rose (Minneapolis: University of Minnesota Press, 1999), 50.

40 Louis Schwartz, *Milton and Maternal Mortality* (Cambridge: Cambridge University Press, 2009), 213.

41 *Ibid.*, 213. For the still-influential case that "Milton's allegory is undoubtedly faulty" because it gives abstract concepts "material agency" in the poem, see Samuel Johnson, "Life of Milton," in *The Lives of the Most Eminent English Poets*, ed. Roger Lonsdale, 4 vols. (Oxford: Clarendon, 1978), vol. 1, 291. See also Joseph H. Summers, *The Muse's Method: An Introduction to Paradise Lost* (Cambridge, MA: Harvard University Press, 1962), 31–39.

42 Su Fang Ng, *Literature and the Politics of Family in Seventeenth-Century England* (Cambridge: Cambridge University Press, 2007), 148–49.

43 See Lana Cable, *Carnal Rhetoric: Milton's Iconoclasm and the Poetics of Desire* (Durham: Duke University Press, 1995), 58.

44 Thomas Bayly, *The Royal Charter Granted Unto Kings by God Himself and Collected Out of His Holy Word in Both Testaments* (London, 1649), 92.

45 See *Sir Gowther*, in *The Middle English Breton Lays*, ed. Anne Laskaya and Eve Salisbury (Kalamazoo: Medieval Institute, 1995), 120–36.

46 Barbara Kiefer Lewalski, *Paradise Lost and the Rhetoric of Literary Forms* (Princeton: Princeton University Press, 1985), 60.

47 See K. W. Gransden, "*Paradise Lost* and the *Aeneid*," *Essays in Criticism* 17 (1967): 281–303.

48 Virgil, *The Aeneid of Virgil*, ed. R. D. Williams, 2 vols. (London: Macmillan, 1972), vol. 2, 8.578.

49 Fallon, *Milton among the Philosophers*, 182.

50 Victoria Kahn, *Wayward Contracts: The Crisis of Political Obligation in England, 1640–74* (Princeton: Princeton University Press, 2004), 22.

51 For the antipapal puns in the passage, see John N. King, *Milton and Religious Controversy: Satire and Polemic in Paradise Lost* (Cambridge: Cambridge University Press, 2000), 82–83.

52 John Rumrich, "Milton's God and the Matter of Chaos," *PMLA* 110 (1995): 1040.

53 "play, n.," OED 5b.

54 Patricia A. Parker, *Inescapable Romance: Studies in the Poetics of a Mode* (Princeton: Princeton University Press, 1979), 145.

55 Empson, *Milton's God*, 97.

56 For the political connotations of this unorthodox view of a meritocratic heaven, see David Loewenstein, *Representing Revolution in Milton and His Contemporaries: Religion, Politics and Polemics in Radical Puritanism* (Cambridge: Cambridge University Press, 2001), 226.

57 See *CPW* 6:212–18; and Michael Bauman, *Milton's Arianism* (Frankfurt: Peter Lang, 1987).

CHAPTER 7. CHILDREN OF PARADISE

1 Thomas N. Corns, *Regaining Paradise Lost* (London: Longman, 1994), 57.

2 Scott Maisano, "Descartes avec Milton," in *The Automaton in English Renaissance Literature*, ed. Wendy Beth Hyman (Farnham: Ashgate, 2011), 42.

See also Mandy Green, who describes their "coming to consciousness as fully formed adults" in *Milton's Ovidian Eve* (Farnham: Ashgate, 2009), 28.

3 Margaret Olofson Thickstun, *Milton's Paradise Lost: Moral Education* (Houndmills: Palgrave Macmillan, 2007), 158.

4 Christine Froula, "When Eve Reads Milton: Undoing the Canonical Economy," *Critical Inquiry* 10 (1983): 326–27.

5 Robert Filmer, "The Anarchy of a Limited or Mixed Monarchy," in *Patriarcha and Other Writings*, ed. Johann P. Sommerville (Cambridge: Cambridge University Press, 1991), 145.

6 Filmer, "Observations on Mr. Hobbes' *Leviathan*," in *Patriarcha and Other Writings*, 188.

7 Su Fang Ng, *Literature and the Politics of Family in Seventeenth-Century England* (Cambridge: Cambridge University Press, 2007), 85. See also Philip C. Almond, *Adam and Eve in Seventeenth-Century Thought* (Cambridge: Cambridge University Press, 1999). For the argument that Eden was among the most important of the "origins, points of departure, and moments of inception [that] were produced as a solution to an array of questions endemic to seventeenth-century England," see Alvin Snider, *Origin and Authority in Seventeenth-Century England: Bacon, Milton, Butler* (Toronto: University of Toronto Press, 1994), 3.

8 Hugo Grotius, *De Jure Belli ac Pacis*, ed. William Whewell, 3 vols. (Cambridge: Cambridge University Press, 1853), vol. 2, bk.1, ch. 16. See Helen Thornton, *State of Nature or Eden? Thomas Hobbes and His Contemporaries on the Natural Condition of Human Beings* (Rochester: University of Rochester Press, 2005), 1–8.

9 Thomas Bayly, *Witty Apophthegms* (London, 1669), 7.

10 *Ibid.*, 78.

11 Augustine, *The City of God*, trans. John Healey (London: 1610), bk. 14, ch. 26, 529.

12 See Augustine's account of his own childish sin of stealing pears merely "for pleasure," in *Confessions*, trans. Henry Chadwick (Oxford: Oxford University Press, 1998), bk. 2, ch. 3, sec, 8.

13 Augustine, *City of God*, 14.26.529

14 William Poole, *Milton and the Idea of the Fall* (Cambridge: Cambridge University Press, 2005), 21–24.

15 Irenaeus, *The Demonstration of the Apostolic Preaching*, trans. J. Armitage Robinson (New York: Macmillan, 1920), 82.

16 Clement of Alexandria, *Exhortations to the Heathen*, in *The Ante-Nicene Fathers: Translations of the Fathers Down to A.D. 352*, eds. and trans. Alexander Roberts and James Donaldson, 10 vols. (Buffalo: Christian Literature Publishing, 1885), vol. 2, p. 203. For Milton on Clement, see Walter H. Wagner, "A Father's Fate: Attitudes Toward and Interpretations of Clement of Alexandria," *Journal of Religious History* 6 (1971): 209–31.

17 Theophilus of Antioch, *Theophilus to Autolycus*, in *The Ante-Nicene Fathers*, 2:104.

18 Jacob Boehme, *Mysterium Magnum*, trans. John Ellistone (London, 1656), 72. For the likelihood that Milton knew Boehme's works, see Margaret Lewis Bailey, *Milton and Jakob Boehme: A Study of German Mysticism in Seventeenth-Century England* (Oxford: Oxford University Press, 1914), 135. For the ambivalent role of sexuality in Boehme's account of the fall, see James Grantham Turner, *One Flesh: Paradisal Marriage and Sexual Relations in the Age of Milton* (Oxford: Clarendon, 1987), 142–48.

19 Boehme, *Mysterium*, 79.

20 *Ibid.*, 84.

21 *Ibid.*, 93; repeated at 101, 157, 158, 177.

22 For Traherne's knowledge of Irenaeus and the church fathers, see Patrick Grant, "Original Sin and the Fall of Man in Thomas Traherne," *ELH* 38 (1971): 40–61. Grant was unaware of British Library MS Add. 63054, which I discuss later, but it would have confirmed his speculation that Traherne shared Irenaeus's sense of Adam as a child.

23 Thomas Traherne, "Innocence (II)," *Centuries, Poems, and Thanksgivings*, ed. H. M. Margoliouth, 2 vols. (Oxford: Clarendon, 1958), vol. 2, line 52.

24 Thomas Traherne, *Commentaries of Heaven*, British Library MS. Add. 63054, f. 38r.

25 "resent, v.," OED I1b. This obscure and now obsolete usage implies experiencing or feeling something with extreme sensitivity.

26 Traherne, *Commentaries*, f. 37v.

27 *Ibid.*, f. 38r.

28 Thomas Traherne, "The First Century," in *Centuries, Poems, and Thanksgivings*, 1:3.

29 The ongoing discovery of his manuscripts has upended the former view of Traherne as a reclusive mystic. British Library MS Add. 63054, for example, shows that he engaged in regular debates with the Anabaptist leader John Tombes (f. 193v.b), while Lambeth Palace MS 1360 has multiple entries on Bacon, Boyle, Gassendi, and Descartes (see, for example, fol. 249r).

30 Joanna Picciotto, *Labors of Innocence in Early Modern England* (Cambridge, MA: Harvard University Press, 2010), 36–37.

31 Gerrard Winstanley, *Fire in the Bush*, in *The Complete Works of Gerrard Winstanley*, ed. Thomas N. Corns, Ann Hughes, and David Loewenstein, 2 vols. (Oxford: Oxford University Press, 2009), vol. 2, 220.

32 Winstanley, *The New Law of Righteousness*, in *The Complete Works*, 1:534.

33 For hierarchy as the Satanic perspective, see Diane Kelsey McColley, *Milton's Eve* (Urbana: University of Illinois Press, 1983), 40, and Neil Forsyth, *The Satanic Epic* (Princeton: Princeton University Press, 2003), 134–35.

34 See Turner, *One Flesh*, 241.

35 See Kevis Goodman, "'Wasted Labor'? Milton's Eve, the Poet's Work, and the Challenge of Sympathy," *ELH* 64 (1997): 415–46; and Picciotto, *Labors of Innocence*, 464–507.

36 Thickstun, *Milton's Paradise Lost*, 122.

37 Stanley E. Fish, *Surprised by Sin: The Reader in Paradise Lost* (Berkeley: University of California Press, 1967), 9.

38 John Leonard, *Naming in Paradise: Milton and the Language of Adam and Eve* (Oxford: Clarendon, 1990), 23.

39 Jan Amos Comenius, *Orbis Pictus: A Facsimile of the First English Edition of 1659*, trans. Charles Hoole, ed. John E. Sadler (London: Oxford University Press, 1968), 94.

40 Edmund Spenser, *The Faerie Queene*, ed. A. C. Hamilton, Hiroshi Yamashita, and Toshiyuki Suzuki, 2nd ed. (London: Longman, 2001), 6.7.16. This is the description of Arthur, who falls asleep and is surprised by the traitorous knight Turpin.

41 Kristin Pruitt McColgan, "'The Master Work': Creation and Education in *Paradise Lost*," *Milton Quarterly* 26 (1992): 31.

42 Roger Ascham, *The Scholemaster* (1570), in *The English Works*, ed. William Aldis Wright (Cambridge: Cambridge University Press, 1904), 214. See also Pierre de Primaudaye, *The French Academie* (London, 1618), 219.

43 Samuel Hartlib, *Londons Charity Inlarged, Stilling the Orphans Cry* (London, 1650), 10.

44 John Locke, *Some Thoughts Concerning Education*, ed. John W. Yolton and Jean S. Yolton (Oxford: Clarendon, 1989), 56.

45 Michael Allen, "Divine Instruction: *Of Education* and the Pedagogy of Raphael, Michael, and the Father," *Milton Quarterly* 26 (1992): 114.

46 See Karen L. Edwards, *Milton and the Natural World: Science and Poetry in Paradise Lost* (Cambridge: Cambridge University Press, 1999), 72.

47 Leonard, *Naming in Paradise*, 12, 27. See also Barbara K. Lewalski, "Innocence and Experience in Milton's Eden," in *New Essays on Paradise Lost*, ed. Thomas Kranidas (Berkeley: University of California Press, 1969), 100.

48 Milton, *Ad Patrem*, 50–52: "Denique quid vocis modulamen inane juvabit, / Verborum sensusque vacans, numerique loquacis? / Silvestres decet iste choros, non Orphea cantus."

49 For a Lacanian reading, see Claudia M. Champagne, "Adam and His 'Other Self' in *Paradise Lost*: A Lacanian Study in Psychic Development," *Milton Quarterly* 25 (1991): 48–59. However, Champagne's emphasis (following Lacan) on the "lack" (48) and "void" (49) that Adam seeks to fill imposes an un-Miltonic sense of insufficiency on God's creation.

50 For an argument that *Of Education* applies to Raphael's instructional method, while *Areopagitica* applies to Michael's, see Kathleen M. Swaim, *Before and After the Fall: Contrasting Modes in* Paradise Lost (Amherst: University of Massachusetts Press, 1986), 17–25. See also Murray W. Bundy, "Milton's View of Education in *Paradise Lost*," *Journal of English and Germanic Philology* 21 (1922): 127–52; George Williamson, "The Education of Adam," *Modern Philology* 61 (1963): 96–109; Ann Baynes Coiro, "'To Repair the Ruins of Our First Parents': *Of Education* and Fallen Adam," *SEL* 28 (1988): 133–47; and Angelica Duran, *The Age of Milton and the Scientific Revolution* (Pittsburgh: Duquesne University Press, 2007), 93–110.

51 Michael Schoenfeldt, "'Commotion Strange': Passion in Paradise Lost," in *Reading the Early Modern Passions: Essays in the Cultural History of Emotion*,

eds. Gail Kern Paster, Katherine Rowe, and Mary Floyd-Wilson (Philadelphia: University of Pennsylvania Press, 2004), 60. See also Turner, *One Flesh*, 265.

52 See Alastair Fowler (ed.), *Milton: Paradise Lost*, 2nd ed. (London: Longman, 1998), 463n.618–20. See also A. D. Nuttall, *The Alternative Trinity: Gnostic Heresy in Marlowe, Milton, and Blake* (Oxford: Oxford University Press, 2007), 198.

53 Empson, *Milton's God*, 106.

54 For an argument that the exchange reflects the youthful Milton-Diodati relationship, see Karen L. Edwards, "Raphael, Diodati," *Of Paradise and Light: Essays on Henry Vaughan and John Milton in Honor of Alan Rudrum*, eds. Donald R. Dickson and Holly Faith Nelson (Cranbury: Associated University Presses, 2004), 123–41.

55 Mary Nyquist, "The Genesis of Gendered Subjectivity in the Divorce Tracts and in *Paradise Lost*," *Re-membering Milton*, eds. Mary Nyquist and Margaret W. Ferguson (London: Methuen, 1988), 123.

56 *Ibid.*, 123.

57 *Ibid.*, 120.

58 McColley, *Milton's Eve*, 78.

59 Regina M. Schwartz, *Remembering and Repeating: Biblical Creation in Paradise Lost* (Cambridge: Cambridge University Press, 1988), 100.

60 Dominican Laurent, *Somme des Vices et Vertus*, trans. William Caxton (Westminster, 1485), sig. H2r.

61 Richard Younge, *Apples of Gold from the Tree of Life* (London, 1654), 3. See also Joseph Hall, *Contemplations upon the History of the New Testament* (London, 1661), 495.

62 Fish, *Surprised by Sin*, 9.

63 George Sandys, *Ovid's Metamorphosis Englished, Mythologized and Represented in Figures* (Oxford, 1632), 106.

64 *Ibid.*, 89; Patricia A. Parker, *Inescapable Romance: Studies in the Poetics of a Mode* (Princeton: Princeton University Press, 1979), 117.

65 *Ibid.*, 120.

66 McColley, *Milton's Eve*, 77.

67 Diana Trevino Benet, "'All in All': The Threat of Bliss," *All in All: Unity, Diversity, and the Miltonic Perspective*, eds. Charles W. Durham and Kristin A. Pruitt (Selinsgrove: Susquehanna University Press: 1999), 54.

68 William Prynne, *Minors No Senators*, 1st ed. (London, 1646), 10.

69 Melissa E. Sanchez, *Erotic Subjects: The Sexuality of Politics in Early Modern English Literature* (Oxford: Oxford University Press, 2011), 219.

70 Jan Amos Comenius, *Didactica Magna*, in *Opera Didactica Omnia*, 3 vols. (Prague: Czechoslovak Academy of Sciences, 1957; repr. of Amsterdam, 1657), vol. 1, ch. 6, sec. 5, 35.

71 Nuttall, *Alternative Trinity*, 128.

72 John Hollander, *The Figure of Echo: A Mode of Allusion in Milton and After* (Berkeley: University of California Press, 1981), 16.

73 Henry Reynolds, *Mythomystes* (London, 1632), 110–11.

74 The downgrading of reason has been prominent in much of the "New Milton Criticism," for example, Victoria Silver, *Imperfect Sense: The Predicament of Milton's Irony* (Princeton: Princeton University Press, 2001), 50–52.

75 Thomas Bayly, *The Royal Charter Granted Unto Kings by God Himself and Collected Out of His Holy Word in Both Testaments* (London, 1649), 48.

76 *Ibid.*, 40.

77 Waldock, *Paradise Lost and Its Critics*, 52. For Adam's "half-nobility," see C. S. Lewis, *A Preface to Paradise Lost* (Oxford: Oxford University Press, 1961), 126.

78 William Kerrigan, *The Sacred Complex: On the Psychogenesis of Paradise Lost* (Cambridge, MA: Harvard University Press, 1983), 70. See also Shari Zimmerman, "Milton's *Paradise Lost*: Eve's Struggle for Identity," *American Imago* 38 (1981): 250.

79 John T. Shawcross, *John Milton: The Self and the World* (Lexington: University Press of Kentucky, 1993), 14. For a similar argument that Eve represents Freudian narcissism "finally resolving into object-love only in mothering . . . a fall into adulthood," see James W. Earl, "Eve's Narcissism," *Milton Quarterly* 19 (1985): 14.

80 Goodman, "'Wasted Labor'?," 432.

81 Dennis Danielson, "Through the Telescope of Typology: What Adam Should Have Done," *Milton Quarterly* 23 (1989): 123.

82 *Ibid.*, 124.

83 Coiro, "To Repair the Ruins," 134.

84 See Turner, *One Flesh*, 306–07.

85 Fish, *Surprised by Sin*, 329.

EPILOGUE

1 James I, *The True Law of Free Monarchies*, in *The Political Works of James I*, ed. Charles Howard McIlwain (Cambridge, MA: Harvard University Press, 1918), 85.

2 "Report of the Attorney General and Solicitor General," in *The Statutes at Large; Being a Collection of All the Laws of Virginia*, ed. W. W. Hening, 13 vols. (Richmond: J and G Cochran, 1809), vol. 1, p. 530.

3 Gerrard Winstanley, *A Declaration to the Powers of England (The True Levellers Standard Advanced)*, in *The Complete Works of Gerrard Winstanley*, ed. Thomas N. Corns, Ann Hughes, and David Loewenstein, 2 vols. (Oxford: Oxford University Press, 2009), vol 2, p. 8.

4 Gerrard Winstanley, *The Law of Freedom in a Platform*, in *The Complete Works*, 2:315.

5 Roger Williams, *George Fox Digg'd Out of his Burrowes* (London, 1676), 76.

6 For accounts of these early Quaker leaders, see Rosemary Moore, *The Light in their Consciences: The Early Quakers in Britain, 1646–66* (University Park: Pennsylvania State University Press, 2000).

7 Thomas Ellwood, *The History of the Life of Thomas Ellwood*, 2nd ed. (London, 1714), sig. B6v.

8 See, for example, Mary Penington, *A Brief Account of Some of my Exercise from my Childhood*; Elizabeth Andrews, *An Account of the Birth, and Education*; and Elizabeth Stirredge, *Strength in Weakness Manifest*, all excerpted in David Booy (ed.), *Autobiographical Writings by Early Quaker Women* (Aldershot: Ashgate, 2004).

9 William Empson, *Some Versions of Pastoral* (Norfolk: New Directions, 1960), 249.

10 *Ibid.*, 253, 255.

11 The quotation was one of many reported by Newton's contemporary, the historian Joseph Spence, in Ernest Rhys (ed.), *Spence's Anecdotes, Observations, and Characters of Books and Men* (London: Walter Scott, 1890), 70.

12 For Quaker involvement with the Royal Society, see Geoffrey Cantor, "Quakers in the Royal Society, 1660–1750," *Notes and Records of the Royal Society of London* 51 (1997): 175–93. For Newton's heresies and their relation to his physics, see Stephen D. Snobelen, "To Discourse of God: Isaac Newton's Heterodox Theology and his Natural Philosophy," *Science and Dissent in England, 1688–1945*, ed. Paul Wood (Aldershot: Ashgate, 2004), 39–65.

13 Locke, *Two Treatises on Government*, ed. Peter Laslett, 2nd ed. (Cambridge: Cambridge University Press, 1992), bk. 2, sec. 6, p. 55.

14 *Ibid.*, 2.6.74; John Locke, "Atlantis," in *Political Essays*, ed. Mark Goldie (Cambridge: Cambridge University Press 1997), 255.

15 Locke, *Two Treatises*, 2.6.56.

16 John Locke, *An Essay Concerning Human Understanding*, ed. Roger Woolhouse (London: Penguin, 1997), ch. 4, sec. 7, pp. 16–17. For Locke on innate principles, see *Ibid.*, 1.2.27.

17 *Ibid.*, 4.7.11.

18 John Locke, *An Essay on the Poor Law*, in *Political Essays*, 191.

19 Andrew O'Malley, *The Making of the Modern Child: Children's Literature and Childhood in the Late Eighteenth Century* (New York: Routledge, 2003), 22.

20 Seth Lerer, *Children's Literature: A Reader's History from Aesop to Harry Potter* (Chicago: University of Chicago Press, 2008), 98.

21 Isaac Watts, *Divine and Moral Songs, Attempted in Easy Language, for the Use of Children* (London, 1829), ix.

22 *Ibid.*, ix–x.

23 *Ibid.*, 56, 12.

24 Eliza W. Bradburn, *The Story of Paradise Lost For Children* (London, 1828), 5, 8. See Jonathan Sircy, "Educating Milton: *Paradise Lost*, Accommodation, and the *Story of Paradise Lost, for Children*," *Milton Quarterly* 45 (2011): 172–86.

25 Patricia Meyer Spacks, "'Always at Variance': Politics of Eighteenth-Century Adolescence," *A Distant Prospect: Eighteenth-Century Views of Childhood* (Clark Memorial Library, Los Angeles, 1982), 6.

26 *Ibid.*, 13.

27 Stanley Fish, *How Milton Works* (Cambridge, MA: Harvard University Press, 2001), 329.

Index